The History of Inclusion
in the United States

The History of

INCLUSION

in the United States

Robert L. Osgood

GALLAUDET UNIVERSITY PRESS ✦ *Washington, D.C.*

Gallaudet University Press
Washington, D.C. 20002

http://gupress.gallaudet.edu

Photograph permissions: p. 51—courtesy of Dallas M. Barker; p. 65—courtesy of the John F. Kennedy Library; p. 68—reprinted with permission from Burton Blatt and Fred Kaplan, *Christmas in Purgatory: A Photographic Essay on Mental Retardation* (Syracuse, N.Y.: Human Policy Press, 1969), pp. 97, 99; p. 73—reprinted from *MR 67: A First Report to the President on the Nation's Progress and Remaining Great Needs in the Campaign to Combat Mental Retardation* (Washington, D.C.: U. S. Government Printing Office, 1967), 9; p. 113—reprinted courtesy of the *Temple Times*; p.135 —courtesy of William Stainback; p. 135—courtesy of Susan Stainback; p. 145—reprinted with permission from Rud Turnbull, Ann Turnbull, Marilyn Shank, Sean Smith, and Dorothy Leal, *Exceptional Lives: Special Education in Today's Schools*, 3d. ed. (Upper Saddle River, N.J.: Merrill Prentice Hall, 2002), 77; p. 159—courtesy of Doug and Lynn Fuchs; p. 161—courtesy of James M. Kauffman.

Cover—left, students at the South Carolina School for the Deaf and Blind by and courtesy of Dede Ward; right, courtesy of the Department of Communications and Public Information, Montgomery County Public Schools, Maryland.

Library of Congress Cataloging-in-Publication Data

Osgood, Robert L.
  The history of inclusion in the United States / Robert L. Osgood.
    p. cm.
  Includes bibliographical references and index.
  ISBN 1-56368-318-0 (alk. paper)
  1. Inclusive education—United States—History. 2. Special education—United States—History. I. Title.
  LC1201.O74 2005
  371.9'52—DC22

                                                    2005040060

Contents

Introduction

Since the enactment of PL 94-142, the *Education for All Handicapped Children Act of 1975*, the United States has undergone a profound transformation in its efforts to provide a "free and appropriate education" for school-age individuals with disabilities. The original legislation has been revised several times, most notably with the Individuals with Disabilities Education Act (IDEA), passed in 1990. Further revisions of IDEA, combined with the extensive reach of the Americans with Disabilities Act (also passed in 1990), have contributed to today's complex and ambitious approach to special education. As of 2002, there existed thirteen categories of disability recognized under federal law, and persons from birth through the age of 21 are entitled to a wide variety of educational programs and support services through public schools. Consequently, special education has become a significant and highly visible component of American education, directly or indirectly affecting the lives of virtually every student and teacher in the nation's public education system.

These developments have not occurred without debate, controversy, or struggle. Indeed, special education—even long before 1975—has drawn an enormous amount of attention, energy, and concern among educators, legislators, advocacy groups, parents, and other citizens. At the heart of this discussion lies the fundamental issue of just how special—or exclusive—the education of exceptional children should be. Since the 1800s, the question of whether children with disabilities should be taught alongside, or separate from, children not so identified has generated tremendous discussion—and heat. Such discussions have

followed the transition of the location of special education from families and institutions into the public schools, and from segregated to
integrated settings within the schools themselves.

The current framework for these conversations is situated in the
term *inclusion.* The use, and hence meaning, of this term varies widely
depending on the user, the context, and the purposes involved. Despite
such confusion, inclusion without a doubt has become a primary focus
of discourse involving special education policy and practice. It wields
far-reaching repercussions on issues of school organization and administration; classroom management; teacher recruitment, training, and
retention; and especially on planning and implementing instruction for
all students, not just those identified as disabled. In addition, its significant but often inconsistent, even confusing relationship to other terminology used extensively in special education, such as *mainstreaming,*
normalization, integration, and *full inclusion,* makes any analysis of the
history and significance of the concept as problematic as it is worth-
while. Consequently, an exploration of how this term has evolved over
time, and how the very concept can, does, and most likely will affect
special education now and in the future, is crucial to effective implementation of current legislation, policy, and practice as well as optimal
development of the field itself.

This book constitutes an attempt to understand more thoroughly
and accurately what inclusion is, how it came to be, and where it might
go. The widespread use of the term *inclusion* is actually a quite recent
development in the long history of special education in the United
States; this is perhaps surprising given its ubiquity and importance in
current educational discourse. Even so, discussions and debates regarding this key idea in the field have *always* been topics of discussion in
special education. Since the 1800s, when individuals with disabilities
first were segregated in the public schools for instructional purposes,
there have been consistent calls for closer contact of such children with
their nondisabled peers and for their more equitable, "normal" treatment in instructional settings. Moreover, the closely related issues of
who actually should be considered disabled, and who should ultimately bear responsibility for planning and providing their education, have
been the subject of constant discussion and inquiry.

Of particular interest to the evolution of inclusion as an idea has been the expansion of its core questions into broader realms of thought and practice. In its earlier stages, the debate's focus on the propriety of segregating or integrating children with disabilities in regular classroom settings was on the classroom itself: Do these children belong there; if not, why not; and if so, how can it be accomplished? By the late 1960s, however, the scope of the debate had begun to expand beyond individual classrooms and schools to include reconsiderations of the comprehensive structures of special education and of its relationship with general education. Within the past twenty years, the debate has included numerous, substantive demands to question the need for any sort of separate "special education" at all, to advocate a single, fully inclusive general education system that provides a free and appropriate education for *all* children in the regular classroom regardless of ability. Thus the notion of integration, always at the heart of these discussions, has extended from classrooms, schools, and programs to matters related to principles and structures.

Understanding how these issues have evolved is vitally important because special education has become an enormously influential public education enterprise that struggles continually with its relationship with regular, or general, education, especially regarding the degree of its separateness in both structure and execution. In 1902, the annual meeting of the National Education Association formally introduced the term "special education" to America's professional educators, reflecting the advent of what at the time was a new yet undeniably significant trend in public schools: the establishment and support of a multitude of specialized, segregated classes and programs that assumed responsibility for most, and usually all, of the instruction of students identified as disabled. Combined with the school programs of the residential institutions for deaf, blind, and mentally disabled persons, these settings established a tradition of segregated instruction for exceptional children.

Most of the decades-long debate over the relative merits and drawbacks of segregated and integrated settings for the education of students with disabilities has derived from and been referenced to the education of students with mild disabilities—especially those with mild mental retardation (EMR), and later those identified as learning disabled (LD). (In particular, the literature discussing integration in the context of children with mild mental retardation is vast and has been present for decades—due in large part to the centrality, and significant numbers, of children formally or informally identified with mild mental disability in the development of segregated as well as integrated special education programs in public schools.) Such categories of disability—termed "judgmental" by Reynolds, Wang, and Walberg— bore the brunt of criticism in terms of the dubious assumptions and outcomes of identifying, categorizing, and labeling students in need of special education services. Yet also crucial to an understanding of how inclusion had developed as an idea were discussions regarding the segregation and integration of other categories of exceptionality. Included in these were students who were blind, those with physiologically based disabilities, those with multiple disabilities, as well as those exhibiting serious behavior disorders—categories now considered low-incidence disabilities. In addition, a great deal of discussion has occurred regarding the proper placement and instruction of children identified as gifted and talented, which while never considered a disability per se has acquired considerable status as an exceptionality worthy of consideration for specialized educational services. And finally, the condition of deafness, one of the earliest conditions to benefit from specially designed programs within public school systems, has been discussed and addressed in public schools in a variety of ways. It is especially noteworthy because many in the deaf community do not consider deafness a disability and also believe strongly that segregated educational settings for deaf children are appropriate and necessary in order to preserve traditions of deaf culture and community. These issues deserve closer attention, for they suggest to us how issues of exceptionality, identity, and community may intertwine with notions of integration to give special educators and regular educators much to contemplate as they consider the merits of inclusion.[1]

Evolving Definitions and Terminology in Disability

Throughout the almost 200-year history of formal special education in this country, little about the field or its practice has remained static.

This certainly holds true for the terminology used to define and explain its characteristics and activities. Special education and the overarching construct of disability are both deeply rooted in constantly evolving or redefined assumptions, conditions, and understandings related to science, culture, society, and certainly education. Consequently, the descriptors, nomenclature, and labels that describe theory, purpose, and practice related to disability have undergone considerable alteration—even when describing similar phenomena. As is consistent with gradual, evolutionary change, specific moments when the transition from one established terminology to another took place are difficult to pinpoint or identify. Yet the shifts have been significant because they reflect not only dissatisfaction or discomfort with previously accepted terms and their implications but also anticipation of the possibilities and promise that new ones suggest. Such changes are common in the development of an idea such as inclusion, where a multiplicity of intellectual, social, practical, and ethical concerns interact with human experience to create disequilibrium and generate reinvention.

The most obvious and important of such changes are found in the labels used to identify and describe what we now call categories of disability. Over time, there have been three kinds of changes related to category labels. The first relates to changes in specific labels that still refer to the same or quite similar disabling conditions. The second refers to changes in labeling that reflect shifting understandings of or sensibilities toward a particular disabling condition or conditions, such that the new label reflects these new understandings. The third involves new labels that reflect different understandings of the relationship of various kinds of disability with each other. These generalized distinctions are most certainly not mutually exclusive and often overlap; nevertheless, they capture some of the important features that demonstrate the fluidity of disability as a construct as well as the evolution of medical, social, and psychological knowledge and perceptions over time, very much the result of research, experience, and shifting social and cultural standards.

Such changes are most readily seen in the generalized category of mental or cognitive disability. Alterations in the terminology of mental disability have occurred in both the name of the generic condition as well as in the various classifications describing the severity of its presence in individuals. The general term *idiocy* was used widely during the 1800s to refer to persons who, it was believed, demonstrated obvious and deep-seated intellectual incapacity, to the point where an independent, functional life in and of a community was deemed almost impossible. The term thus implied a severe involvement of disability, and it came to distinguish intellectual functioning from other mental conditions such as mental illness and immorality. By the latter 1800s, the term *feeblemindedness* attained currency, referring to the same condition but also encompassing more mild, less apparent intellectual incapacity. By the early 1900s, and with the advent of standardized intelligence tests, more specific gradations of mental retardation or feeblemindedness became widely accepted. Labels of specific levels of cognitive disability at the time included *moron, imbecile,* and *idiot,* suggesting grades from mild to moderate to severe involvement, respectively. In addition, terms such as *backward, borderline, subnormal,* and *dull normal* (or *dullard*) defined further gradations of presumed cognitive disability, located between normal functioning and that of the moron. *Morons* were considered especially problematic in terms of both identification and treatment, as their typical absence of distinguishing physical characteristics as well as their common ability to seem to others as being in the normal range of intellectual functioning in work and community settings masked their alleged genetic deficiencies and antisocial tendencies.

Over time, the labels attached to these gradations changed, yet the general distinctions among levels of functioning remained relatively consistent. Eventually the labels mild, moderate, and severe mental retardation became nearly universally accepted as descriptors for generalized levels of functioning. *Mild* referred to those individuals who did not function at the same level as their chronological-age peers, especially in academic work and school settings, but were capable of making progress in such endeavors, performing essential life skills on their own, and living relatively independent lives as adults. Persons with moderate mental retardation were seen as more delayed relative to their chronological peers, less capable of—or in need of—academic instruction, but able to be trained in certain basic life skills as well as in certain kinds of structured living and employment arrangements that were less complex or intellectually demanding. Severe involvement referred to those individuals exhibiting no capacity for academic work, extreme differentiation from the capabilities of their age-mates—including the absence of speech—and requiring partial or full assistance for even the most basic life skills, such as dressing and personal hygiene; in short, someone almost entirely dependent on care from others. Relatively recently, the categories of mild, moderate, severe, and profound were widely used; recently severe and profound have become fused in the view and usage of many in the field. In addition, these gradations are defined by intelligence quotients (IQ), with mild generally falling in the 60–70 range, moderate in the 40–60 range, and severe and/or profound being applied to persons with measured IQs of less than 40.

Concurrent with these developments in classification constructs and terminology were significant changes in the generic terms used for cognitive disability. From idiocy to feeblemindedness in the 1800s and early 1900s, descriptors for the generalized condition have moved from *mental defect*, to *mental deficiency*, to *mental retardation*, to *mental disability*, to *intellectual* and/or *cognitive disability*. The terms describing persons identified as having this condition have followed suit: *mentally defective, mentally deficient, mentally retarded, mentally disabled, mentally/cognitively challenged, differently abled.* For a time, the condition of epilepsy was also grouped under mental disability. While the basic three- or four-tier gradation of the condition has remained relatively stable, the labels describing those levels of ability and those persons who exhibit them have been changed, largely to reflect new findings, new perceptions, or new sensitivities, more recently in an attempt to destigmatize those saddled with the label. Such changes also reflect changes in beliefs about the balance between medically based and more socioculturally based constructions of the condition itself.

Similar transitions took place within other categories of disability, with many of the same intentions and influences driving them. In the realm of behavioral disability, terms have moved from *moral insanity* to *moral imbecility*, to *incorrigibility, miscreance, delinquency, emotional disturbance*, and *behavioral disorder*. *Speech defect* has moved to *speech disorders*, then broadened to include *speech and language disorders* and *communication disorders*. Physical disability has exhibited descriptors such as *deformed, crippled, physically defective, orthopedically impaired,* and *physically disabled* or *physically challenged.* Entirely new categories have been constructed in the past few decades in an attempt to address research findings and school experiences of teachers and students; these include *autism, learning disabilities,* and *attention deficit hyperactivity disorder* as among the most prominent and compelling in school contexts. Paralleling, and to a great extent interacting with, all these terminological transitions were efforts to move from perceiving disability as a negative, problematic feature of a person's being (deficit-driven or problem-driven) to one that sees disability as a distinction but not necessarily a detriment to a person's life and character, such that their problems are not so much a personal deficit but rather a function of social reaction and prejudice toward their difference. Related to this are recent efforts to avoid using the disability to define the person and instead to consider disability as but one feature of a person's total being, and one that is not nearly as important as a person's other qualities; such efforts are embodied in the movement defined as "person-first" language.

Changes in the terms used to describe choices about including or excluding children with disabilities are equally intriguing and instructive. From the early 1900s into the 1960s, the terms *integration* and *segregation* were used almost exclusively in research and professional discussion related to this issue. By the early 1970s, other terms emerged, perhaps to some extent an adjustment to the widespread application of these two terms to considerations of race and the controversy over racial desegregation and integration of the public schools. During the 1970s, the term *zero reject* was used to some extent in exploring ideas of including exceptional students—especially those with more severe multiple disabilities—in public schools and integrating them more extensively in regular classrooms. By 1974, *mainstreaming* had become the term of preference; before the end of the decade, it had taken firm root as the key word for those involved in research, advocacy, policy development, professional training, and classroom practice to describe efforts to more fully integrate students with disabilities in schools. Then, as special education entered the 1980s, calls for more purposeful, aggressive efforts to integrate virtually every child, regardless of the severity of the disability, increased, giving rise to the terms *full* or *complete mainstreaming.*

By the mid-1980s, a few references to the idea of *progressive inclusion* had appeared. Later, during the highly charged debate over the Regular Education Initiative initiated in the late 1980s, the term mainstreaming was still being widely used, as was progressive inclusion. It was not until the early 1990s that the terms *inclusion* and *full inclusion* had superseded mainstreaming as preferred terminology for the ongoing debate. Notably, the simultaneous use of mainstreaming and inclusion—which to some mean the same thing but to others mean quite different things—has contributed to the, at times, muddled, frustrating, and often antagonistic nature of the debate as it has entered the twenty-first century. Also important is the term *normalization,* which became popular in the United States in the late 1960s and early 1970s and continues to describe a generalized framework for more integrative approaches for persons with disabilities not just in schools but in the community, the workplace, and throughout society. Through it all, the longstanding concept of *integration,* while fading in direct usage as formal terminology, remains the fundamental focus of the various debates regarding placement and responsibility for instruction of exceptional children as well as over the proper form and structure of special education itself.

Understanding the nature and forces behind these changes is vital to appreciating, understanding, and interpreting debates about integration and inclusion, because it contextualizes the ever-shifting perceptions and constructions of disability and its impact on the operations of schools as well as on the teaching-learning process. That fluidity has been reflected in discussions about integration and segregation as topics move back and forth among practical concerns in the classroom, the processes of teaching and school administration, and more philosophical or ideological frameworks. To understand that much has changed, yet that in many ways the essential characteristics of the debate have remained, is to go a long way to making sense of what has been said and what has been done in special education over an extended period of American history.

Core Issues in the Inclusion Debate

Although the terminology has changed over time, several key issues have remained at the center of discussion, continuing to help shape the nature and direction of this important debate. Particular research questions, commentary, and lines of argument that special educators and other stakeholders in the education of children with disabilities have examined typically focus on one or two of these issues but incorporate aspects of others as well; they certainly overlap with and affect each other in many significant ways. These issues include:

+ *Efficacy:* Are segregated or integrated settings more effective in helping all students—those with disabilities and those without— achieve and succeed academically, socially, and emotionally? The question of "what works best" has been examined and debated at least since the 1930s but has intensified in the face of concerns about research methodology and bias as well as about educational priorities and goals.

+ *Efficiency and Economy:* How do these settings compare in terms of facilitating the efficient education of students in schools or other settings, the efficient operation of those institutions supporting them, and the effective distribution and use of finite financial and other resources? The practical implications of integrative approaches, especially in times of heightened concern about classroom management and battles over entitlement to scarce resources, have deeply troubled many stakeholders in special education since the field's beginning.

+ *Territory:* Who should be responsible for making decisions, planning programs, delivering instruction, and evaluating the success of students and programs? In what ways, if any, do such decisions challenge traditional and preferred delegations of space and authority and raise legitimate concerns over accountability and professional expectations of privilege and autonomy? Issues of autonomy, territory, authority, and professional prestige have profound implications for any attempts to implement more inclusive approaches in schools.

✦ *Community:* How crucial is the establishment and nurturing of a sense of community among students in classrooms? Community-building is a key goal of inclusion advocates, but the status and image of disability—especially of a more severe nature—can make achieving this goal as complicated and challenging as it is desirable. Issues of community challenge inclusive approaches in other ways; many in the deaf community, for example, see inclusion as a very real threat to their sense of community and identity.

✦ *Legality:* How have changes in state and federal laws undercut the legal basis for segregationist practices and established fundamental benchmarks for the civil and educational rights of children with disabilities? Especially since 1954, the law has responded to powerful advocacy on behalf of children with disabilities and greatly restricted legal grounds for segregated settings except under certain limited conditions. Even though laws have played a forceful role in maintaining the momentum of the movement toward inclusion, they have also established demands and expectations on schools and school districts that slow-moving, often financially strapped institutions have had great difficulty meeting, creating widespread criticism as well as stimulating efforts to work around legal mandates.

✦ *Power and Identity:* In what way is the debate over inclusion an actual if subsumed function of the power relationships among the disabled and the nondisabled? Persons with disabilities have long been "otherized" in social, intellectual, political, and economic circles, and distrust or contempt has been a real—if often coded—stance toward the disabled throughout the history of special education, not to mention social history in the United States. The extent to which arguments in favor of inclusion represent an attempt to repudiate seeing the disabled as the "other," and those against inclusion constitute a veiled but purposeful means to continue the marginalization of persons with disabilities in school and in society is a crucial yet volatile issue, one that can generate considerable skepticism and alienation between the generalized factions.

✦ *Axiology:* To what extent are integration, mainstreaming, and inclusion moral or ethical, rather than legal or practical, issues? Moral and ethical arguments in favor of inclusion have emboldened and sustained its advocates while serving as a powerful engine for change. Nevertheless, the inevitable clashes between ethical imperatives and practical considerations have slowed the movement and generated sharp critique of its intentions as well as its alleged failure to appreciate the real lives of school professionals and students. While perhaps stronger in tone and content now than ever before, these clashes have been part of discourse in the field for over fifty years.

While distinct in many ways, these issues share three questions central to their exploration: *Where* shall such education take place? *Who* should be responsible for it? And *what*, if anything, is so truly special about special education that separate educational settings are necessary?

Contents of the Book

The History of Inclusion in the United States is just that: It examines the development of the idea and its essential elements over time. The current term, inclusion, has meaning for us now, but most of the book in fact covers periods of time when that term was used rarely if at all. As such, the book is actually an examination of the *ideal* of authentic physical, educational, psychological, and interpersonal integration of children with disabilities in regular education settings: how it started, who has supported it and why, who has questioned it and why, and what our responses as a society have meant to the education of all students, whether formally identified as disabled or not. Chapter 1 provides a brief overview of the emergence of segregated facilities for persons with disabilities in the United States and the establishment of separate special education programs in American public schools by the early 1900s. Chapter 2 examines the development of special education between 1930 and about 1960, looking at the expansion of programs, changes in the understandings of disability, and the origins of debate regarding the propriety of segregated programs for exceptional children. Chapter 3 covers the years 1960 to 1968; during this period, segregated special education grew steadily in size, scope, and power, and the role of the federal government increased dramatically. More importantly, considerations of the rights of the disabled heightened, as did more critical examinations of the field. The next chapter, Chapter 4, looks at how continuing changes in attitudes toward disability, in understandings about who might be labeled disabled, and in beliefs about the quality or even necessity of segregated education generated considerable and extensive debate in the field. These deliberations led to calls for more self-reflection and more integrative alternatives from those both in and outside of special education; they also accelerated the process of various state laws and court decisions paving the way for the landmark PL 94-142 in 1975, an act that firmly sanctified and in many ways facilitated the move toward greater integration of special and regular education.

Chapter 5 looks at the period 1976 to 1984, when public schools struggled to meet the challenges of the Education for All Handicapped Children law and a few scholars and practitioners began championing much stronger collaboration, cooperation, and interdependence between special educators and regular educators through professional development and pilot educational programs. Chapter 6 then focuses on the debate over the Regular Education Initiative, a generalized, somewhat amorphous umbrella term for efforts to blur the distinctions of power and separate identity among special education and regular education students, teachers, and programs. In Chapter 7, the specific cases of giftedness and deafness are examined in terms of their contributions to and impact on the idea of inclusion, highlighting how considerations for children with these labels complicated both the ethical and practical aspects of the debate. Chapter 8 outlines recent developments in the idea of inclusion, summarizes the current lines of contention in the debate over its viability, considers what the impact of the *No Child Left Behind Act* will be on special education, and explores what the history of the field might tell us about its prospects for the future and about possibilities for framing inclusion in a way that can be accepted by most of the stakeholders involved.

While this study covers over 100 years of educational development and examines several important topics related to the lives of children with disabilities in school, it is important to note at least three intentional limitations of the study itself. First, it concentrates almost exclusively on developments in the United States. Nations such as Canada and regions such as Scandinavia were intensely involved in considering the advisability of integration and inclusion for exceptional children, and each has its own interesting and instructive history in this regard. However, this study draws mostly on the work of American scholars and educators and looks at how their work not only shaped the idea of inclusion within the context of specific American realities and conditions but also how their ideas have affected developments in the nation's public schools and other educational institutions.

Second, the concepts of integration and inclusion in this study are applied specifically to the construct of disability and the practice of special education for students with disabilities. Clearly, integration and inclusion both have much broader applications beyond the construct of disability: race, class, gender, ethnicity, sexual orientation, and religion are just some of the constructs for which these terms hold their own special meaning, history, and promise. While there are occasional instances where inclusion as considered within the disability framework intersects with one or more other such constructs, this study again focuses primarily on disability and education in order to render its scope manageable. In addition, such limits allow more thorough investigation of the discussions regarding the educational implications of inclusion, discussions that are of critical importance to the relatively limited but absolutely authentic and important world of students, teachers, parents, and others involved in special education of the past, present, and future.

Finally, this by no means is intended as a comprehensive history of American special education itself. During the course of the research for this book, it became crystal clear how sophisticated and complex special education is in all of its manifestations, applications, and interconnections, and a decent complete history of the field would reflect that. The goal with this study has been to focus, as much as possible, exclusively on a cornerstone idea in special education that is but one part of special education's whole. Nonetheless, the idea of inclusion is crucial to any understanding of the field's history; furthermore, it constitutes a uniquely powerful perspective for helping anyone who is interested in special education to understand its remarkable historical, practical, social, intellectual, and ethical dimensions.

It is also crucial to note the author's perspective and context in preparing this book. My intention is to present a balanced, authentic picture of how the debate over the integration of students with disabilities in regular classrooms has proceeded over time. Admittedly, I began this project as someone who fervently believed that the full integration of all children in regular schools and classrooms, regardless of any attending labels, was not just a possibility but a must. I consider the notion that certain students could be excluded from regular settings against their will and that of their parents an anathema, especially given the long, tragic history of segregation in schools based on all kinds of dubious if not contemptible rationales. I have assumed that schools and teachers were in fact quite capable of doing more to accommodate children with disabilities, and that integration of all children in schools is not only inherently more effective, it is an ethical imperative.

Nevertheless, during the course of this research, I have come to appreciate the vast complexity of the debate and all the various sub- and side-issues involved. It has been an arduous learning process to reaffirm what I have known all along but struggled to acknowledge: that others see the world of special education much differently than I do, and that the convictions and sensitivities of others involved in the debate can and do run counter to positions I had taken as obvious. While I still hold to my convictions, I nonetheless now understand that other voices and other perspectives may not share those convictions; or at least they frame and prioritize them differently. As noted, this book attempts to present a balanced and fair history, but this history is written by one who exits the process with greater humility and less certitude than when entering. Perhaps that is a good thing, perhaps not; it is my hope that readers of this work will share my interest in the topic, my concern for hearing and valuing the voices of all the stakeholders involved in the debate, and my dedication to using this information to make the education of all children more humane, more compassionate, and more valuable, now and in the future.

1

Special Education to 1930:
The Rise of Segregation

The current extensive involvement of American public schools in the education of children with disabilities constitutes a relatively recent development. Significant intellectual, physical, and behavioral differences among individuals have of course been observed for literally thousands of years, mostly in the form of modality deficits, physical appearance, severe and obvious mental disorders, and abnormal public and private behavior. Yet the various categories of disability, the understanding of their nature, and the approaches to the formal instruction used in the past of those so labeled might strike us today as uninformed, confused, and even crude, for the history of the recognition and treatment of disability reveals that until quite recent times, there existed a wide range of constructions, reactions, coping mechanisms, and levels of acceptance or rejection regarding the disabled. As a result, any attempt to explain the extent of integration or inclusion of persons with disabilities in the mainstream of society prior to the mid-1900s is limited by some fundamental differences between then and now of what the definition of disability is and who has it.

Early On

A survey of general historical overviews of the understanding and treatment of disability underscores the difficulty of ascertaining the extent to which individuals with disabilities were identified and then integrated, accepted, or even tolerated in society. These histories, almost all of which focus on Europe and the United States, typically examine the pronouncements and activities of philosophers, religious leaders, physicians, and other interested parties as well as the practices of organized groups or societies. Generally, these overviews describe a wide range of conditions found among the various populations that manifested some sort of physical, mental, or behavioral abnormality; they then explain the various ways in which social groups or particular individuals responded to those afflicted. Responses to the presence of such individuals, according to these histories, ran the gamut from passive acceptance or ignoring to various forms of stigmatization, segregation, isolation, banishment, or even extermination. Physicians and religious figures were at the forefront of identifying and labeling the conditions and their causes as well as suggesting or practicing appropriate methods of treatment or other responses. Attracting particular attention were individuals exhibiting deafness, blindness, epilepsy, congenital deformity, and obvious cognitive impairment (mental retardation, insanity, or "mental alienation"). While the overviews do acknowledge certain positive developments—including the attribution of divinity to certain disabled individuals—for the most part, they establish patterns of response grounded in fear, suspicion, contempt, and cruelty. The lack of clarity and understanding of the nature of the conditions themselves, the frequent ascription of the cause of such conditions to demonic or satanic possession, and the fundamental realities of a universal existence lived mostly in chronic poverty, disease, malnutrition, and debasement ensured that social responses to such individuals would rarely elicit tolerance or compassion.[1]

Definitive changes in the identification, construction, and social and medical responses to disability in Europe began occurring before the seventeenth century. Significant efforts to educate deaf individuals had taken place in Spain and France beginning in the 1500s. The development of sign language and the published successes of pioneers in deaf education challenged prevailing beliefs about the hopelessness of disability, opening a sense of possibility that would lead to similar efforts on behalf of the blind and the mentally disabled. Nevertheless, disability remained firmly entrenched at the margins of society, and those who were publicly identified as disabled held—and were offered—little if any hope.[2]

Underscoring the discomfort and disdain with which most visibly disabled individuals were viewed was the common practice of institutionalizing those with any clearly manifested characteristics of perceived disability. Such institutions had evolved from hospices and other efforts to "cloister" the disabled for purposes of protection of and isolation from society; these began in the Western world as early as the fourth century A.D. and included hospices and hospitals for the blind and the mentally disabled. By the seventeenth century, thousands of institutions housing sufferers of leprosy existed in Europe. During the 1600s, two of that continent's most notorious institutions—London's Hospital of St. Mary's of Bethlehem, or "Bedlam," and the Biçetre in Paris—came into being, incarcerating a wide range of persons and outcasts suffering from numerous conditions such as poverty, mental illness, and physical disability. Salpetriére was later founded in Paris as the women's "lunatic" hospital. Thus, cloistering and institutionalization designed to isolate and segregate disabled and/or despised individuals or groups had a long history in Europe prior to and even concurrent with the colonization of North America. Meanwhile, structured and deliberate efforts to educate the deaf arose in Europe during the 1500s, with similar efforts for the blind beginning by the 1700s.[3]

Developments in the United States

In colonial North America, these traditional views and practices regarding the disabled and other marginalized groups took root. Conditions such as deafness, blindness, abject poverty, "unusual" behavior, mental illness, and intellectual disability certainly existed, and persons exhibiting one or more of these qualities were typically stigmatized, ostracized, or otherwise isolated from the mainstream. The means or methods of such isolation varied: Families would house their "afflicted" members within the family, keeping them hidden and protected; other individuals might be "warned out" or "placed out" of a locality or community in an effort to expel the individual and the condition. Others might find themselves supported by the community but housed at home or in an isolated, often wretched setting. As in Europe, accusations of witchcraft frequently befell the disabled, and the typical view of them as demonic, dangerous, and contemptible persisted.[4]

Institutional care for people with disabilities in colonial North America did not arise in any organized fashion until the latter part of the eighteenth century. The Pennsylvania Hospital began admitting mentally "disturbed" patients to a "mad ward" in 1752. These patients were typically placed in a basement setting and "treated" with traditional methods developed in Europe: shackling, isolation, and accepted medical practices such as bloodletting and natural "cures." In 1773, the colony of Virginia opened a hospital designed solely for the mentally ill and disabled in Williamsburg; this institution served as the only one of its kind until the founding of a similar hospital in Kentucky in 1824. Such institutions sought to provide at least some relief to other kinds of institutions, such as prisons and almshouses, which housed persons with disabilities but were poorly equipped to deal with them. For most colonial Americans, however, the family home and these other facilities served as locations to house, segregate, and otherwise deal with disabled members of the community until the early 1800s.[5]

Nevertheless, Enlightenment thought, combined with advances in the education of persons with disabilities—especially the deaf and the blind—helped forge more compassionate and optimistic, although by no means inclusive, attitudes regarding disability. Encouraged by European successes in educating the deaf, the blind, and "idiots," American reformers worked to establish both private and public institutions that would provide treatment and formal instruction to persons with disabilities. The nation's first institution for the deaf, the Connecticut Asylum, For the Education and Instruction of Deaf and Dumb Persons, was founded in 1817 in Hartford, largely through the efforts of Thomas Hopkins Gallaudet. Another American who was deeply involved in a variety of causes for social reform, Samuel Gridley Howe, spearheaded the organization of the Massachusetts Asylum for the Blind, which opened in 1832, and the Massachusetts Asylum for Idiotic and Feebleminded Youth, first established as an experimental school in South Boston in 1848.[6]

As the first of their kind in the United States, each of these institutions benefited dramatically from the tireless work of their founders while coming into being amid intense scrutiny and skepticism on the part of the public. Both Gallaudet and Howe engaged in considerable research on European practices, not only in terms of institutional administration and organization but, more importantly, on specific methodologies for instruction. Armed with this knowledge, Gallaudet and Howe were able to convince donors, legislators, and others interested in the work of the value of institutions and the potential for teaching students previously considered uneducable. The extensive publicity surrounding the success that Howe and others had in teaching a deaf-blind child, Laura Bridgman, solidified the notion that educating the disabled was not only feasible but also exemplified the finest humanitarian and Christian impulses of this era of optimism and reform. In addition, Howe insisted that although such institutions may be isolated from the outside world, they nevertheless should be considered an important part of the educational structure. "Institutions for the blind, deaf, and dumb, and for the feeble-minded," he claimed in a speech in 1853, "were not properly asylums, but public schools; and the pupils have as much right to the benefits as such as ordinary children in the common schools." Indeed, Howe noted that such asylums should be considered "the last . . . but still a necessary link" in the common school system.[7]

Over the next several decades, the number of such institutions, both public and private, grew steadily. By the early 1900s, most states had at least one residential facility for the deaf, the blind, or the mentally disabled, and many had separate institutions for each of the three populations. However, the purposes of these institutions shifted over time even as their numbers increased. The humanitarianism and optimism regarding instruction embodied by Gallaudet, Howe, and other pioneers gradually shifted toward more negative constructions and understandings of mental disability. Meanwhile, the institutions for the deaf moved away from a more positive view of the deaf experience, which was grounded in the respect for and emphasis on a proud deaf culture and the use of sign language as the primary mode of communication. This view gave way to an emphasis on oralism, which called for greater

integration with the hearing world and expressed more negative views
of deafness as a disability and affliction rather than a positive quality or
characteristic. Assertions regarding the danger and contaminating
effects of disability gained in popularity and influence throughout the
latter half of the nineteenth century; prominent voices such as Isaac
Kerlin, Alexander Johnson, Walter Fernald, and Alexander Graham Bell
lent stature and credibility to such views. As a result, the twentieth century began with the disabled facing near as much ostracism, contempt,
and misunderstanding as ever. In the world of mental disability, that
meant continued segregation and isolation from the mainstream; for
the deaf community, it meant continuous and intensive efforts to meld
that community into the mainstream and the abandonment of a
unique deaf culture. In both cases, it meant calls for the eventual elim-
ination of the condition through potent mechanisms of social control,
including physical isolation from society, legal restrictions or prohibi-
tions on marriage, and advocacy of various social policies designed to
restrict the potential for procreation among those deemed "defective." [8]

Special Education in the Public Schools

As the 1800s drew to a close, another major actor entered the realm of
special education for persons with disabilities: the public schools. Institutions for the disabled had grown dramatically in number and stature
during the nineteenth century, yet that growth was limited compared
with the ascension of the public school as an influential and ubiquitous
manifestation of social policy and practice. Almost nonexistent in 1800,
public school systems in the United States—especially those in the
largest urban centers—had become firmly established by 1900. With
that growth came the realization that children with all kinds of disabilities, both obvious and "hidden," found their way into public school
classrooms. Beginning in the mid-1800s, schools began to develop ways
to address the presence of disability in classrooms, which incorporated
current thought and beliefs on disability but also responded to the particular needs of schools as institutions and bureaucracies. Influenced by
other factors such as the child study movement, progressive education,
and the rapid diversification of the American populace, schools devel-

oped a variety of programs and approaches designed to accommodate and cope with disabled children in the schools. Segregation for these children was advocated by the vast majority of school professionals and researchers, who relied on two fundamental arguments: that segregation was necessary for efficient classroom and school operation, and that separate programs for disabled children was in their best educational and psychological interests. In the multitude of commentary and justification that has been offered in the name of special education, these two claims almost always appear, often in juxtaposition.

The development of large, complex public school systems originated in the largest American cities during the early 1800s. As urban schools became more heavily populated and their student populations more diverse, efforts began to fashion efficient bureaucracies and administrative mechanisms that would facilitate instruction in the classroom and improve school management. In 1847, the Boston public schools initiated its graded school approach, where students were assigned to specific grades according to their chronological age. By the late 1800s, graded schools constituted the preferred model for urban school systems in the United States. The graded school represented an attempt to streamline school organization by establishing a prescribed educational ladder that students could ascend in mass numbers at a predictable pace. Consequently, students found themselves grouped in classrooms with other children who were close in age but could vary dramatically in background, interests, skills, abilities, and preparation.

As might be expected, such settings—especially in classrooms with upwards of eighty or ninety students under the charge of a single teacher—proved highly problematic in terms of both instruction and management. The common school movement and the adamant belief that school attendance was vital to ensuring proper acculturation of all schoolchildren strongly encouraged enrollment of all children of school age who were "capable of instruction." However, in the classroom, the differences of disabled children, especially allegedly aberrant behavior and failure to keep pace academically with the majority of students, were seen by teachers and administrators as causing unacceptable levels of inefficiency and frustration. For example, in Boston, even before the implementation of graded schools, teachers complained about academically weak and ill-behaved children—most of whom were identified as being of immigrant backgrounds—and strongly urged the creation of separate schools to which they could send them. Educators argued that to segregate them would be not only to their benefit but also to that of the more capable students, who would then be able to receive more of a teacher's time and attention. These were among the earliest examples of teachers and administrators calling for segregated settings for children who were different, uncooperative, or unsuccessful in school; large urban school districts throughout the country would experience such demands throughout the nineteenth and into the twentieth centuries (and they have yet to go away).[9]

Such conditions and concerns led to the establishment over the next several decades of a wide range of separate settings for students who, it was believed, overtaxed the efficient operation of schools and classrooms. In 1838, Boston established "intermediate schools," also known as "schools for special instruction." These would continue until 1879, when they were reorganized and renamed "ungraded classes." Ungraded classes included students from multiple grade levels who exhibited a remarkably wide range of ages, backgrounds, and abilities; the settings were designed to relieve pressures on regular classrooms and to provide at least a modest attempt to address the academic and behavioral challenges ungraded class students presented. Other cities, including Cleveland and New York, experimented with specialized settings in the 1870s; these primarily served children who were truant, "incorrigible," or otherwise presented serious behavior problems. Into the early twentieth century, generic ungraded classes remained popular as settings—often referred to as "dumping grounds"—for children whose particular condition may have gone undefined but who nonetheless generated sufficient concern or contempt among teachers to prompt their removal from the regular classroom.[10]

These nationwide developments in student differentiation paralleled the dramatic influx of persons from overseas who emigrated to the United States. This influx contributed to a steady increase in the numbers of children attending school, especially in urban areas. Immigrant children brought to often crowded classrooms a wide range of languages, educational experience, and cultural values, which all too often led to academic and behavioral struggles in school, in turn bringing about much of the differentiation among students noted above. Boston's location of their intermediate schools exclusively in immigrant neighborhoods, and the rapid growth of those schools during the first wave of mostly Irish immigration between 1840 and 1860, exemplified the presumed connection between immigrant background and school failure.

As the nineteenth century progressed, doctors, researchers, and educators increasingly alleged a more direct connection between immigrant background and actual intelligence (not just school performance). As the more tolerant and optimistic perceptions of the character and curability of the mentally disabled faded in favor of more negativistic views, the rise of anti-immigration sentiment—especially after 1880—intensified, and suspicions about the connections between the two strengthened. Research during the era repeatedly demonstrated the hereditary nature of mental disability; much of this work was grounded in "family studies" that skirted the immigration issue. Even so, the notion that mental disability was inherited, and that it was frequently apparent in families of the "foreign-born," became commonplace. Such sentiments were bolstered significantly in the early 1900s by the work of Henry Herbert Goddard, perhaps the most preeminent researcher of mental disability at the time. During the early 1910s, Goddard used the recently developed standardized Binet intelligence tests and administered them to immigrants arriving at Ellis Island in New York Harbor. His results, which claimed to demonstrate that the great majority of immigrants from certain regions of Europe were in the "moron" range of intelligence—if not lower—shocked the country and firmly embedded the connection of certain ethnicities with mental disability in the minds of the public. This connection found comfort in the intense anti-immigrant atmosphere of the early twentieth century and validation in the reputedly "scientific," "objective" findings of standardized intelligence tests.[11]

The Emerging Special Education Structure

The first formal public school setting for a clearly defined exceptional population again is found in Boston. In 1869, the city opened the School for Deaf-Mutes, renamed in 1877 as the Horace Mann School for the

Deaf. It was a recognized component of the public school system and the first public day school for deaf children in the United States. The initial class specifically designated for children with mental retardation is generally credited to Providence, Rhode Island, which initiated the class in 1896. Within just a few years, other cities followed: Day schools for deaf children opened in Erie, Pennsylvania, in 1874 and in several Wisconsin cities during the 1880s. Between 1898 and 1910, special classes for children with mental retardation opened in Springfield, Massachusetts; Boston; Philadelphia; New York; Chicago; Baltimore; Detroit; and Los Angeles among others. The growth and development of such classes accelerated significantly during the 1910s and 1920s with the advent of intelligence testing as an allegedly scientific and objective means of identifying children who belonged in a special class.[12]

Between 1900 and 1920, several other segregated settings designed to serve specific conditions or disabilities in public school systems opened nationwide. These included open-air classes for chronically ill children, especially those with tuberculosis; speech sessions and programs for students with various speech disorders; classes for children with serious vision and/or hearing impairments; classes and separate schools for children with severe behavior or truancy problems; classes for children with limited or no proficiency in English; and in some cities, special programs for children identified as gifted. These joined the special classes for children with mental retardation, and in many cities, the continuing ungraded settings, to form significant programs of special education in most major American cities by 1930. In 1932, for example, the number of mentally retarded children in special classes alone reached over 75,000 nationally in 483 cities in 39 states.[13]

Such substantial differentiation into a wide range of programs required some sort of formal identification process. For children with obvious physical, sensory, or severe behavioral disabilities, the process was relatively simple; determining who truly belonged in a special class for "mental defectives," however, was not by any means. Consequently, describing the prevalence, characteristics, and even basic categories of those considered mentally defective proved complicated and problematic. Before mental testing was accepted as a common practice, the process was subjective, casual, and widely inconsistent; with the introduction of mental testing, it became rigid and oversimplified. Categories such as "backward," "dull normal," "dullard," "borderline," and "moron" overlapped and substituted for each other among districts, researchers, and public agencies, making determinations of prevalence and characteristics difficult. Nevertheless, research conducted then and since suggests that the special classes for the mentally disabled were majority male, often to a great extent; that they included students primarily from working-class, hence usually immigrant, backgrounds; and that they served children of all races. Student composition in special classes did vary widely, though, and was heavily dependent on the demographic makeup of the city and even individual neighborhoods. (The same was true for the disciplinary or delinquent classes.) Prevalence rates proved especially difficult to determine, given the inconsistent processes of identification and classification. Typically, studies and data from the early 1900s show the prevalence of students who were "feeble-minded" or "defective" would vary from less than one percent to more than three percent, depending on the community and whether marginally "defective" students were included in the count.[14]

Rationales for Segregation

This startling rise in the number and scope of separate classes for children with various exceptionalities took place during a period when an enduring, widespread, and mostly unchallenged belief held sway, which stated that the segregation and even isolation of these children was in the best interests of pedagogy, school management, and social control. In his seminal 1924 text on the education of the handicapped, psychologist and special education pioneer J. E. Wallace Wallin advanced five detailed "reasons for training mentally deficient and seriously backward children in special and ungraded classes," clearly segregated from the regular classroom. First, he noted the "benefits which accrue to the regular grades and the normal pupils from the removal of the subnormals." Wallin maintained that mentally disabled students "represent . . . an unassimilable accumulation of human clinkers, ballast driftwood, or derelicts which seriously retards the rate of progress of the entire class and which often constitutes a positive irritant to the teacher and other pupils." He claimed their inability to do the work led to serious behavior problems, and that spending inordinate amounts of time trying to help them keep pace "would seem like robbing bright Peter to pay dull Paul. . . . This constitutes one of the strongest practical arguments in favor of the policy of organizing separate classes for children who cannot possibly keep up with the pace of the regular grades. . . ."[15]

Wallin also argued that segregated settings would benefit the disabled child: "In the special classes deficient children are relieved of the . . . disheartening, cruel, and unjust competition with their superior fellows. . . . They also escape from the taunts, jeers, jokes, and gibes sometimes suffered at the hands of their normal playfellows . . . In the special class . . . they will encounter an atmosphere of mutual understanding, helpfulness, and sympathy" as well as "more aid and encouragement" and a relief from "a maladjusted curriculum which they cannot master." Wallin concluded by claiming that segregated settings offered numerous benefits "to the regular grade teachers. . . . to society . . . . [and] to the science of education from the scientific study and training of deficients." He emphasized that segregated settings were essential not only to the "subnormal" but also for "the blind, the deaf, or the crippled."[16]

Wallin's comprehensive analysis captured both the content and spirit of similar comments found among most everyone involved in special education at the time, from national scholars and experts to school district administrators and the teachers in the classroom. In a presentation to the National Education Association in 1903, Mary C. Greene, a former special class teacher from London, asserted:

> No argument is required to show that the children embraced in these . . . groups cannot be required to attend the ordinary schools, in continuous association with normal children, except to the disadvantage of all concerned. The cripple would suffer in body; the epileptic and the weak-minded would be unable to keep pace with their school-fellows, or would be a drag upon their progress; the deaf would profit hardly at all; the blind only by the spoken word.

New Jersey educator Meta Anderson's important and widely referenced book *Education of Defectives in the Public Schools*, published in 1917, presented a detailed argument not for segregated classes but for segregated schools altogether, a concept applauded by Henry Herbert Goddard. E. R. Johnstone, superintendent of the influential Training School at Vineland for the "feeble-minded" in New Jersey (where Goddard, Johnstone, and others engaged in widely disseminated and respected research on the mentally disabled and their education), presented a detailed discussion in 1908 before the National Education Association that pointed out the important role of the special class in improving the instruction not only of the disabled but also of those regular children who no longer had to contend with the presence of obvious disability in their classrooms. Johnstone also supported the contention, noted in Wallin's text, that segregated classes could be used as laboratories to study ways to improve instruction for all children. And in addressing the Indiana State Teachers Association in 1917, James T. Byers, secretary of the National Committee for Provision for Feeble-Minded, claimed that the separate "small special class" was the best setting in which to educate feeble-minded children, whom he considered to be "a drag upon you, a drag upon the class, and a drag upon the school, day after day and year after year. . . ."[17]

Other educators offered similar comments in reference to their own immediate locales. Baltimore public school Superintendent James Van Sickle noted that compulsory education compelled school administrators to operate small, segregated classes for "mentally defective children" even though such settings were much more expensive to maintain. The extra expense, he said, was worth it, given that "the presence in a class of one or two mentally or morally defective children so absorbs the energies of the teacher and makes so imperative a claim upon her attention that she cannot under these circumstances properly instruct the number commonly enrolled in a class." In Boston, Superintendent Franklin Dyer followed a similar argument in stating that "it is therefore economical in every way to establish classes for children who are exceptional." In Indianapolis, special class teacher Katrina Myers focused on the alleged benefits for the exceptional child: "For hundreds of our public school pupils, the hope of escape from a life of utter inefficiency lies in the ungraded classes of our public schools . . . . [where now] they can be given training and treatment adapted to their subnormal, individual capacities." Summarizing the universal appeal of segregated settings, a Boston Finance Commission report on the city's public school system assured the public that the segregation of mentally disabled children "is essential for good administration, and . . . is also beneficial to the child." As of 1930, the concept and reality of a segregationist approach to the instruction of children with identified disabilities in the public schools had become accepted in most large American cities and many smaller ones.[18]

Several historians have argued that the primary impetus for a separate special education was the apparent benefits it served teachers, administrators, and other school personnel in facilitating the growth, power, and influence of school systems and easing the already arduous tasks of teaching in the era of a heightened emphasis on and enforcement of compulsory education laws. Joseph Tropea, a sociologist and educational historian, determined that special classes, especially those for students with mental and behavioral disabilities, resulted from the need to reconcile the clashing demands of strictly enforced compulsory attendance laws and the articulated "sentiments" as well from the traditional expectations and desires of classroom teachers through a process he refers to as "backstage" negotiations: "Special classes . . . allowed urban schools to preserve order in the regular classroom, continue past exclusionary practices, and comply with the law." Education and curriculum historian Barry Franklin's analysis of Atlanta's experience in creating special classes argues that special classes were but one feature of that city's attempt to engage in Progressive-era educational reform through curriculum differentiation—a manifestation of a tracking approach to prepare students for predetermined types of employment and levels of social stratification. John G. Richardson, an historian and organizational analyst, echoing Tropea, describes the special class as "an organizational strategy born of the enduring conflict between the ideal of a common schooling and the practical demands for efficiency in meeting this ideal," closely tied to the development of both intelligence testing and vocational education. While acknowledging the role of an authentic concern for the educational and social needs of children with disabilities, Marvin Lazerson, an expert in urban educational history, still concluded that "the humanitarian concerns of special education become secondary to the desire to segregate all those the educational system found disruptive." Although considerable evidence challenges the idea that special education arose almost exclusively from bureaucratic, organizational, and control impulses in relation to more humanitarian and child-centered concerns for the youngsters directly affected, the fact remains that these two fundamental features drove the development of a segregated special educational structure in cities across the country.[19]

Analyses of the origins of segregated special education in public schools tend to focus on the *special class,* which typically was the term reserved for settings for children identified as mentally disabled, and on the separate classes, schools, or programs for children with severe behavioral problems. Even so, other populations of students with disabilities also required settings that teachers and administrators believed demanded segregated instruction. Classes for chronically ill children—primarily those with tuberculosis—used open-air environments and a curriculum modified to include substantial rest periods, seen as not possible or necessary in the regular classroom. Classes for vision-impaired students required specialized lighting, texts, and equipment; those for hearing-impaired students gave significant attention to lipreading and other communicative skills not considered valuable or appropriate for "normal" students. Speech-improvement classes represented an early attempt at a pull-out program, with those students spending most of their time in regular classrooms but engaging in speech therapy activities in a removed setting, typically two or three times a week. Also popular were separate classes and schools for physically disabled or "crippled" children, although the need for segregated instruction was, for the most part, limited to physical education and issues related to physical access. These settings support the idea that segregation was seen as appropriate even by those less concerned with efficiency or control and more concerned with the well-being of the disabled child.

It should be noted that segregation of students with disabilities was by no means always seen as the wisest approach. For example, beginning in 1898, a few notable districts, including Batavia, New York; Newton, Massachusetts; and Winnetka, Illinois, attempted to operate what was often called the "Batavia Plan" or the "Winnetka Plan," where "assistant or unassigned teachers" would work with individual students by giving "special attention" and individualized instruction to "laggards" or "retarded pupils." Such in-class special education was combined with efforts to reorganize the curriculum in these classes to allow the regular teacher to work more closely with individual children. In addition, as early as the mid-1800s, the Boston schools entertained the idea of having students who were sent to the ungraded classes or schools for special instruction intermingle with the regular class children, so that the segregated students could "become in all respects the *subjects* of influence, and not the *leaders* of it"; others suggested that integrating ungraded class children with students in regular classes would encourage emulation of the regular students and provide a "healthy moral incentive." Almost forty years later, an assistant school supervisor in Boston argued that separation of vision-impaired students aggravated their sense of abnormality and insisted that when a vision-impaired student "mingles with other children . . . such nicknames as 'blinky' and 'blindy' disappear." While statements and programs advocating closer contact between regular class students and their disabled peers did exist, they were nonetheless quite rare.[20]

It is also important to recognize that segregation of children with disabilities did not occur nearly to such an extent in the vast numbers of small-town and rural schools across the nation. Well into the twentieth century, formal special education in public schools was almost exclusively an urban phenomenon. Smaller districts—facing limited resources for differentiated curriculum or special equipment, lack of well-trained teachers, far fewer students in a classroom or grade, weaker enforcement of compulsory attendance laws, and limited expertise with which to identify students with disabilities—did not engage in building extensive and expensive special education programs until student numbers and district resources permitted or demanded it. In the thousands upon thousands of one-room schoolhouses and other ungraded schools in the United States in the early 1900s, teachers typically engaged in traditional practices of ability grouping within a class, peer instruction, and outright exclusion or expulsion of children whose behavior proved too problematic as mechanisms for coping with significant intellectual, physical, and behavioral differences among students who today, or in urban districts at the time, might well have been labeled disabled. Ironically, these very techniques are similar to methods employed today in classrooms across the country as schools attempt to once again bring as many students with disabilities as possible into the regular classroom—and keep them there as much as possible.

Nevertheless, the definitive trend from the late 1800s on was to identify students with disabilities and remove them from the regular classroom. The precedent of the segregated institution carried over into growing urban schools systems, which began to hear calls for segregated settings for certain children as soon as classroom realities and the size and diversity of the student population exposed the complex nature of student difference and its significant effects on efficient classroom instruction and school administration. Public school students who exhibited a wide range of intellectual, physical, and behavioral challenges to school efficiency, and who clearly required resources and instruction substantially different than the great majority of students, found themselves increasingly being assigned—on a permanent basis, more often than not—to separate classes that carried different names, exhibited different environments, and employed different means of instruction among themselves but shared one fundamental characteristic: existence on the margins of public schooling. As the twentieth century unfolded, segregation continued as the preferred model for decades as special educators and their allies engaged in the serious and purposeful business of developing their own educational world within the public school system.

2

1930–1960: Special Education Comes of Age

There has been considerable controversy over the policy of 'segregation' of exceptional children from the normal school population. . . . If a child can be accepted by a regular class and can profit by instruction in the regular class, with needed special services brought to him there, he may well remain there. If, however, his enrolment [sic] in the regular class is detrimental to his own development or that of the other children, then he should be placed where his growth can best be furthered. Thus, the education of exceptional children accepts special services in regular grades, special classes, and special schools as possible means for the appropriate education of each child.

—*National Society for the Study of Education, 1950*

BETWEEN 1930 and 1960, the world of special education, both in and beyond the public schools, changed dramatically. During these three decades, the number of children identified as disabled and placed in a special education setting steadily increased; research on the etiology, diagnosis, and treatment of a wide range of categories of disability expanded and became more sophisticated; and public as well as professional attitudes shifted remarkably in response not only to that research but also to legal decisions, public advocacy, and extensive experience in schools. Slowed temporarily by the Depression of the 1930s, special education nonetheless developed a momentum, a structure, and a core of assumptions and knowledge that by the beginning of the Kennedy administration in 1961 would propel it to an important position in educational practice and public consciousness. At the heart of this expansion was continued debate concerning the propriety and effectiveness of segregated settings for special education students.

Status as of 1930

In 1930, President Herbert Hoover convened a White House Conference on Child Health and Protection. As part of that conference, the Committee on the Physically and Mentally Handicapped prepared a report on "The Handicapped Child," which was published in 1933 as Section IV of the full conference report. "The Handicapped Child" consisted of more than 400 pages of statistics, description, analysis, and recommendations related to the education and treatment of the nation's disabled children, representing the most thorough discussion yet of the national investment in special education. The report included detailed discussions of "the deaf and the hard of hearing," "the visually handicapped," "the crippled," "internal conditions" (tuberculosis, heart disease, intestinal parasites), "problems of mental health," and "problems of mental deficiency." It also offered a discussion on "vocational adjustment."[1]

The committee estimated that there were at least 10,000,000 handicapped children in the United States classified under these various conditions. The report did not include consistent data on the number of public school children enrolled in special education; rather, it focused on ascertaining prevalence rates in the population and on the size of residence populations in institutions. It did report 2,785 visually handicapped pupils in public schools, but did not indicate how many were taught in classes designed especially for them. It also reported 13,282 "crippled" students assigned to 500 special schools or classes in eighty-three cities with populations of 10,000 or more. The committee estimated that 7.89 percent of all children were "mentally and physically atypical" to the point of "requiring special class provision."[2]

In 1930, Stanley Davies published *Social Control of the Mentally Deficient,* a text that would be widely read and discussed over the next several decades. Davies reported that in the school year 1926–1927, there were 51,814 "subnormal and backward children enrolled in the special classes of 218 city day school systems reporting from 33 States." Davies also cited a survey undertaken for the 1927–1928 school year by Ohio

State University professor Arch O. Heck, who reported at least 3,996 "special and ungraded classes throughout the country, enrolling in all, 78,014 children, of whom approximately two-thirds are definitely subnormal." Davies was adamant that the public schools be involved in special education: "The position of the public school in the mental deficiency program is unique. No other agency can begin to make so effective a contribution to the social control of mental deficiency. No other agency, by its neglect of this problem, can leave so much damage to be repaired by other agencies." He argued that failure to provide special education for the mentally disabled would cause society to "[pay] for this, either by supporting these persons for the rest of their days in institutions, or more likely, in a larger bill of crime, delinquency, pauperism, and social degeneracy." Although their tone differed to a large extent, both the White House Conference committee and Davies clearly articulated the view that special education in public schools deserved and demanded a crucial investment of public interest and resources.[3]

1930–1950

Of crucial importance to the expansion of public school special education programs was the enabling legislation passed by the various states beginning early in the century and continuing into the 1940s and 1950s. These laws typically permitted local districts to establish specified classes or programs for children with disabilities; some required that certain programs be established, and other laws provided funding to support local efforts. Such laws also addressed the operation and policies of the residential institutions for the disabled, the establishment of special day schools for other kinds of disability (e.g., behavioral disorders related to delinquency) and, more importantly, requirements regarding service to children with disabilities in public schools and in particular settings within those schools.

This enabling legislation followed decades of compulsory attendance laws that either made no mention of disability at all or specifically exempted (or more to the point, excluded) children with obvious disabilities from their reach. Yet despite such restrictions, children with obvious disabilities were most certainly finding their way into the public schools. By the 1920s, a few states such as Massachusetts stipulated that "mental or physical condition" should not necessarily constitute a reason for exempting a child from attendance at a state-sponsored educational facility. Nevertheless, children with recognized disabilities—especially those who were seen as especially problematic for the efficient delivery of instruction to the vast majority of "normal" students—continued to be subject to exclusion, with various states permitting such exclusion if approved by the state superintendent of instruction, the state board of education, the local school board, or a physician. For example, Michigan allowed the exclusion of a child if a doctor signed a certified statement that "a child is so physically handicapped that he should not attend school . . . or on the basis of mental handicap . . . that the child is incapable of benefiting from public school attendance." Such generic qualifications clearly allowed school officials a great deal of latitude in sanctioning the dismissal of a disabled child from public school responsibility. Even so, laws pertaining to the inclusion or exclusion of children with disabilities from the public schools varied widely from state to state in terms of age limits, conditions of the child, and conditions permitting exclusion.[4]

The Depression of the 1930s created significant obstacles to the development of special education. Extremely limited resources were less likely to be directed to the disabled; for example, in 1932, the state of Indiana abandoned a summer institute for the training of special class teachers in response to a "retrenchment in the public school system" that reduced the need for teachers of special, or "opportunity," classes. Some historians see the period as a time of continued development and progress; others assert that dismal conditions and administrative contradictions and struggles plagued special education throughout the decade, with special and regular education drifting further and further apart and the status and resources of special education students, classes, and teachers sinking even lower. Efforts during the decade clearly emphasized employment of the "normal" population first, limiting employment and vocational training opportunities for the disabled. State legislatures slowed their activity in passing laws supporting or at least permitting the development of special education programs. There was a relatively slight but notable drop in special education enrollment, especially in the number of cities supporting special education programs, from 1936 to 1940. Nevertheless, there were still eighty more cities with special education in their schools serving more than 23,000 more students in 1940 than in 1932, even with drops in overall school enrollment. The structure and scope of special education, while buffeted by the Depression and its own aging process, nonetheless continued its significant development. [5]

By the late 1940s, much had changed. In 1949, Elise H. Martens, a recognized leader in the field who had been engaged in research on special education since the 1920s, conducted a survey of special education legislation throughout the United States. Published by the U.S. Office of Education, the survey examined the nature and extent of state laws pertaining to the education of exceptional children nationwide, revealing not only the wide variance in status of and policies toward special education among the states but also the extent to which it had become embedded in the public school mission. Martens wrote, "'Special education,' as here used, refers to all those instructional services which are specially planned for children of elementary and secondary school age who are physically handicapped, seriously retarded in learning ability (often called mentally deficient or subnormal), or emotionally maladjusted." She also stated that, in her opinion, gifted children should also be included in special education, "but, since present State laws take little cognizance of the State's responsibility to make special provisions for these, there is little to say about them in this report except to point out the urgent need of doing something about it." She noted that "special education" did not include "remedial instruction . . . for children of approximately normal ability and behavior who . . . fall short of expected achievement," nor did it apply to "the differentiation of curriculum that takes place for that large group of children who are slow in their learning process but not seriously below average." To Martens, special education "is reserved for those physical, mental, or emotional deviations that demand some radical change in the school program."[6]

Using these general guidelines, Martens stated that "special education for the handicapped may in some cases involve full-time special instruction at school. In other cases it may be limited to an hour or two per day (more or less) of specialized instruction under a special teacher, with membership in a regular class for the rest of the day," or it may involve teaching the child in a hospital or at home. Consequently, it did "not call for a rigidly defined procedure, but is exceedingly flexible in its plan of operation." Thus, while the laws she examined did not mandate that special education take place in separate settings, her definition of special education itself and her description of options clearly suggested that segregated instruction constituted the most widely used—and expected—model. In summarizing her findings, Martens wrote,

> In general, it might be said that five-sixths of our States have now taken the step of legally recognizing the place of special education in local school districts as an essential feature of the State's educational system. Two-thirds of them have taken the additional step of legally specifying a plan for some degree of State aid to local districts maintaining such programs. Almost half of them give added emphasis to the importance of the work by legally specifying the appointment of consultative and supervisory personnel in the State education department.

This evolution, from simple permissive legislation allowing districts to establish special education programs to more extensive state involvement in both planning and, most importantly, funding such programs, represented an important development in special education policy and practice by mid-century.[7]

Martens concluded her analysis with a list of ten recommendations for the improvement of special education. These included statements that all exceptional children should be identified and attend school; that they had a right to appropriate educational services from an early age through adolescence, whether in school, home, or hospital; that each state should provide leadership, guidance, and especially sufficient funding to local districts as they develop special education programs; and that the state "should encourage the preparation of well-qualified personnel" to ensure that exceptional children are "well taught and well prepared for life adjustment." Martens acknowledged that the nature of "good legislative practice" can and does change but that the "principles that have just been proposed are offered as a bill of rights for exceptional children and as basic tenets for State legislation." Martens' work both encouraged and reflected the movement of special education toward becoming a more accepted and central feature of public education in the United States.[8]

Public schools sought other ways to respond to this growing need. Some school districts engaged in cooperative ventures with private schools, programs, and organizations to provide special education services for public school students, sometimes for lack of resources, sometimes for lack of interest. Cities such as Buffalo, Nashville, and Chicago and states such as Arkansas, New Jersey, and Rhode Island worked with local parent groups to establish and maintain such endeavors, beginning in the 1940s. In addition, special education scholars as well as local and state school administrators published pamphlets, articles, and other materials offering advice for parents, teachers, and other interested parties on how best to provide services to children with disabilities.[9]

Underscoring special education's emergence as an important feature of public education was the 1950 publication of *The Education of Exceptional Children*, part II of the forty-ninth yearbook of the National Society for the Study of Education (NSSE). This comprehensive overview of the field, as applied to all recognized categories of exceptionality, suggested by Dr. Harry Baker of the Detroit Public Schools on behalf of the International Council for Exceptional Children (ICEC), brought together the thoughts and writings of many of special education's most prominent and prolific figures. The volume's stated purpose was to "furnish valuable guidance to teachers in regularly organized classrooms, to school administrators and supervisors, and to the parents of children requiring unusual educational programs and facilities" while simultaneously "stimulat[ing] further progress in the development of teacher-training programs . . . and facilitat[ing] the work of all classes of teachers in dealing with pupils whose learning experiences are rendered ineffective by educational handicaps of different kinds." In his introduction, noted special educator Samuel Kirk suggested that the yearbook's purpose was to "describe the procedures and special services which have been found effective in meeting the needs of exceptional children within a school system." Like Baker, Kirk felt strongly that the information would help not only teachers in the various special classes and programs but also would assist regular classroom teachers "in adapting instruction to the needs of pupils within their own class-rooms. It is important that the regular classroom teacher be sensitized to the problems faced by exceptional children . . . and to know what to do with the many borderline children who will always be found in the regular classrooms."[10]

The volume's first chapter, "Basic Facts and Principles Underlying Special Education," authored by the entire Yearbook Committee, acknowledged that "from one point of view . . . every child is excep-tional, since every child's individual abilities and disabilities differ from those of every other child." Even so, the authors stipulated that "in this discussion . . . the term 'exceptional' is applied only to those who are so markedly different in physical mental, emotional, or social traits that they need special educational treatment or services." It estimated that nationwide, 10 to 12 percent of children of elementary- and secondary-school age would be considered 'exceptional' and in need of special educational services," putting that number at approximately four mil-lion children. These included students with physical handicaps (crip-pled, impaired hearing and vision, speech handicaps, or other types, including tuberculosis, epilepsy, and endocrine disorders), children with "mental deviation" (both well below and well above average), and children with emotional or social maladjustments. All such children required "special facilities for their optimum development." It added: "The goals of education for them are the same as those for all children. The difference lies in the means or techniques by which those goals can be realized and in the way in which they find expression in the individ-ual's life." Although the number of children requiring special education was believed to be around four million, the committee cited statistics showing that only 365,000 children were, in fact, benefiting from such services in the public schools during the 1947–1948 school year. This was substantially more than the nearly 314,000 reported in 1940; but even when counting the children housed in various institutions, the total of 425,000 in some kind of formal educational program was "still far from . . . the desirable goal." (The underserving of children in need of special education continued as a troubling issue for decades.)[11]

Marten's survey and the NSSE yearbook helped set the stage for a series of discussions and developments that would prove crucial to the growth and changing nature of special education during the 1950s. State government became more and more involved and directive in mandating, fashioning, and supporting financially special education in the public schools. Both philosophical discourse and scholarly research focused on the advisability and practicality of segregated and integrated settings for special education programs in classrooms and schools. And each of these general developments were energized and shaped by significant changes in national perceptions of disability: Beliefs about what the disabled were capable of, and what they were truly like, altered considerably not only in light of increases in public awareness and advocacy but also as a function of experiences in schools and workplaces.

Public Schools, Special Education, and the "Integration" Debate

The concurrent expansion of public school involvement and investment in the education of exceptional children featured the continued growth of a variety of specialized settings for students with disabilities. The special class for children with mental disabilities remained a cornerstone of special education but was by no means its only manifestation. By 1948, more than 439,000 children were enrolled in various special settings, including 108,440 in special classes for the mentally retarded; 182,344 in programs (typically pull-out, partial-day) for children with speech impairments; 47,227 in special classes and schools for the physically disabled and chronically ill; 26,948 in special settings for the deaf and hard of hearing; 13,366 in programs for children with vision impairments; 37,800 in programs for the "emotionally disturbed and socially maladjusted"; 2,819 in "other" placements; and even 20,712 in programs for gifted students (although giftedness was not considered a disability, but an exceptionality requiring separate instructional settings). Data from 1956 showed that "between 1948 and 1953 the enrollment of children in special schools and classes increased 47 percent, that the number of school districts providing special education services increased 83 percent, and the number of teachers in special education programs increased 48 percent." As the number of categories and separate settings increased, considerable discussion and debate arose regarding the advisability and effectiveness of separation as a fundamental policy and practice in special education instruction. During the 1940s and 1950s, this debate was typically framed as one of *segregation vs. integration.*[12]

As noted in the previous chapter, the belief that segregated settings constituted the best approach to special education for all concerned went unchallenged for the most part. Despite occasional comments proclaiming the value of social contact between disabled and nondisabled children, most everyone involved in the education of exceptional children saw segregation as appropriate and desirable for all concerned: administrators, teachers, and all students in public schools regardless of ability or condition. Nevertheless, concerns about the repercussions of segregationist practices never disappeared and, in fact, grew significantly stronger and more frequent between 1930 and 1960.

Such concern found voice among parents and practitioners who questioned the efficacy of segregated settings and who were troubled not only by the effects segregation would have on the academic and social development of students but also by the impact and messages of a segregationist philosophy in a democratic society. For example, parents in East Haddam and Norwalk, Connecticut, expressed diverse opinions over the opening of special classes; some supported it, while others viewed them as "unjust condemnation of pupils" and saw "the non-promotion and segregation as definite problems." In a more comprehensive assessment of the impact of segregation, Dr. Alan Challman, director of the child study department of the Minneapolis Public Schools in 1941, observed, "complete segregation of a subnormal group has the effect of calling attention to the retardation . . . . [T]o place a child in complete segregation does stigmatize and verify the lack of mental ability and this acts as a mental hazard in many ways. . . ." Challman also criticized the special classes themselves, noting they lacked a "recognized academic status" and held a reputation as a place where 'they don't learn 'em nothing,'" preventing promotion and adversely affecting a child's self-concept. "The principle of segregation," he stated flatly, "is bad."[13]

At its twenty-second annual meeting in 1945, the ICEC held a panel discussion entitled "Segregation versus Non-Segregation of Exceptional Children." The panel considered not only special versus regular classes in the pubic schools but also the value of segregated special schools compared with regular schools as sites for delivery of special education services. The panel's staunchest opponent of segregation was Howard Lane, a member of the Detroit Police Department. Lane argued that:

> segregation gives any human being a skewed culture. The handicapped needs special understanding rather than special classes . . . .Even greater than the abnormals' need for normal associates is the need of the bulk of human beings to know the dull, crippled, blind, deaf, mildly neurotic child well enough to accept him and not regard him as a being pathetic or discomforting or something to be kept out of sight. . . . Special education today is in the unenviable position of tempering evil winds to the most closely shorn victims of outmoded and inadequate educational provision for all children.

Lane's observations focused on the primary concerns regarding segregation: that it stigmatized and isolated children in special classes and deprived them all of mutual and beneficial exposure, contact, and cooperation. In addition, others expressed concern that segregation was inherently antidemocratic because it "labels" certain pupils who then fail to gain "a sense of belonging" and are "deprived of social experience that would be a stimulus to further development." Another member of the ICEC panel, I. M. Robb of the Morrison School for Mentally Retarded in Ontario, Canada, asserted that "modern educational philosophy assumes the right of every child to be educated according to his ability and social needs. It would seem right, therefore, that, with our knowledge of modern educational methods a more scientific treatment than segregation be afforded all children within a school."[14]

Most special education professionals at least acknowledged that segregation was in many respects a flawed approach. "Segregation is justified only to the extent that the program can be administered in no other way," wrote one practitioner in 1940. "Subnormal pupils should mix with average and superior pupils for such activities as assembly programs, physical education, club activities, and in any fields where individuals may be found to have ability, such as art, music, shop, and homemaking." Boston special education teacher Katherine Coveny reported in 1942 that the Boston schools had worked hard to involve special classes and their students much more fully in the mainstream of the regular schools and had done so successfully. John W. Tenny, a member of the ICEC panel, shared that assessment, commenting that special class pupils should "participate with pupils of the regular grades in all classes and activities where they can do so with profit and safety to themselves." Even so, such integration was seen as being limited to arenas that did not require adaptation to the needs of the exceptional child. "In general," asserted Tenny, "the atypical children attending a regular class should be expected to participate in the regular activities of the class and to meet class standards." Fellow panel member Bess Johnson concurred: "Dumping a handicapped child into a pool of normal children where he must sink or swim should not be permitted until all teachers have been trained to be life savers. Teach the handicapped child to swim first." Alan Challman suggested "compromises to cut down isolation," including having children with disabilities "take whatever subjects they can with the regular group" and locating remedial work for "slow" but nondisabled children in the special class, creating a fluid class population that might prove problematic for teachers but would represent "a program for better pupil mental health ... you can not better anything without changing something, even though the change may be difficult." Some educators cautioned that decisions about whether or not to segregate a child or group of children should typically be made on the basis of the child's needs, not those of the institution; others argued that integration was advisable only if convenient for the school. Wrote ICEC panel member Edward Stullken, principal of the Montefiore Special School in Chicago:

> In general, it is best not to segregate any individual by placement in a special group, if he may receive as good or better training in a normal group of pupils .... The exception to the rule is encountered when the detriment to the interests of the group outweighs the benefit derived by the individual from his association with the regular group.

Clearly a strong ambivalence about segregating children with disabilities lingered, driven by a need to reconcile the consequences of isolating exceptional children with the assumption that special education indeed needed to be truly special—and hence separate.[15]

For some children with less-severe physical or behavioral disabilities, integration had seemed even in the past viable and desirable, at least to a certain extent. The 1950 NSSE yearbook in general advocated involving children with vision and hearing impairments, epilepsy, physical disabilities, and behavioral disorders with their regular education peers wherever and whenever possible, usually in nonacademic activities and settings. Children with a slight or even moderate hearing loss, according to the yearbook, could participate within regular classrooms that possessed the requisite technology and trained staff; those with moderate hearing impairments could spend considerable time in the regular class and be pulled out for lipreading training. Even students in special classes for those with more significant hearing loss should be given opportunities to participate with "normal" children in other aspects of school life such as assembly, recess, and lunch. The same was true for students with substantial vision impairment; and children with physical disabilities, epilepsy, or even behavioral disorders should not, the yearbook proclaimed, automatically be prohibited from regular classroom participation. It described a continuum of services for several such disabilities, arguing that special schools, special classes, resource rooms, and the regular class could all be made available to a child depending on opportunity and need. The key to inclusion in regular settings was whether the child had the intellectual ability to achieve at the level of the regular class and whether the school could provide adequate training for teachers and sufficient appropriate technology or services in the regular classroom.[16]

Recognition that integrating certain students with low-incidence and/or severe disabilities was indeed possible and appropriate continued through the 1950s but was by no means universally accepted. Anna Engel, who had served in the Department of Special Education of the Detroit public schools, encouraged attempts toward integration but noted that children with more severe or low-incidence disabilities would still require "a strong special education program" consisting of a core of specialists for various disabilities as well as a range of specialized equipment and teaching techniques that may demand segregation. Maurice Fouracre of Teachers College argued that children with visual, hearing, or physical impairments needed and deserved specialized services and that attempts to provide these in the regular classroom would likely mean that such students would "not have equal opportunity" with their normal peers, "even when all the provisions are made . . . in the same class . . . and with the same teacher." F. E. Lord of the ICEC noted that special classes during the decade had been accepting "children with greater and greater disabilities," including those with cerebral palsy and severe mental retardation. He praised teachers for their willingness "to expand your services" but cautioned about potential and even current problems of "dumping" where placement even in special classes within the public schools did not ensure appropriate instruction. Hence, even the "integration" of children with disabilities requiring highly specialized interventions in classes with those of a more "mild" nature created concerns for teachers, administrators, and students.[17]

Much of the impetus for discussing the relative merits and drawbacks of segregated special education arose from what came to be known as efficacy studies. Efficacy studies have been a feature of special education research since the 1930s, when the earliest research comparing the performance of students with disabilities in a special class with that of such students in a regular class took place. At least a dozen of such studies were published before 1960, almost all of them focusing on children with mild mental retardation. Generally speaking, the findings of these studies were mixed at best. Some indicated special class placement was not as effective as the regular class for students with disabilities in terms of academic achievement but was more effective in terms of providing positive social experiences. Others came to different conclusions. Several critics assailed these studies for what they considered serious methodological flaws, especially in terms of selecting populations for the study and overgeneralizing from limited evidence. At any rate, some who questioned the practice of integration argued that, in the absence of convincing evidence that segregated settings were better for students with disabilities, segregation could not be automatically justified and accepted. Others countered that there was sufficient

FIGURE 1. A typical normal child. You would love to teach this child. His head size is supposed to symbolize normal intelligence. The presence of ears indicates normal range of hearing. A dot for the eyes implies normal vision and a straight line for the mouth signifies average speech. Straight arms and legs suggest normal motor control. Satisfactory emotional adjustment is indicated by the absence of a symbol which you will readily note in certain cases below.

MR Mentally Retarded
G   Enlarged head to show deviation
V   Visual impairment
H   Hearing loss
Sp Speech defect, impairment or limitation
Mo Motor limitations
E   Emotional problems

FIGURE 2. Symbolic presentation of deviations which are significant enough to influence instruction and adjustment of the child.

These stick figure illustrations originally accompanied F. E. Lord's article "A Realistic Look at Special Classes—Extracts from the President's Address," which appeared in the May 1956 issue of *Exceptional Children*. These crude

FIGURE 3. A class of children with hearing impairments. You are on your own now to make your own interpretations. The question marks signify a good possibility of aphasia or some other disability which is confused with impaired hearing. Presence of ears indicates that the child is hard of hearing as distinguished from deaf. The teacher of this class has many questions which she would like to have investigated scientifically.

FIGURE 4. A class of crippled children. Degrees of impairment are not indicated, but you can be sure that they are here. If you are acquainted with such classes, you must recognize this as a familiar scene. The teacher of this class is faced with a multitude of problems. What kind of special training does the teacher of such a class need?

renditions representing various disabilities and their captions are shocking and truly illustrative of his arguments and the attitudes of the times. Copyright 1956 by the Council for Exceptional Children. Reprinted with permission.

evidence that special classes at least provided a safer, more supportive environment, thus demonstrating their value. (Efficacy studies, although now more sophisticated and varied, remain a central referent for those discussing the merits and drawbacks of integration to this day.)[18]

Nonetheless a general consensus existed that segregation, while flawed, was by far the lesser of two evils. The argument was made frequently that being included in a regular setting was no guarantee of being authentically integrated into the classroom community, and that segregation provided benefits for the child that could not be realized any other way. Harley Wooden, superintendent of the Michigan School for the Deaf, exclaimed that

> The exceptional child—especially certain types—possesses needs of which neither the regular classroom teacher nor normal classmates have any understanding. Consequently to place such a child in a normal environment may lead to disastrous educational retardation and emotional and social maladjustment, for the simple reason that physical presence with a normal group is no guarantee against segregation. In fact it often results in its worst form, namely that of *impossible* intellectual competition and social isolation.

The child's inability to keep up with her or his classmates was seen as inevitably leading to a child's being labeled a failure as she or he struggles with the consequences of an inappropriate education and a hostile, unwelcoming environment. "This," argued Philip Cowen of the ICEC panel, "is even more undemocratic that the worst segregation." Others emphasized the positive side of segregation. Bess Johnson maintained that "to segregate a child, for a short time, often gives him [a] chance to develop a sense of security and the ability to face the problems presented by living with so-called normal children. Segregation of several types of physically handicapped children for education and treatment, for a necessary period of time, is psychologically sound. . . ." Referring to the theme of democracy again, Maurice Fouracre stated explicitly that "educational equality demands the consideration of individual differences and needs and the provision of special services to meet those needs." Handicapped children, he asserted, "do not profit from the group education techniques used in most of our schools for teaching children of average ability." Other researchers called attention to studies showing that children with disabilities in regular classrooms were likely to suffer rejection and isolation within the classroom setting much more frequently than children not so labeled.[19]

Such rejection, it was thought, underscored the judgment that physical proximity did not necessarily lead to true integration, nor did a primarily separate setting condemn an exceptional child to permanent isolation. As John Tenny pointed out,

There are some who consider any setting apart of pupils, no matter how slight, as segregation. It would appear to me, however, that segregation is better understood not as a plan or an organization but rather a frame of mind. Teachers in a residential school, if so minded, can provide for pupils so many contacts with the regular community that segregation is avoided. Conversely a teacher having an atypical child in a regular classroom might make that child an island of isolation and segregation.

Harley Z. Wooden, Superintendent of the Michigan School for the Deaf

The forced combination of regular class children and those with significant, identified disabilities in order to satisfy either "an administrative expediency of segregation or a blind ideal of non-segregation," without paying sufficient attention to "a thorough understanding of the particular child involved," was a serious mistake, according to Harley Wooden. Ultimately, proper determination of placement required teachers and administrators to "maintain a balance between the interests of the pupils needing special education and the interests of the great majority of the pupil personnel of the school." Authentic integration of exceptional children with their nondisabled peers was seen as desirable, but only when the needs of both the children and the school administration could be met. "Although it has never been a mark of distinction for a child to be placed in a special class room," argued an Iowa supervisor of special education in 1944, "this is perhaps better for him than to have us attempt to ignore reality, than to make no special provisions for a child's handicap, and to subject him to continued failure. . . ."[20]

Assumptions persisted that delivery of effective special education typically demanded separate settings well into the 1950s. In a stinging, comprehensive 1956 critique of integrationist tendencies during the 1950s, Arthur S. Hill, education director of United Cerebral Palsy and an associate editor of the flagship journal *Exceptional Children*, said efforts to employ more "child-centered" approaches to special education and to see exceptional and normal children as more alike than different reflected "the 'goo' of wishful thinking." Hill challenged attempts to render special education more like general education, claiming that

> In too many instances . . . our leaders in education continue to ignore the reality of learning differences and refuse to consider the obvious needs for differentiated school services. . . . It is time to discard platitudes and speak in realistic terms. Generally speaking, exceptional children *are* much like other children, but educationally they present specific problems of learning and physical adaptation. If it were not so, there would be no need for differentiated educational services.

Hill also lamented the various fragmented and uncoordinated special education programs, stating that it was "no longer sufficient to provide isolated special education services that are differentiated according to obvious impairments, but rather a coordinated program for children with many kinds of learning problems in which pupils may be taught according to their major educational disabilities." His desire for a more coherent, comprehensive, and distinct structure for special education included a call for greater reliance on residential schools to deliver instruction.[21]

Hill's primary concern was what he saw as the ascent of two questionable and dangerous clichés: "Get them into the normal stream of society" and "integrated program of special education." He charged that the former had been used to misplace children with physical disabilities in regular classes, leading to them becoming "misfits in the occupational world. Special educators may be well advised to screen more carefully the children who are to be returned to the regular schools and classes." Hill then labeled *integration* a "nebulous ideal" with a "positive rather than negative connotation. Nevertheless, it is merely a word, with many meanings and interpretations." He claimed that

> In some places integration merely means the assignment of handicapped children to one or more class periods with unhandicapped children. Where this occurs the result easily may be the disintegration of children and their learning experiences. . . . In other places integration means the location of special classes in ordinary school buildings. . . . Its integration depends upon the acceptance of the units by all the members of the faculty, the school administrator, the children in the school, and the patrons of the school.

Dismissing the pursuit of a "cliché" for its own sake, Hill cautioned that "the only integration about which special educators should be concerned is the integration of the children for whom they are responsible." Adherence to this cliché and a narrow vision of how integration might be achieved had limited special education's progress and effectiveness. "Undoubtedly," he asserted, "many unrealistic and undesirable measures are being adopted in the name of 'integration.'"[22]

Hill's implicit alarm about trends toward more progressive and integrative approaches to special education suggested that indeed such efforts were beginning to gain ground. During the 1940s, the purposeful efforts to put Boston special class children in much closer contact with their regular class peers and the notable positive comments regarding integration during the ICEC panel discussion demonstrated significant interest in the idea of a special education more interwoven with regular education. Hill's charge that "they are more alike than different" had become a popular view and was validated by comments to that effect in the 1950 NSSE yearbook and elsewhere. In 1953, Samuel Kirk published a definitive analysis of education for the mentally handicapped; in that article, he downplayed the differences between special and regular education. He stated that "essentially the curriculum is the same" for "normal" and "subnormal" children and that "all that is necessary for a special class program" is for any "good teacher" to "[adapt] instruction to the level of learning of her children." Thus, Kirk claimed, special education is not a program of its own (*"special* or *regular"*) but rather *"regular plus special."* Kirk's view was that the two branches of education should be more closely articulated; his implication was that teachers and administrators should see special education as more a complementary than alternative program. Three years later, F. E. Lord, ICEC President and a special education coordinator in Los Angeles, applauded the development of "auxiliary services" for exceptional children, which allowed them to spend much more time in regular classes as well as "the use of consultants to work with children with special problems while they are enrolled in regular classes." Like Kirk, Lord challenged the notion of a competitive special education. He encouraged the development of programs that would supplement, but not replace, special classes and celebrated what he termed "the increasingly popular approach of integrating the education programs for normal and exceptional children." Two years later, Norris Haring and associates advanced a "Philosophy of Integration" that also applauded the evolution of "a more integrative" approach to special education. Haring et al. claimed that "educators are becoming more favorable in their attitude toward the integrated placement of exceptional children which, of course, has resulted in more of these children being educated in the regular classroom." Ambivalence regarding the "proper" approach clearly persisted.[23]

Institutional Care

Even as the public schools enrolled more and more children with disabilities, the private and public residential institutions for persons with disabilities continued to house thousands throughout the United States. Since the late nineteenth century, the focus of such institutions

depended largely on the kind of population it housed: Institutions for
the deaf and the blind featured relatively strong educational programs,
whereas those for the mentally disabled became more custodial as the
institutions came to serve more and more individuals who were classified as "low functioning." Although the earlier "institutions for the feebleminded" became "state schools" or "training schools," and many of
them moved to the "cottage plan" featuring housing in smaller groups
and basic vocational training, they nonetheless de-emphasized the
"educational function" in favor of "their custodial and protective
responsibility." By 1950, states also supported institutions serving crippled children as well as people with epilepsy and juvenile delinquents.
Within all such institutions, the wide range of ages and severity of disabilities made provision of formal schooling problematic, and the educational functions of each became clouded by the institutions' multiple
roles as school, hospital, penal institution, and warehouse. Whereas in
some states, the department of education held the supervisory role for
such institutions, in others, that control was exercised by correctional,
welfare, or health agencies. This diffusion and inconsistency in supervision, operation, and purpose inhibited any concerted efforts to stan-
dardize objectives or programs for the "patients," "inmates," or
"residents" among the various institutions.[24]

Nevertheless, institutions continued to serve a considerable number
of persons with disabilities, and that number increased dramatically
during the 1950s. In 1948, just over 62,000 individuals lived in residential schools for the blind, the deaf, the mentally disabled, and the emotionally disturbed; ten years later, that figure had grown to more than
86,000. This included a more than 30 percent increase in the number of
residents of institutions for the mentally retarded and a remarkable 64
percent growth of the institutionalized population for the emotionally
disturbed and socially maladjusted. Accordingly, a construction boom
began during the decade; in 1970, 75 percent of the residential institutions serving the disabled had been built after 1950. Even so, conditions
of overcrowding, which had plagued all such institutions since the
1800s, continued to be a serious problem, contributing to discussions
about the nation's failure to provide special education services to a large
majority of those who needed them.[25]

Organizations of and for Persons with Disabilities

Another manifestation of special education's coming-of-age at mid-century was the continued growth and influence of organizations dedicated to the study of disability and to the support of persons identified as disabled or exceptional. Professional organizations of this description had been functioning for generations. The American Association on Mental Deficiency, founded by a group of state institution superintendents as the Association of Medical Officers of American Institutions for Idiots and Feeble-Minded Persons in 1876, was the preeminent association dedicated to research on mental retardation; for generations, its leadership and membership had been involved in the study of mental disability and the development of social policy toward the mentally disabled. The National Association of the Deaf, founded in 1880, was one of many national, regional, and local organizations serving the deaf community; many of these were composed exclusively of deaf people. Professional organizations for the study of blindness and the education of the blind had existed since the 1870s; by the 1940s, both the National Federation of the Blind and the American Foundation for the Blind, as well as other organizations, offered proactive leadership and educational activities on behalf of blind people. And in 1922, a group of educators attending a summer conference at Teachers College, Columbia University, organized the ICEC, the first umbrella organization addressing multiple issues of all recognized categories of disability. Through publications, conferences, lobbying, and support for research and educational programs, these and many other professional organizations generated much wider and visible concern for disability in general and special education in particular.[26]

Lay associations had also begun organizing and engaging in educational and political activity by the early 1950s. The most visible of these was founded as the National Association of Parents and Friends of Retarded Children (NAPFRC). Although the NAPFRC was formally organized in 1950, local groups of parents dedicated to the improvement of education and services for the mentally retarded had been meeting and planning at least since the 1930s in states such as Ohio, Washington, and New York. Their initial purpose was to provide mutual sympathy and support in dealing with the neglect and ignorance that parents of mentally disabled children confronted on a routine basis; the focus was on pooling resources and speaking as a unified voice in dealing with the lack of concern and respect the parents believed institutions and public schools exhibited toward their children. Begun in relative isolation, local organizations began to gain awareness of each other through other groups like the ICEC and the American Association on Mental Deficiency (AAMD). Parent groups gained further attention at the AAMD conventions in 1947 and 1949; and in 1950, the AAMD convention featured two separate programs on parent organizations. With this momentum and increased public awareness, the NAPFRC was formally launched in 1950. The following year, its name was changed to the National Association for Retarded Children (NARC). These various professional and lay organizations would prove instrumental in spearheading changes in public perceptions of mental retardation in particular and disability in general, leading to fundamental transformations in the debates and discussion over the proper approaches to administration and instruction in special education.[27]

Images of Disability

The continued focus on institutions and the growth of parent and professional organizations both drew from and contributed to notable changes in the image of disability and the disabled, especially in the areas of physical disability and mental retardation. After the 1920s, the standard belief that mental retardation was inherited, untreatable, and responsible for a range of social pathologies came under serious question, with the assertion that environmental factors played a much more significant role than previously thought gaining significant ground. During World War II, it became much more apparent that the disabled, especially the deaf and the mentally retarded, were capable of successfully performing jobs in factories and other workplaces, which had been held previously by men who had joined the armed forces. In addition, major technological breakthroughs in various devices used to improve the lives and capabilities of the disabled occurred, and disabled veterans returning from the war heightened the visibility of disability and enhanced sympathy for and appreciation of it.[28]

Also of significance in the evolution of images of disability were articles and photographic essays appearing in the print media that portrayed the lives of the disabled in greater detail and with greater empathy and concern for those affected. During the 1940s, photographs of Letchworth Village, a well-known facility for the mentally disabled in New York, appeared, depicting the respected institution in a negative light. Meanwhile, a series of exposes, many based on information reported by conscientious objectors working at residential institutions for the mentally retarded, reported on the terrible, nearly inhuman conditions of residents in several unnamed institutions nationwide. The abuses and incompetence recorded in these articles shocked policy makers and the public while painting the disabled as all-too-real victims, doing so in an era where the institution was widely considered a viable option for both educating and housing persons with serious disabilities.[29]

During the 1950s, the public became much more aware of the nature of mental retardation and its impact on families with the publication of "confessional literature": books and articles written by well-known personalities who told of members of their families who were mentally retarded. Pearl S. Buck's *The Child Who Never Grew*, which first appeared in *Ladies' Home Journal* in 1950, and Dale Evans Rogers's *Angel Unaware*, published in 1953, each described the struggles their families faced in learning of their child's disability and in securing appropriate medical advice and intervention on their behalf. The frank discussion of these works and others like them elevated mental retardation out of the margins of society and into mainstream, middle-class America; thousands of similarly situated parents found the stories comforting and liberating. As a result, interest in mental retardation in particular, and disability in general, increased substantially, bringing the issues of treatment of and education for persons with disabilities to a more central location in public discourse. Dale Evans Rogers's subsequent promotion of and financial support for the NARC proved highly beneficial for that organization's visibility—and clout. And the consequent shift in image of a mentally retarded person, from one of "menace" to one of a childlike innocence, or "child of the shadows," or "eternal child," rendered the topic more palatable and compelling.[30]

Joining the testimonial or confessional literature were persons who either spoke as a disabled person or who claimed to speak on behalf of the disabled. As early as the 1930s, Henry Latimer, a distinguished blind person whose *The Conquest of Blindness: An Autobiographical Review of the Life and Work of Henry Randolph Latimer* was a featured publication of the American Foundation for the Blind, explained the rationale for more extensive use of day schools for and greater integration of blind children into society. In the mid-1950s, Salvatore G. Di Michael, at the time the executive director of NARC, published a lengthy document claiming to be "speaking for mentally retarded children to America." The document covered a wide range of topics related to the role of NARC, society's treatment of the mentally retarded, and suggestions for improving the status of persons with mental disabilities. Parents and advocacy groups were also becoming more vocal and adamant, as exemplified by an advocacy group for persons with severe disabilities that convinced the Nashville public schools to establish a program for students with severe disabilities in that city. "WHAT CRIME HAVE THESE CHILDREN COMMITTED—that they cannot have these special classes?" they demanded to know. "Why should a small group bar our children from their rightful American heritage?" (emphasis in the original). In contrast, a polite publication entitled *Your Deaf Child: A Guide for Parents*, written by a Northwestern University professor of audiology named Helmer Myklebust, advised parents not to expect any integration of their deaf child with regular class students, that a segregated day school or a residential school were the only viable options. While still relatively muted, the voices of and for the disabled were beginning to emerge with greater frequency and force.[31]

Minority Status and the Disabled: Entering the Civil Rights Era

The concepts of segregation and integration were of course not limited to discussions of special education during the 1950s. The *Brown v. Board of Education of Topeka* decision by the Supreme Court in 1954 constituted one of the most crucial events in American social and intellectual history during the twentieth century, and its sweeping applications and implications were not lost on special education advocates and professionals. As with public education in general, most of the decision's impact on special education would manifest itself after 1960. Even so, broad sociological questions about the segregation and status of minorities in the United States that were instrumental in shaping the court's decision would be applied more and more to persons with disabilities. Such applications would have a dramatic, fundamental impact on discussions regarding the appropriate settings for the education of exceptional children.

One such discussion arose even before the *Brown v. Board* decision. In 1953, John Tenny published an article in *Exceptional Children* entitled "The Minority Status of the Handicapped," stating bluntly that the disabled in the United States found themselves "in a minority status not greatly different from the status of more commonly identified minority groups." He noted the social distance between the handicapped and nonhandicapped; their "unfavorable" portrayal in literature, drama, and "slapstick humor"; their segregation in the schools—in regular classes as well as special programs—comparing it directly to the segregation of "the Negro"; and their "vocational disadvantage over and above that involved in the nature of the handicap." Tenny did observe that there were differences: The status of handicapped children was better than that of the adult; the handicapped did not benefit from community and neighborhood support that, he claimed, helped members of other minority communities; and they were not perceived as creating "social-crisis threats" (an obvious change from their status as "menace" or "burden" of previous generations). Tenny suggested a series of "action programs" to help the disabled improve their social status, including better funding for services and research, better training of "specially prepared teachers," and the development of "intergroup programs," which he labeled "a program of cautious social engineering to reduce prejudice and discrimination." Such programs would make teachers more aware of the conditions facing persons with disabilities and help them facilitate contacts between their exceptional students and various social programs, working to "understand society with its various minority-majority situations and with its prejudices and discriminatory acts." The movement would ultimately "help minority groups to evaluate and improve their own roles to appreciate their right to be different."[32]

In 1958, special educators Norris Haring, George Stern, and William Cruickshank developed a workshop for teachers designed to improve the attitudes of all educators toward students with disabilities. Their workshop employed many of Tenny's ideas involving the intergroup approach. On the basis of their workshop experience, the authors concluded that the troubles teachers had in accepting children with disabilities were similar to those encountered by the majority in attempts to accept and assimilate Blacks. With school integration involving exposure to students who were different, the similarities were striking:

> In both instances a rejected and feared minority group is involved. The absence of specific experiences in either case causes diffuse anxiety. The effect of a formal attempt to modify attitudes . . . seems only to increase the anxiety and to provide a specific focus for the expression of rejection and the development of organized resistance. . . . The confusion of fantasied imaginary conflicts . . . associated with anxieties stemming from anticipation of the unknown is much more difficult to resolve.[33]

By 1960, the nature of the debate over integration had moved well beyond whether segregated programs worked for the children and teachers involved, although such discussions remained at the core of the debate. Hereafter, concerns over the ethical, moral, and legal propriety of segregation and integration, tied to revised considerations of the status, reputations, and capabilities of persons with disabilities in school and society, advanced to the forefront of the work of special education as it gained steadily and dramatically in its size, funding, and impact.

3

1960–1968: Challenging Traditions in Special Education

[T]he progress we can make . . . is in some degree a function of the ideological climate of the times. . . . The cultural climate dictates what can be done, but we can also have a hand in creating the most favorable climate. . . . [I]t is incumbent upon all of us as individuals, as human beings, to work toward the development of the kind of cultural climate . . . which will bring us closer to the acceptance of the kind of philosophy and ideals which will provide for the mentally retarded, and indeed for all who are less fortunate, the necessities to which they as human beings are entitled.

—*William Sloan, President, AAMD, 1963*[1]

As the United States entered the 1960s, American public schools faced challenges in several areas. Discussions regarding social and economic inequality led to intense national soul-searching, with the sweeping implications of the Supreme Court's 1954 *Brown v. Board of Education of Topeka* decision affecting developments in law, politics, social policy, and certainly education. The federal government under President John F. Kennedy determined that much greater involvement on its part was necessary to stimulate action and ensure the enforcement of law, the protection of civil rights for all Americans, and the fulfillment of the promise of public schooling. Among educational professionals, questions about the rigor and direction of curriculum and instruction dominated educational discourse after the launch of the Sputnik satellite by the Soviet Union in 1957, leading to reform efforts in the teaching of most subject areas, especially science and mathematics. As deliberations about the appropriate purposes, character, and methodology of education intensified, special education found itself linked, directly and indirectly, to changes in the teaching of content and subject matter, the organization and structuring of schools, and the classification and categorization of students.

From 1960 through 1968, special education would continue its dramatic evolution, encountering significant challenges to its assumptions, structures, and operations. It maintained its remarkable expansion in terms of its number of programs offered and students served, even while special educators constantly maintained that an unacceptably low percentage of students who needed special education services were actually receiving them. The introduction and solidification of learning disabilities as a recognized category of disability rearranged and expanded the identified population of children with disabilities; the linking of disability with poverty, cultural deprivation, and minority status substantially altered views on the etiology and diagnosis of disability, especially in the area of mental retardation, shifting the ways in which discussions of special education services and purposes were framed. The number of people with disabilities housed in residential institutions kept increasing, leading to severely overcrowded conditions and serious charges that care and treatment of the residents all too frequently was cruel and inhumane. Such developments took place in the context of rapidly expanding federal involvement as well as heated debate about the propriety of segregated schools and settings, including those for students with disabilities.

Expanding the Federal Role in Special Education

Special education's development in the United States during the 1960s was shaped by a multitude of significant social and educational initiatives. Among the most fundamental of these was the dramatic change in the nature and extent of involvement of the federal government— generated under the leadership of President Kennedy—in developing public awareness and shaping policy toward disability, especially in the area of mental retardation. In 1958, during the previous administration of President Dwight D. Eisenhower, Congress passed two laws directly supportive of special education: PL 85-905, which authorized loan services for captioned films for the deaf, and PL 85-926, which provided federal support for training teachers for children with mental retardation. Passage of both laws benefited from the intervention professional and advocacy groups, notably the International Council for Exceptional Children (ICEC; renamed the Council for Exceptional Children in 1958). The National Defense Education Act, also passed during the 85th Congressional session, allowed greater opportunity to develop "categorical support for education of the handicapped." The necessary precedent for more extensive involvement in special education on the part of the federal government thus had been well established by the time Kennedy took office.[2]

Kennedy's interest in special education derived largely from personal considerations. His sister Rosemary had been identified as mentally retarded, and the Joseph P. Kennedy, Jr. Foundation, named in honor of his brother, had been supporting research in mental retardation for some time before his election. Urged on by family members—especially his sister, Eunice Kennedy Shriver—and with the support of the National Association for Retarded Children (NARC), Kennedy in 1961 appointed a Panel on Mental Retardation delegated to examine ways "to consider a national approach to the prevention and management of mental retardation." In presenting a rationale for the panel's creation, the president argued that "We, as a nation, have far too long postponed an intensive search for solutions to the problems of the mentally retarded. That failure should be corrected. . . ." Within a year, the panel, which included several prominent special educators, doctors, and others associated with NARC and the American Association on Mental Deficiency, had produced a report entitled *A Proposed Program for National Action to Combat Mental Retardation*. The report provided guidance to the development of federal programs in special education for the next several years, establishing goals, guidelines, and parameters for expanded research and legislation as well as increased federal funding in education, personnel training, and residential care.[3]

Although the panel dissolved soon after issuing the report, the

President Kennedy and the 1961 poster children for the National Association for Retarded Children at the White House. With the children are, from left, Eunice Kennedy Shriver; the girls' mother; Leonard Mayo, chair of the president's Panel on Mental Retardation; President Kennedy; and Vincent Fitzpatrick, president of NARC.

Kennedy administration's proactive involvement in special education remained strong and continued into the years of the Johnson administration following Kennedy's assassination in 1963. The centerpiece of Kennedy's legislative initiatives was both PL 88-156, which focused on supporting state initiatives, and its companion PL 88-164. This was a comprehensive act that established a Division of Handicapped Children and Youth within the U.S. Office of Education; authorized funding for continued and expanded training of special education personnel; and provided support for more research, research facilities, demonstration projects, and dissemination activities in mental retardation and other areas of exceptionality. The administration also directly or indirectly supported related efforts through the National Institute of Mental Health, the National Law Center of Georgetown University, and the Advertising Council. Kennedy also appointed a Special Assistant to the President on Mental Retardation and continued his direct collaboration with NARC right up until his death. In 1966, President Johnson established a permanent Committee on Mental Retardation; his administration also backed the Elementary and Secondary Education Act (ESEA, PL 89-10), a sweeping law which included grants to states to support the education of children with disabilities, and under PL 89-105 continued support for research and demonstration projects in special education. Most significant was PL 89-750, the amended Title VI of the ESEA, which established the Bureau of Education of the Handicapped and provided grants to states for special education at the preschool, elementary, and secondary levels. By the late 1960s, federal planning, action, and funding had profoundly expanded government commitment to and public awareness of issues related to the education, care, and treatment of persons with mental retardation. As a result, public sympathy, concern, and desire for action in support of disabled children elevated special education to a heightened status in the public discourse while facilitating the expansion of special education services at state and local levels. Although much of the concern and activity was indeed focused on mental retardation, other categories of exceptionality directly benefited from such attention and effort.[4]

Expansion of Institutions for the Disabled

While governmental activity generated significant, mostly positive publicity and discussion regarding special education and exceptionality, residential institutions—for so long the locus of education and treatment for individuals with the most serious and obvious disabilities—became the subjects of intense scrutiny. The number and size of such institutions continued their relentless growth into the late 1960s; as more and more families began to institutionalize their severely disabled family members—with the increased awareness and acceptance of disability generated during the 1950s and 1960s offering encouragement and opportunity to do so—the institutions, reflecting as well the population boom and enhanced postnatal survival rates, grew faster than at any other time in history. Physicians and other professionals felt more comfortable in recommending institutionalization, even as conditions became much more crowded and unhealthy. By 1966, over 127,000 school-age children were enrolled in institutions, an increase of over 40,000 since 1958.[5]

Such pressures and attention revived and accelerated efforts to investigate living conditions in institutions and to hold their administrators and overseers accountable for any problems. Reminiscent of the exposes of the 1940s, investigations during the 1960s proved harshly critical of the quality of education and care at institutions nationwide. Robert F. Kennedy's critique of two New York state institutions (Rome and Willowbrook), Robert Edgerton's expose of Pacific State Hospital in California, and especially Burton Blatt and Fred Kaplan's extensive photographic essay *Christmas in Purgatory* once again shocked professionals, politicians, and the public and led to profound criticism, soul-searching, and policy re-evaluation. By the late 1960s, calls for dismantling the dependency on segregated institutions and instead encouraging a more normalized, community-based approach to caring for and educating this particular population of persons with disabilities gained significant ground. Concurrent and subsequent state and federal legislation and dollars encouraging just such an approach soon followed; consequently, states began the complicated and challenging process of "depopulating" their institutions, reducing their crowded conditions and rendering the institutions themselves more manageable. This radical transition from an institution- to community-based approach to the care, treatment, and education of persons with disabilities both drew from and contributed to the policy of "normalization," an approach imported from Europe during the 1960s that would have a powerful impact on discussions about the integration of the disabled into society characterizing the special education debate during the 1970s.[6]

Advocacy by the NARC

The decade also saw the dramatic expansion of the voice and influence of the most prominent disability advocacy group at the time, the NARC. Empowered by support from popular public figures such as

Classroom scenes from
Christmas in Purgatory.

Dale Evans Rogers and by involvement with the President's Panel on Mental Retardation, the NARC took center stage in much of the conversation concerning rights and policy related to disability. In 1963, the organization published "in the public interest" a Bill of Rights for retarded children, essentially a restatement of its Educational Bill of Rights from 1953. The document asserted the right of "every retarded child [to] opportunities for the fullest realization of his potentialities, however limited, . . . affection and understanding from those responsible for his care . . . . [and] help, stimulation, and guidance from skilled teachers, provided by his community and state as part of a broadly conceived program of free public education." Three years later, NARC issued another statement outlining the organization's "basic aims" and "current prime objectives." In addition to extensive discussion of the need for high-quality institutional care and treatment, the document detailed its efforts to bring "every retarded child," but especially those classified as "trainable," into quality public school special education programs. The statement discussed NARC's cooperative efforts with the ICEC and the U.S. Office of Education to provide such instruction and to ensure a ready supply of competent special education teachers. In particular, the document emphasized the organization's determination to "help States meet their obligations [by helping to interpret] Federal laws to laymen and professionals so that the schools can utilize public funds to initiate or improve their special education programs. . . . NARC will continue to collect, evaluate and develop appropriate instructional materials to assist parents and teachers." NARC clearly saw its mission to not only improve the general status of the mentally disabled in society but also to represent their interests to governments charged with providing an appropriate formal education.[7]

Further Changes in Constructs of Disability

These widespread, sweeping developments in the perception and practice of special education played out on a national stage and involved important elements of the national media as well as governmental and professional circles. Yet equally significant to the development of special education during this period were changes in the understandings and taxonomies of disability itself, changes that brought discussion and debate in narrower circles of educational research, policy, teaching, and administration. Two features of this development had important implications for discussions regarding the inclusion of children with disabilities in regular education settings during the 1960s: the advent of *learning disabilities* as a recognized—and popular—category of disability, and the direct linking or conflation of disability with broader social conditions of poverty, cultural deprivation, and minority status.

The path toward the identification of learning disabilities as its own distinct category of exceptionality began in earnest with the work of Alfred Strauss and Heinz Werner at Wayne County Training School in Detroit during the 1930s and 1940s. Strauss and Werner were interested in investigating the notion of "brain injury" among children. Those deficits appeared strongest in distractibility, behavior, perception, and indications of physiological damage to the brain and/or nervous system. The research of Strauss, Werner, Henry Head, Kurt Goldstein, and others, while controversial, strongly suggested that significant numbers of children exhibited cognitive dysfunction and problems in school performance that could not be explained by traditional constructs of mental deficiency.[8]

Over the next several decades, research into neurological dysfunction leading to mild to moderate disability, still widely referred to as "brain-injury," caught the attention of a number of researchers and practitioners as well as parents; for example, by the 1950s, classes specifically targeted for brain-injured children had been established in Milwaukee and considered in Minnesota. By the early 1960s, the category of "brain-injured children," or alternative terms such as "aphasoid," or "perceptually handicapped," had become widely recognized and accepted among professionals, parent groups, and schools; efforts to establish classes specifically designed for such children occurred across the country. Finally, in a keynote address before a conference sponsored by the Fund for Perceptually Handicapped Children in Chicago in April 1963, noted special educator Samuel Kirk of the University of Illinois described the status of the research to that point and proposed the term *learning disabilities* to describe the behaviors of children who were experiencing such troubles in school. The term struck a chord, and parents in attendance soon formed the Association for Children with Learning Disabilities. The term was used subsequently to indicate a syndrome associated with a wide range of mild to moderate disabling conditions and kinds of poor performance among school children. Learning disabilities would soon become a widely used descriptor for such children and find itself at the center of discussions about how easily and successfully regular classrooms can accommodate children with disabilities, especially those whose condition was considered only mildly disabling.[9]

Further development of a more sophisticated, complex, and instructive understanding of disability emerged from the continuing, often heated debate over the relative impact of biological and environmental factors on the etiology and identification of disabling conditions, especially mental retardation. Linkages between disability and minority status arose from earlier beliefs about the hereditary nature of "feeblemindedness," with doctors, educators, and the general public for the most part convinced that feeblemindedness was almost completely determined by heredity and largely confined to particular ethnic groups, impoverished classes, or "inferior" races. By the 1960s, however, considerable numbers of researchers, doctors, and educational practitioners believed that environmental factors such as living conditions, physical and intellectual resources, cultural deprivation, and child-rearing practices played powerful roles in either causing mental retardation or leading professionals to misdiagnose a child as retarded. While Tenny and Haring et al. had compared the social status and public perception of persons with disabilities with those of racial and ethnic minority groups during the 1950s, special educators and policy makers in the following two decades noted a direct connection, even considerable overlap, among those identified as disabled and minority populations.[10]

In a lengthy monograph published in the May 1958 issue of the *American Journal of Mental Deficiency*, Seymour Sarason and Thomas Gladwin documented in great detail what they saw as the clear connections between the construct of mental retardation and the sociocultural environments of children identified as such. "[Mentally retarded] individuals, of somewhat staggering numbers in our population, come largely from the lowest social classes, or from culturally distinct minority groups, or from regions with conspicuously poor educational facilities or standards," they argued. They then drew a distinction between mental *retardation*, which they viewed as largely being a product of such environments, and mental *deficiency*, which they viewed as a more organic and unalterable cognitive dysfunction. However, in the typically limited and narrow processes of diagnosis and identification common to most public schools, that distinction was not made; consequently considerable numbers of children were identified as mentally retarded and placed in special classes when, according to some, they were not *disabled* but *disadvantaged*.[11]

The conflation of disability and sociocultural disadvantage resonated with special educators and others interested in the evolution of special education, especially in an era that focused on efforts to achieve equal opportunity in schools and society for minorities and other disadvantaged groups. In 1960, Burton Blatt alluded directly to Sarason and Gladwin's work when he challenged the prevailing definition of mental retardation as "basically a physical or constitutional defect." Blatt argued instead that many children placed in special classes for mentally retarded children were there due to "functional rather than constitutional causes," citing what he considered the significant numbers of children—and actually described by Samuel Kirk as early as 1952—"from low cultural levels who are approximately normal at an early age [who] may later become mentally retarded because of their cultural environment or other unknown variables." Blatt accepted the distinction between cultural-familial mental retardation and organically based mental deficiency and urged further study of "the nature-nurture issue." The relation among minority status, poverty, and disability has remained a central topic of research and discussion since, as well as a central concern of the President's Committee on Mental Retardation.[12]

Challenging Traditions of Segregation: Schools

From the late 1950s through the mid-1960s, special education continued its steady growth even while its advocates constantly expressed concern

In its report *MR 67: Mental Retardation, Past and Present,* the President's Committee on Mental Retardation urged President Kennedy to help find ways to bring mental retardation services to "low income, disadvantaged neighborhoods, both urban and rural."

over the number of students who, it was believed, needed special education but were not receiving it. Between 1958 and 1966, the number of formally identified students receiving special education services either in schools, institutions, or other settings more than doubled, from just under 976,000 to more than 2,106,000. Nearly 1,979,000 of those children in 1966 were enrolled in public school programs for the visually handicapped, hearing impaired, speech impaired, crippled or "special health," emotionally disturbed and socially maladjusted, mentally retarded, or "other" (including severe learning disabilities, brain-injured, "culturally restricted," or unreported). That figure also included 312,100 students in "gifted" programs, demonstrating an increased willingness to consider giftedness as an exceptionality worthy of special (and segregated) education. During that same period, the number of persons enrolled in residential schools for children who were deaf, blind, hearing or vision impaired, mentally retarded, or emotionally disturbed rose from 86,412 to 127,200, an increase of almost 68 percent. In those eight years, the number of school districts operating special education programs of some sort increased from 3,641 to 6,711, with the number of teachers assigned to special education in schools and institutions moving from just over 71,000 in 1963 to 82,000 three years later.[13]

A variety of reasons helps explain such dramatic increases in the number of students, teachers, and programs in special education during the 1960s. To begin with, two decades of establishing and strengthening permissive as well as mandatory state legislation that called for more thorough searching and identification of children with disabilities had clearly had an effect; more children requiring special education were being located in the community, brought to school, and accommodated in special programs. Making this easier were the increased tolerance and understanding of disability and the concurrent willingness of families to acknowledge a child's disability and seek help for it. The aftereffects of World War II—with the heightened visibility of disabled persons and greater recognition of their potential for contributing to society—combined with the testimonials and encouragements of noted members of the community to facilitate this.

Another likely factor was the continuing effort to develop and implement more sophisticated procedures and instruments for diagnosing and classifying disabling conditions among children. Continued refinement of intelligence and other psychometric testing, more accurate and reliable instruments determining modality and other sensory deficits, and procedures involving more complex approaches to determining disability—including greater experience on the part of teachers, administrators, and parents—meant that students could be identified with greater confidence. And as awareness of the options and possibilities offered through special education increased within school systems, referrals to such programs—both appropriate and inappropriate, as had always been the case, no doubt—likely increased as well. The added category of learning disabilities would have a tremendous impact on the number and kind of students referred to special education, but that effect did not show significantly until several years after the formal affirmation of the category in 1963. It should also be noted that some of the numbers, especially those alleging so many children being under-served, were at best educated guesses that were not necessarily indicative of a real increase in the number of eligible children.

Data from 1963 also showed the extent to which children with various disabilities were in fact integrated at least to some extent in schools at the time in the United States. According to the data, every student with identified speech disorders spent at least some time in the regular classroom. The majority of students with "visual handicaps," both partially blind and totally blind—more than 52 percent—spent at least some time in regular classes, as did 62 percent of students with hearing impairments (although it should be noted that more than 85 percent of totally deaf students spent all their time in fully segregated classes, schools, or institutions). In contrast, only 11.5 percent of children identified as "crippled and special health problems" participated to any degree in regular class settings; for children identified as emotionally disturbed and socially maladjusted, that figure was slightly more than 26 percent. Fewer than 2 percent of students identified as "middle range" mentally retarded ever joined in regular classroom activities. These figures included all children of school age, so many of these students were being educated in institutions, hospitals, at home, or other segregated, nonpublic school locations.[14]

Despite this remarkable growth, special education professionals remained convinced that it was insufficient in relation to need and demand. Data reported for 1966 claimed to show that only 35 percent of children requiring special education services were receiving it, based on enrollment figures and prevalence estimates. The percentages of students being appropriately served by category included 57.5 percent for the visually impaired, 56.3 percent for the speech-impaired, 46.8 percent for the mentally retarded, 31.1 percent for gifted children, and only 17 percent, 12 percent, and 7.8 percent for hearing-impaired, emotionally disturbed, and "crippled" children, respectively. Romaine Mackie, a prominent compiler and analyst of special education statistics, spoke for most in the special education profession when she wrote, "It has been demonstrated that most handicapped children can have satisfying, productive lives if they receive appropriate education, training, and care. Thus, America cannot afford to ignore the gap that remains." The result was further entrenchment of special education as a unique, separate entity in public education with its own structures, settings, funding, and training—in short, as a force to be reckoned with, one that was gaining increasing recognition and acceptance by practitioners, administrators, legislators, and the public.[15]

By the early 1960s, a definitive structure for special education placement in public schools, institutions, and other settings had become fairly well established. Data compiled by Mackie in 1963 showed 1,570,370 children enrolled in public school special education programs. Of those 456,145, or approximately 29 percent received instruction in a full-time special class or special day school; 986,509, or almost 63 percent, spent part of their school day in a special program and part in regular classes. The balance of these students were educated at home, in a hospital, in a sanatorium or convalescent home, in a residential school, or not reported. Mackie and other proponents of special programs argued that more students needed to be in special programs, either part-time or full-time, thus acknowledging the advisability of placing more and more students at least part of the day in segregated settings. However, she too recognized that differentiating students with disabilities from other "children who have special needs such as the environmentally deprived, migrants, and children of cultural minority groups" was a difficult and complicated process that needs to be factored into developing more school programs "within and outside of special education. . . . New concepts call for distinction between those who are handicapped by capacity . . . and those who are only functioning as handicapped due to their environments." Mackie noted that while too many children who required special education were not receiving it, others were perhaps capable of greater participation "in some of the streams of general education" because of improvements in America's schools. Thus the challenge to special education was to develop, expand, and sustain distinct special education programs while doing a better job of determining who among America's schoolchildren truly needed them. To that end, many states published guidelines for districts and parents outlining procedures and offering suggestions for identification, classification, and instruction.[16]

In a 1962 examination of the structure of special education in American schools, Maynard Reynolds proposed a pyramid-like framework for describing the various levels and programs then serving students with special needs. His framework suggests that even in the early 1960s there was a strong recognition that many students with special needs could be served in the regular classroom, especially if provided with consultation or supplementary teaching services. With a base labeled "most problems handled in Regular Classroom," Reynolds's pyramid ascended to special assistance in the regular classroom to resource room, part-time special class, full-time special class special day school, and upward to residential institutions, hospitals, or treatment centers. His scheme noted that as a child moved up the pyramid, the more severe his or her disability would likely be; it also noted that the flow upward toward more isolated settings should occur "only as far as necessary" and should move downward to more integrated settings "as soon as possible." Reynolds provided no data on the number of students at each level, in part because he commented that there was—and should be—considerable fluidity of student movement among the stages and overlap among the stages themselves. "The strategy proposed here," he wrote, "requires variety and range in programs for all handicapping areas, continuing assessment procedures to assure changes in placement at appropriate times, and coordinated planning and placement services covering all levels." While acknowledging that "it is . . . inexcusable to delay or deny special services when they are needed," Reynolds also argued that "it can be a disturbing experience for a child to be placed in a special class or any other type of special program. . . . The prevailing view is that normal home and school life should be preserved if at all possible." Reynolds's view thus clearly, if indirectly, challenged the then-common view that the most effective way to improve special education services to students with disabilities was to organize more segregated settings and place the students in them.[17]

The intensive process of growth for special education may have felt comfortable to its professionals, but parents involved in the process struggled to accept what had become to them a powerful and mysterious force. Parents of students with disabilities faced the assumed superior expertise of teachers, administrators, and medical personnel regarding their children as well as the difficult and uncertain prospects of formal schooling for children who up to that time had often been marginalized or ignored. A representative survey published during the decade showed a considerable amount of satisfaction, but it also expressed disempowerment, anxiety, and uncertainty among parents regarding the education of their children. The survey revealed that the majority of parents felt "that their child's present school situation represents the best possible school arrangement that could be obtained" and held positive views of special education teachers. Some parents, however, held quite negative views about that placement. The survey also noted that relatively few parents had "any real understanding of the nature of difference in curriculum between the special group and a regular classroom" and that their assumptions about special education were "essentially a remodeled perception of what regular schooling was for them. . . . The interpretation of the rationale, curriculum and specialized techniques of special education has not been brought to parents in any degree of depth."[18]

Concerns about Segregation in Special Education

Before startling the nation with the publication of *Christmas in Purgatory*, Burton Blatt published one of the first significant comprehensive critiques of special education of the 1960s. In an article entitled "Some Persistently Recurring Assumptions Concerning the Mentally Subnormal," Blatt examined several basic assumptions then prevalent about the special education of children with mental retardation using a "fact or fiction" framework. As noted earlier, he questioned the prevailing notion of mental retardation as being a permanent "physical or constitutional defect" and offered some detailed discussion of how manifestations of apparent mental retardation in the classroom may actually have been a result of poverty or cultural deprivation associated with minority status and hence be improvable. In addition, Blatt offered a critique of special classes, asserting that the quality of education typically offered in special classes is poorer and certainly less imaginative than that in regular classes and calling for "an infusion of bold, creative thinking into the field. Experimentation with new and unorthodox methods and materials must be encouraged." Blatt also challenged assumptions that mentally retarded children tended to be more "physically limited" and unavoidably much more prone to delinquency and crime than their nondisabled peers. In raising these concerns, Blatt hoped "to reduce the rigidity of a profession that resists change; to provoke the creative to seek answers; and to instill a healthy unrest in all who work with the mentally subnormal." His critique clearly established possibilities for seeing children with mental retardation as being less distinct, distant, or harmful, and for envisioning a special education that was less marginalized within and thus more compatible—and potentially more integrated—with the complex world of general education.[19]

The 1960s produced a multitude of studies and commentaries that questioned the efficacy of special classes in achieving the goals of special education. This body of research, which had occurred to a limited degree for decades, examined special classes from the perspectives of academic achievement as well as social and emotional adjustment, focusing mostly on special classes for students with mental retardation. Studies investigated whether such students learned more and/or faster in segregated settings or in regular classes, and they looked at which type of setting helped mentally disabled students develop stronger social skills, achieve greater self-confidence, or gain greater social acceptance among nondisabled peers.

The results of such investigations proved conflicting and ultimately inconclusive. Several scholars claimed that their research failed to prove the common assumption that students with mental retardation in special classes achieved greater success academically than those still enrolled in regular classes; in fact, several studies showed the opposite. Some research claimed to show that regular class placement provided a healthier environment for the social and emotional development of mentally retarded children; others claimed to demonstrate that such placement typically led to rejection of such students by their normal peers, effectively reproducing a segregated, isolated environment for such children in the regular classroom. Still others found that there were no significant differences in either academic achievement or social/emotional adjustment between the two settings. Almost all suggested further research.[20]

The absence of definitive answers regarding comparisons between segregated special classes and regular class placement for children with mental disabilities was not lost on prominent special educators. G. Orville Johnson, an eminent scholar who had engaged in some of the 1950s efficacy research, noted the enormous amount of time, resources, and expectations invested in running segregated special classes, but pointed out what he considered strong evidence that special classes were inferior in terms of academic achievement and not significantly better in personal and social development. Then, in a passage that was cited and reproduced repeatedly over the next twenty years, he argued:

> It is indeed paradoxical that mentally handicapped children having teachers especially trained, having more money (per capita) spent on their education, and being enrolled in classes with fewer children and a program designed to provide for their unique needs, should be accomplishing the objectives of their education at the same or at a lower level than similar mentally handicapped children who have not had these advantages and have been forced to remain in the regular grades.

The skepticism about the propriety and effectiveness of segregation represented a small but ultimately potent perception in special education, one that by the end of the decade would capture the mind and question the soul of the field.[21]

Lloyd Dunn's Challenge to Special Education

Such ambivalent, even troubling research outcomes challenging the very value of segregated special classes played a significant role in the preparation of one of the most seminal documents in American special education: Lloyd Dunn's "Special Education for the Mildly Retarded— Is Much of It Justifiable?" Published in the September 1968 issue of

Exceptional Children, Dunn's article linked the efficacy research with issues of ethics and equity in both special and general education and concluded that in far too many cases, the reliance on special classes for children identified as mentally retarded—in Dunn's view, often mistakenly so—was not only ineffective, it was indefensible. "I have loyally supported and promoted special classes for the educable mentally retarded for most of the last 20 years, but with growing disaffection," he confessed. "In my view, much of our past and present practices are morally and educationally wrong. . . . Let us stop being pressured into continuing and expanding a special education program that we know now to be undesirable for many of the children we are dedicated to serve."[22]

Dunn presented a series of what he considered serious concerns about special education as then currently practiced. First, segregation itself troubled him deeply. Dunn cited research and court decisions that he believed clearly demonstrated segregation's deleterious effects on the education of children. He directly compared segregation's impact on minority children with that on children with disabilities, noting how thousands of minority children had been erroneously identified as disabled and then shoveled off to segregated, euphemistically labeled "special education" settings, which courts would likely deem as inherently racist, unequal, and unacceptable. Dunn maintained that the homogenous academic grouping found in special education and tracking programs—like those which had recently been declared discriminatory and unconstitutional by a Washington, D.C. judge—constituted academically inferior environments for essentially the same reason that race-based segregation was found unconstitutional: Separate, segregated programs are inherently unequal. Dunn cautioned that court cases could well emerge from overt segregation of minority children in special education programs—a prediction that proved accurate—and concluded that special education was to a great extent merely a transfer of disadvantaged children from one segregated setting to another.[23]

Consequently, Dunn flatly stated that far too many children from minority and/or underprivileged backgrounds were being misidentified as mentally retarded or emotionally disturbed on the basis of cursory identification procedures and inappropriate use of intelligence testing. Dunn argued that those children—of whom he estimated 60 to 80 percent were from "low status backgrounds"—were then placed in segregated, inherently inferior special education settings "at the expense of the socioculturally deprived slow learning pupils themselves," raising "serious educational and civil rights issues which must be squarely faced."[24]

Dunn's critique extended to the diagnosis and identification processes in special education that he believed led to essentially useless and certainly stigmatizing labeling of students. He argued that the entire process was far too facile and was vested in the wrong hands, namely psychologists who administered some cursory intelligence testing, with "the purpose . . . to find out what is wrong with the child in order to label him and thus make him eligible for special education services. In large measure this has resulted in digging the educational graves of many racially and/or economically disadvantaged children." Dunn wrote that these labels then have highly negative effects on the attitudes and practices of teachers responsible for the education of these children as well as on the students themselves. He also maintained that the consequent segregation for special education services "probably has a serious debilitating effect upon [the disabled child's] self image. . . . We cannot ignore the evidence that removing a handicapped child from the regular grades for special education probably contributes significantly to his feelings of inferiority and problems of acceptance." In addition, he argued, regular classes by this time had become much more able to accommodate children with mild retardation due to team teaching, flexible grouping, more stimulating curricula, better training and specialization among teachers and staff, and more sophisticated technology. Dunn also referred directly to the efficacy literature, which he stated failed to demonstrate the value of special class instruction for mentally retarded children. Such evidence against special classes convinced him that schools needed "to find better ways of serving children with mild learning disorders than placing them in self-contained special schools and classes."[25]

Dunn then offered a detailed vision as to how special education could reinvent itself along more effective, and certainly more ethical, lines. He describes an "intuitive" and "clinical" approach that focused

on the teacher's assessment of the child's educational needs and a labeling process that emphasized not the child's deficit but rather the appropriate educational approach to be taken. He suggested expanding the
opportunities for itinerant and resource room teaching that would
make trained special educators available to all children in school and
would involve those teachers much more in regular classroom activities. He presented a detailed approach to curriculum development that
emphasizes environmental modifications, motor development, sensory
and perceptual training, speech and communication training, person-
ality development, social interaction training, and vocational training.
Such an approach, he asserted, would be advantageous to all children
with disabilities, not just those with mild mental retardation, and in
fact would enhance the holistic education of all children in school. In
concluding his article, Dunn called on all educators to accept the complex and difficult challenges of restructuring special education:

> Teachers and state and local directors and supervisors of special edu-
> cation have much at stake in terms of their jobs, their security, and
> their programs which they have built up over the years. But can we
> keep our self respect and continue to increase the numbers of these self
> contained special classes for the educable mentally retarded which are
> of questionable value for many of the children they are intended to
> serve?[26]

While Dunn's article has been the mostly widely cited, it was by no
means the only commentary from that era that questioned traditional
practices and fundamental assumptions of special education. Particularly since 1960 critics not only challenged the efficacy of special classes
but also expressed great unease, even distaste, for other standard features, most notably programs rooted in segregation; the process of
identifying and labeling students; the assumption that *better* special
education most commonly meant *more* special education; and the stark
separation of training programs for special education and general education teachers. Critics of special education also shared the desire to
imagine, design, and ultimately implement alternative approaches to or
paradigms for the education of students with disabilities that would

most likely involve a fundamental restructuring not only of special education but of entire public school systems as well. By the early 1970s, many prominent educators both within and "outside" the field of special education were in open revolt against what had become an entrenched and mostly segregated system of special education. Such critiques helped shape the 1970s and beyond as a period of intense self-reflection and calls for fundamental change in the structures and practices of the field. Subsequently, litigation and legislation pertaining to the care and education of persons with disabilities that dramatically altered the legal bases and expectations for teaching students with disabilities proliferated, setting the stage for the eventual passage of PL 94-142, the Education for Handicapped Children Act, in 1975.

4

1968–1975: Mainstreaming as the Alternative to Segregation

LOYD DUNN's article, which openly questioned so much of special education's tradition and character, stimulated the kind of critique and self-reflection in the field that Dunn undoubtedly hoped it would. Over the next several years, a number of scholars and practitioners in special education reacted to Dunn's critique by examining their perceptions of not only segregationist practices but also the status and future of the field. Their analyses and reflections often focused on special classes for children with mental retardation yet were typically applied and extended to important fundamental elements of special education in general. Such topics included diagnosis and labeling, the limitations and ethical concerns of segregation, the nature and extent of training teachers of exceptional students, the extent to which students with more severe disabilities might be able to participate in regular education programs, and ultimately the true motives of special educators who argued for continued expansion of special education services and development of a separate special education structure. While there continued to be staunch defenders of traditional policies and practices in special education, the voices of those demanding new structures and approaches gained considerable strength, backed by important court decisions and legislative action that led directly to PL 94-142.[1]

New Conceptions of Special Education

Between the publication of Dunn's article in 1968 and the passage of PL 94-142 in 1975, a plethora of articles, essays, and studies discussing integration and segregation in special education were published, primarily but not exclusively in scholarly education and special education journals. Dozens of such pieces appeared during this intensely active time in the field; even so, a few managed to capture the essential elements of the debate and were therefore cited often and in detail in print and conference discussions for years to come. In addition to the Blatt, Johnson, and Dunn articles of the 1960s, seminal, frequently cited literature condemning segregation in special education included Florence Christoplos and David Renz's "A Critical Examination of Special Education," James J. Gallagher's "The Special Education Contract for Mildly Handicapped Children," Milton Budoff's "Providing Special Education without Special Classes," Arthur Kraft's "Down with (Most) Special Education Classes," and another Orville Johnson article, this entitled "Special Education for the Inner City: A Challenge for the Future or Another Means for Cooling the Mark Out?" Evelyn Deno and Stephen Lily wrote two of the most widely cited articles criticizing the entrenched, segregationist structure of special education in their respective articles "Special Education as Developmental Capital" and "Special Education: Teapot in a Tempest." These authors represented a variety of backgrounds and areas of expertise: College professors, research institute scholars, psychologists, school administrators, and teachers all found a voice in the professional literature's critique of segregation and special education.

A primary tenet for many critics was that segregation of any student for whatever reason was ethically indefensible, especially given the by-then widely acknowledged connection between special education and the school lives of many children from minority or otherwise disadvantaged backgrounds. Dunn made this point concisely: As noted earlier, he argued that there were too many "deprived" children "from low status backgrounds" being assigned to special education. Another common view was that the practice of segregation in special education reflected the relative ease of banishment and marginalization of certain students compared with the difficult, complex task of restructuring regular classrooms to effectively accommodate more students with special needs. The assumption was that teachers and parents preferred the ability grouping and segregation of exceptional students due to "social and personal values," even though no evidence supported such practices, and that segregation also denied children in regular classrooms the opportunity to learn about and from exceptional students. Although viable alternatives to segregation existed, these were routinely avoided because the struggles children with disabilities often experienced in meeting general education goals were deemed "intolerable" by educators in regular classrooms. Other critics reiterated the arguments that segregation was legally and ethically untenable in light of the *Brown vs. Board* decision as well as the conspicuous absence of compelling evidence that segregated settings bore clear, definitive, and long-lasting benefits for either the students with special needs or their nondisabled peers. Arthur Kraft, a psychologist for the Long Beach, California, public schools, asserted that segregation in special classes was antithetical to the schools' efforts to prepare special education students for successful integration into society after completing school. He claimed that most students were dumped into special classes and other special education programs because teachers put pressure on administrators and other school professionals to remove troublesome "problem" children from their charge, and special education was the easiest way to accomplish this. (Recall that this argument has been a fundamental characteristic of special education's assigned role in schools since the mid-1800s.)[2]

Another concern often expressed about special education's practices involved the process of identifying and labeling exceptional children. The concerns addressed not only the practical aspects of the process—how children are selected for testing, and how the presence of a disability or disabilities is established—but also the effect disability labels had on the children, the teachers, and their lives in and beyond the classroom. "Placing any label on any human being does violence to that individual uniqueness which is the joy of humanity," argued James J. Gallagher. "Yet, we do it all the time because it is such a convenient communication shorthand." He acknowledged that labels can serve useful purposes for planning and instruction but reiterated serious reservations about a typically simplistic process that so often caused a high number of minority and disadvantaged children to be stigmatized and segregated from the regular classroom with little or no chance of ever finding their way back. "It is easy to conclude," he wrote, "that the bridge that should exist between special and regular education is, in fact, not really there. The traffic all goes in one direction." Others asserted that the process of labeling a child as exceptional reflected a societal rather than individual orientation, establishing merely that a child has a deficit or a problem that renders her or him unable to achieve the socially determined basic goals of education and legitimating that child's removal from the classroom—with but limited benefit for making decisions about the child's education. Psychologist Jane Mercer's detailed challenge to labeling practices appeared in her widely read 1973 book *Labeling the Mentally Retarded: Clinical and Social System Perspectives on Mental Retardation* and brought the critique of labeling to a much wider professional and advocate audience. Labeling was thus seen by many as a largely unavoidable but deeply flawed feature of special education, one that should not be abandoned but should be used much more carefully and with much greater discretion.[3]

In the 1970s, two reports from the President's Committee on Mental Retardation reiterated the strong connection between minority status, culturally deprived upbringing, suspect labeling, and placement in special education programs, stating the committee's concern that such placement reflected an inherent cultural bias in the identification processes that needed to be eliminated. Such concerns rendered the understanding of mental retardation, emotional disturbance, and other disability categories significantly more complex and problematic in terms of identification and instructional programming. Perhaps even more importantly, it added multiple dimensions to discussions about the efficacy and propriety of segregated settings for students with disabilities, linking as it did the notion of exceptionality with issues of race, class, ethnicity, and privilege within the context of providing equal access to educational opportunity.[4]

The Reform of Special Education

By the early 1970s, the debate over "segregation vs. integration" of exceptional students had extended to the realm of critique and calls for fundamental reform of special education in general. Building on the important reflections of special educators during the 1960s and catalyzed by Dunn's 1968 article as well as the intense response to it, a number of scholars took a sharply critical eye to several features of special education itself: its thinly disguised trend toward empire-building; its relationship with regular education; its dependence on segregated programs and ill-defined curriculum whose demonstrated value and success were tenuous and debatable at best; and its potential role in wholesale efforts at school restructuring and reform.

The traditional measurement of special education's success had been the steady increase in its size, funding, and influence, with the growth of the number of special classes and the percentage of presumably eligible children enrolled in special programs serving as the primary benchmarks of accomplishment. This "proliferation, as though the 'appetite increased by what it fed on,'" as one critic put it, at times seemed to displace the appropriate and authentic identification and education of children with special needs as the ultimate focus of efforts in the field. There had been "a long standing assumption that its success can be judged by how many more children are enrolled in special education programs this year than were enrolled last year or 10 years ago," wrote Evelyn Deno, a scholar at the University of Minnesota who wrote extensively about the need to reform special education. "Too much special education practice seems to assume that we already know what to do and have only to march firmly ahead until enrollment figures match incidence estimates." Christoplos and Renz asserted that "special educators have often taken satisfaction and pride in the rapid expansion of special education programs" but that such sentiments did not mesh with either research estimates or democratic philosophy. "We cannot ignore, therefore, the disquieting possibility that self-perpetuation may be a factor in the continuation and expansion of special education programs"; consequently, "the rapid growth of special classes . . . has but limited justification." Stephen Lilly, another noted critic, lamented what he viewed as the Council for Exceptional Children's (CEC) and U.S. Bureau of Education for the Handicapped's efforts to perpetuate structures and programs "which [encourage] hardening of the categories and proliferation of services of dubious value" and wondered if these organizations avoided reforms that "would introduce uncertainty into a reasonably stable system." To such critics, special education seemed too intent on expanding its size, scope, and influence—and too little concerned about the effects of its structures and practices on tens of thousands of school children.[5]

Special education's status quo also depended to a significant extent on its relationship with general education, one that some considered inappropriate and subservient. Dunn had bluntly stated that special education lived "at the mercy of general educators, who have referred their problem children to us." Orville Johnson charged that "special education is part of the arrangement for cooling out students" and as such was "helping the regular school maintain its spoiled identity when it creates special programs . . . for the 'disruptive child' and the 'slow learner.'" In an even harsher assessment, Deno wrote,

> Special educators or remedial teachers of any stripe must ask them-
> selves whether they are justified in continuing to try to fix up the chil-
> dren that an inadequate instructional program has maimed so they will
> fit better into a system that should be adjusting itself to the learning
> needs of the children rather than expecting children to adjust to them.
> By providing the regular system with a respectable out for its failure to
> give every child equal opportunity to realize his potential, special edu-
> cators may be perpetuating systems that ought to be challenged to
> change.

Over the years, several scholars had criticized the nature of the special class curriculum. Many argued that there was little substantive difference between the special class curriculum and that of the regular grades, only that it was offered at a slower pace and provided fewer opportunities for intellectual stimulation—an approach one critic labeled as "less teaching and more babysitting" and "anemic." Special education, therefore, constituted a system that drew its purpose and meaning from the inadequate, even cowardly treatment of large numbers of "problem" students by general education—a toxic relationship that to critics was ethically and professionally indefensible.[6]

Given such an unsatisfactory relationship and the alleged debilitating effects of purposefully segregating considerable numbers of children, many critics argued that special education needed to dig deep within itself and stake its place as an agent of fundamental change and reform in education. Deno located special education reform within the generalized calls for radical educational reform, which permeated the period of the late 1960s and early 1970s. Determining that "one army of special educators is committed to the point of view that education's mode of address must change drastically if the precious uniqueness of each child's humanity is to be cherished," she called on the field to "conceive of itself primarily as an instrument for facilitation of educational change and development of better means of meeting the learning needs of children who are different." In her view, special education was "in a unique position to serve as developmental capital in an overall effort to upgrade the effectiveness of the total public education effort." Echoing Dunn, Stephen Lilly focused on the predominant group of children identified as mildly disabled: "It is with regard to these children that we as special educators have trouble justifying our practices both socially and morally. . . . It is the position of this writer, based upon consideration of evidence and opinion from many and varied sources, that traditional special education services as represented by self contained special classes should be discontinued immediately for all but the severely impaired. . . ." In other words, special education needed to reinvent itself—not necessarily disappear, but restructure and reprioritize so that most school children could experience better opportunities to develop necessary intellectual and social skills.[7]

Suggestions as to how to realize such fundamental change in special education ranged from the highly conceptual to the specific, emphasizing in particular the need to rethink the labeling process as well as reorganize classrooms to better accommodate a broader diversity of learners. One article suggested jettisoning the use of categories of exceptionality, claiming that considering the children in terms of their behavior rather than their handicap would improve efforts to develop appropriate educational goals and activities. It also stressed the importance of social integration, noting that "inclusion of deviates in regular classrooms" would positively affect the development of attitudes of the "deviant" and "normal" populations toward each other. Another article presented a detailed argument in favor of abandoning the traditional rigid age-grade approach to grouping children in favor of more flexible, "ungraded" groupings that would give teachers and students greater latitude in successfully providing for individualized instruction. Lilly proposed redefining what is meant by exceptionality—that it should refer not to a child's particular "handicap" but rather to a school situation: "An exceptional school situation is one in which interaction between a student and his teacher has been limited to such an extent that external intervention is deemed necessary by the teacher to cope with the problem." Such a definition, he wrote, would require an analysis of the uniqueness of the student, teacher, and classroom situation and encourage an educational response tooled directly to that particular situation. This approach would have a better chance of success within an integrated setting than one that focused on a label rather than a child and that failed to account for specific needs or opportunities. Lilly went even further when he proposed a "zero reject model" for special education, that is, one in which "once a child is enrolled in a regular education program within a school, it must be impossible to administratively separate him from that program for any reason. . . . We need a zero reject system to protect ourselves from our tendency to blame and label children for failure and to prevent acceptance of easy 'solutions' to complex instructional problems." The "zero reject" notion entered the literature of the 1970s as a widely cited model, one to which legislators and advocacy groups for the disabled would refer repeatedly.[8]

Underscoring this shift in perspective to one that was integration-focused and child-centered, Evelyn Deno offered her conception of a "cascade of services," a capsized pyramid structure that emphasizes instructional settings for students that only require segregation unless other efforts within regular classrooms have failed. The pyramid inverted that which Reynolds proposed in 1962, shifting the emphasis from segregated to integrated programs; it became the standard diagram depicting the preferred model of organizing delivery services in special education and remains so to this day. Together with Dunn's extensive suggestions regarding curricular and organizational change, these visions of a new special education provided educators and administrators in both general and special education with much to ponder by the early 1970s. The critics realized the speculative nature of their models but argued adamantly that such change was necessary. As Lilly said of his vision, "Just what the new system would assume is negotiable, but at least it would be built upon a definition of exceptionality which is both truthful and realistic. Let us remove the onus of inadequate education settings from the shoulders of its victims."[9]

Challenging Traditions of Segregation: Institutions

As special education expanded its scope and reconsidered its ways of identifying as well as describing its clientele in a climate of dramatic national reconsiderations of equality, exceptionality, and governmental intervention, the questions of where the education of children with disabilities should take place, who should be responsible for it, and what such education should entail became even more critical. As the two primary locations for special education, residential institutions and K–12 schools continuously considered these issues internally even as others examined these settings and offered a variety of observations, criticisms, and suggestions regarding the roles they should play.

Institutions faced assault from two fronts by the early 1970s: public exposure of the often deplorable and inhumane conditions found within, and solidifying beliefs that such isolated, sheltered, even unreal environments were functionally counterproductive and ethically indefensible. In addition to the exposes noted earlier, institutions and the state governments responsible for their control faced litigation from guardians or other representatives of residents as well as more demanding standards and guidelines promulgated by concerned professional organizations. Litigation brought in Alabama, Wisconsin, and in federal court affirmed the constitutional rights of institution residents; this permitted challenges to institutionalization and the practice of using unpaid resident labor for institutional maintenance. Following the charge given by President Kennedy to vigorously seek ways to improve the quality of life for persons with mental retardation, the United Nations General Assembly in 1971 adopted a "Declaration of General and Special Rights of the Mentally Retarded," and the Accreditation Council for Facilities for the Mentally Retarded was established. The latter developed standards and regulations that, when adopted by the federal government, gave teeth to institutional reform efforts.

Finally, by the late 1960s and early 1970s, the federal government began subsidizing local communities to establish smaller, less isolated residential settings for former residents of institutions who had been forced out of the institutions as the states began to reduce their size.[10]

Institutional reform that reduced resident population, reassigned many of those residents to smaller community-based settings, and brought to bear stricter standards and guidelines for operation was grounded to a large extent in public pressure, court decisions, and government action. Within the world of special education, the move toward the concept of *normalization* also proved fundamental to such reform. Normalization and the concept of *deinstitutionalization* were and are closely linked in both theory and policy in special education and disability rights. Initially developed in Europe, normalization was popularized in the United States by Wolf Wolfensberger, a strong advocate for the mentally retarded and for institutional reform. According to Bengt Nirje, one of the principle's originators, "the normalization principle means making available to all mentally retarded people patterns of life and conditions of everyday living which are as close as possible to the regular circumstances and ways of life of society." This includes "normal rhythms" of the day, week, and year, the "opportunity to undergo the normal developmental experiences of the life cycle," and the chance to "experience the coming of adulthood and maturity through marked changes in the settings and circumstances of their lives." Such activities would include to the maximum extent possible typical patterns of social and sexual relationships, respect and understanding from others, and economic activity. And directly related to the issue of institutionalization, normalization requires "that if retarded persons cannot or should not any longer live in their family or own home, the homes provided should be of normal size and situated in normal residential areas, being neither isolated nor larger than is consistent with regular mutually respectful or disinterested social interaction and integration."[11]

In his book *The Principle of Normalization in Human Services,* Wolfensberger supplied an extended interpretation of normalization and discussed its application to the issue of residential institutions for the mentally retarded in great detail. He described the social construction of the mentally retarded individual as "deviant" and the serious impediments such a construction poses to efforts to normalize the lives of persons with mental retardation and to integrate them authentically and meaningfully into the community. He then offered specific discussions of how the normalization principle would shape decisions about architecture, residential services, mental health, vocational training, care and treatment of persons with severe disabilities, and social and sexual relationships. While acknowledging the complexity and struggle inherent in achieving such goals—and explicitly recognizing the threat that normalization can pose to certain persons and groups—Wolfensberger believed that "overprotecting" the mentally disabled constituted a flawed approach and that all persons should have the opportunity to achieve dignity in the community, often by engaging in activities and practices that involve significant risk. Normalization called on the mentally retarded and their supporters to seek their rightful place in the community, even at the risk of the struggles and complications that all members of the community would face. To Wolfensberger, the traditional isolated, segregated, sheltered residential institution for the mentally disabled diametrically opposed normalization efforts and should be abandoned.[12]

The work of Wolfensberger and his European and American colleagues proved highly influential. The *Principle of Normalization in Human Services* was widely read, and Wolfensberger and his colleagues championed the causes of normalization and community-based services for mentally retarded persons through widespread presentations and publications. His work drew upon and complemented that of the International League of Societies for the Mentally Handicapped, an organization dedicated to the principle of normalization and spearheaded by Gunnar Dybwad. Dybwad was a prominent special educator who had served as a consultant in 1963 to the first special assistant to the organization's president on mental retardation, Dr. Stafford Warren, and as executive director of the National Association for Retarded Children (NARC) from 1957 to 1964. As staunch and highly visible advocates for the causes of normalization and deinstitutionalization, Wolfensberger, Dybwad, the International League, and other scholars successfully challenged the paradigm of segregationist residential institutions, bringing the concepts of normalization and integration to the forefront of debate in special education. This body of literature did not focus on children or schools, instead concentrating on the lives of adults and their possibilities for successful integration into community settings. Even so, by the late 1970s, these principles had become widely—though not universally—accepted as desirable, obtainable, even mandatory goals for all persons with disabilities, with the concept of normalization becoming a central idea in the advocacy for inclusion in schools in order to "normalize" the educational lives of children.[13]

Integrating Children with Severe and/or Multiple Disabilities

By the early 1970s, another controversy in the field had begun brewing: the issue of whether children with severe disabilities should also be brought into the regular classroom. The almost exclusive focus of discussions and research on integration had been children with mild disabilities, especially mental retardation. However, with deinstitutionalization and the movement to employ community-based settings for children with more severe disabilities, the possibility that such children might start attending public schools in significant numbers drew the attention of a number of scholars and practitioners in the field. Even most of those demanding greater integration and fundamental reform in special education expressed their belief that such children still did not belong in the regular classroom. Dunn, for example, explained that his suggested blueprint for change in special education did not advocate doing "away with our special education programs for the moderately and severely retarded, for other types of more handicapped children, or for the multiply handicapped." Stephen Lilly offered a similar caveat before describing his vision of special education reform. Milton Budoff was quite direct:

> All children cannot be accommodated within general education, no matter how flexibly organized. . . . Regardless of the viewpoint of the teaching staff, psychotic, extremely hyperactive, moderately and severely retarded, or multiply-handicapped children may not be

accommodated within the formal academic portions of the school day. . . . They may be assigned a regular class home room and participate in one or more nonacademic assignments, but cannot be bonafidely integrated into the regular class. . . . Essentially intact class programs for children whose behavior and/or learning potential dictates the need for very specialized care and educational help, or who have very limited adult prognoses will still be required.

Psychologist Arthur Kraft was even more blunt, stating that "trainable and low-level educable mentally retarded children should remain in special classes. There can be no bones about this. They are in to stay and will remain so throughout their school career."[14]

Such strong assumptions and convictions were not shared by all critics. In their examination of the potential for integration of children carrying a variety of disability labels, Christoplos and Renz questioned the presumptuousness of those who assumed the regular classroom was no place for children with severe and/or multiple disabilities. Calling attention to the isolation and stigma that segregation allegedly brought to *all* children, the authors emphasized the positive effects of participation in the regular class and challenged the standard claim that the presence of severely disabled children was too disruptive to the regular education students and better for the disabled children themselves:

Even if children with obvious and severe physical exceptionalities are assumed to require highly specialized teaching, unique for each exceptionality (and this assumption is questionable), isolation in special classes is not thereby the only action feasible. Special helping teachers (itinerant or school-based), resource rooms, and other well-known educational manipulations are possible alternatives. *Anticipated interference with social intercourse resulting from regular class placement of exceptional children is an indefensible explanation for their placement in special classes* (italics in the original).

They also confronted what they believed to be the thinly veiled contempt for the disabled:

> Care must be taken lest the discomfort and anxiety of the normal pop-
> ulation at the possibility of having daily and close interaction with
> deviant individuals become its cause of restriction of such interaction.
> That segregation is for the good of the exceptional, rather than for the
> comfort of the normal population, may be a deluding rationalization.

These concerns would become more open and prominent as the move toward the more complete integration of exceptional children contin-ued into the next decade.[15]

As perhaps the most prominent advocacy group for persons with disabilities at the time, the National Association for Retarded Citizens (previously Children) felt compelled to weigh in on the issue of inte-gration and segregation of students with disabilities. In a 1971 policy statement, the NARC noted that "there remains considerable contro-versy and confusion" as to what children should be integrated, and when. While stating that "whenever possible the retarded child should be integrated into the mainstream of regular education," it cautioned that "integration must be accomplished on an individual rather than group basis" and viewed as a "continuum." Along this continuum, the statement observed, children with increasingly more obvious and/or serious disabilities should expect to spend more and more time in seg-regated settings, and "some severe and all profoundly retarded children should receive their basic instruction in self-contained units." The NARC firmly believed that segregation remained a viable, successful, and at times highly necessary approach to placement and instruction in special education.[16]

Issues in Teacher Training

The impact that teacher training and teacher attitudes had on both the extent and effectiveness of attempts to integrate exceptional children into the regular classroom attracted more attention as integration efforts proceeded. Teacher training programs designed specifically to address the instruction of students with disabilities had existed since at least the late 1800s: Between 1949 and 1961, the number of institutions of higher education offering certification programs for teachers of mentally retarded children grew from 22 to 140. Although there was a lack of consistency in the content of such programs, their steady growth continued through the 1960s as the number of special classes steadily increased. Nevertheless, the credentials of teachers actually staffing special classes often fell short of ideal. A 1967 survey of Iowa teachers, for example, revealed that 20 percent of special class teachers did not hold a bachelor's degree, and more that 43 percent had not qualified for an appropriate endorsement in mental retardation. In addition, states were slow to enact legislation that moved beyond bare-minimum requirements for teachers of special classes by requiring extended specialized coursework. Although improvements did occur in the 1960s, one scholar commented that such improvements were inadequate considering the "rapid expansion" of special classes and other special education programs. Concern was also expressed about the high rate of teacher turnover in the special classes themselves, a problem in settings where teacher and student might stay together for several years.[17]

Of greater relevance to efforts to move toward integration of exceptional students in the regular schools were the personalities, attitudes, and professional relationships found among special class and regular class teachers. According to several special educators, very little research on teacher behaviors and attitudes had been conducted prior to the mid-1960s, yet there existed widespread acknowledgement that these factors undoubtedly had a significant impact on the operation and achievement of special classes and other programs for exceptional students. For example, a private school administrator wrote in *Education and Training of the Mentally Retarded* that lower expectations among special class teachers and students contributed to low levels of achievement; special education teachers, by focusing on the "problem" or "deficit" inherent in a child's disability label, were "conditioned to expect less," and that attitude was often transferred, if unconsciously or inadvertently, to the students. A study published in 1972 found that teacher perceptions of exceptional students varied depending on the disability of the child, with "sociopsychological" labels (mental retardation, emotional disturbance) generating more negative and pessimistic perceptions than labels focusing on physical disabilities. That study found no significant differences in attitudes of special education teachers and regular education teachers, implying that extensive training in special education had little discernible effect on teacher attitudes toward children with disabilities. A 1975 study reported that "approximately 60% of both regular and special educators felt that self-contained classes had proven to be more effective than regular classes for the mildly handicapped," but also found that there existed serious communication problems between special educators and regular educators in planning and implementing cooperative instructional programs. It called for continued research on such factors, noting that successful integration of special education students demanded that the roles of teachers in the process be better understood.[18]

Pedagogical and Legal Outcomes

The intense reflection and debate regarding the status and future of special education and its emphasis on segregated programs manifested itself in two highly important realms: policy and practice in the public schools, and legislation and litigation at the state and federal levels. Acting on efforts to integrate exceptional students more fully and authentically in public school settings, a considerable number of school-based and/or district- and statewide initiatives experimented with more inclusive approaches to teaching students with disabilities. Although their success was mixed, general results proved encouraging, setting the stage for more widespread and comprehensive efforts, which, by the mid-1970s, had come to be known as *mainstreaming*. The need for such efforts was guaranteed by a number of important court decisions and legislation pertaining to the education of exceptional children, which upheld the right of children with disabilities to be educated alongside their general education peers to a far greater extent than ever before. These decisions and laws, culminating in the passage of the Education for All Handicapped Children Act (PL 94-142) in 1975, compelled schools and other public institutions to formulate and support such efforts—to move the integration/segregation debate past the question of *whether* and on to the question of *how*.

Between 1970 and 1975, the number of school districts implementing pilot efforts in the integration of special education and regular education, and the literature describing and interpreting these efforts, increased dramatically. According to a 1974 study, four factors proved instrumental in stimulating these efforts: the failure of research to establish the effectiveness of special classes; the recognition of the cultural bias and consequent inappropriate diagnosis of children as disabled, especially those from minority and/or disadvantaged backgrounds; the counterproductive, even debilitating effects of labeling; and court litigation establishing the right of disabled children to an equitable and appropriate education in regular education settings to the maximum extent possible. The state of California took a leadership role in developing integrated special education programs: While no more than ten districts in the state had such programs in 1971, the number of districts formally applying to the state for approval of their programs more than doubled the following academic year. Other districts in the state created their own programs without having to seek state approval. By 1974, at least thirty different programs nationwide had been identified and described in the professional literature; some of these programs were in fact university training models that had ties to local districts.[19]

In addition to specific and concrete school programs, other generic models for and approaches to special education integration were either described or proposed by special educators. Gilbert Guerin and Kathleen Szatlocky of the University of California at Berkeley examined eight California districtwide programs and classified them under four types. These included programmed partial integration, where special class students were programmed into regular classes for specific blocks of time and for certain subject areas; the combination class, where a few mildly mentally retarded children were in regular classes the entire school day, supported by one of the regular class teachers who held a special credential; the learning resource center, where the special class teacher functioned instead as a resource room teacher and the exceptional children, all of whom were assigned to regular classrooms, would meet with her as needed; and the learning disability groups model, where the children with disabilities remained in their assigned regular class and a special education teacher would support them on an itinerant basis. Robert Bruininks and John Rynders of the University of

Minnesota described in detail four different approaches: individually prescribed instruction, an objectives-based program "interlinked with diagnostic tools and teaching materials"; Downriver Learning Disability Center, which emphasized "pupil assessment as an approach to planning instruction"; the Educational Modulation Center, which focused on developing specific skills and instructional materials that would enable an exceptional child to remain in the regular class; and the Harrison Resource Learning Center, which used a resource room model to support the work of disabled children enrolled in a regular class while training University of Minnesota students in the "skills of prescriptive teaching." Donald MacMillan of the University of California at Riverside suggested the combined use of three different approaches—preventive programs, transitional programs, and model regular programs—to help districts answer the question "to what extent, and under what circumstances, can a wider range of individual differences be accommodated in the regular class than is presently the case?" And among the most observed and discussed approaches was the Vermont Consulting Teacher Model, an intensive and comprehensive program whereby special education teachers served as consultants and instructors in preparing regular classroom teachers to not only meet the needs of exceptional children in their classrooms but also to prepare them to successfully accept the authority and responsibility for designing and implementing effective individualized programs for those students.[20]

Although the scores of programs described in the literature varied considerably in terms of specific policies and practices, these descriptions do reveal some features that applied to most of the programs, at least in general terms. Most focused on programs designed for children with mild disabilities, the majority being the educable mentally retarded. Most exhibited considerable flexibility in the ways students could be and were grouped, with many emphasizing organizing learning groups according to learning needs or behaviors rather than specific categories of disability. In general, the programs were designed and implemented at the school or building level, rather than districtwide, allowing for more successful adaptation to the particular needs and dynamics of the students in a particular setting (along the lines Stephen Lilly suggested). Most of the programs also provided significant opportunities for preservice and inservice training, often relying on special educators to guide and counsel regular class teachers. Closely connected with such training was the acknowledged importance of time for planning and communication, with all participants being actively involved in discussion and development. Finally, the majority of these programs not only involved the regular class teacher more directly in planning and instruction for exceptional children; they also vested significant authority over and responsibility for the effective education of special education students in the regular class teachers, so that they would become the primary locus of control and decision-making—often relying extensively on consultation with and support from special education teachers—regarding the educational programming and well-being of students with disabilities assigned to regular classes. These features revealed dramatic shifts in the assumptions, policies, and practices of special education from its traditional emphasis on specialized training and segregated settings.

As noted above, a primary factor in spurring the development of such programs were court decisions and state legislation addressing the rights of exceptional children to an education in a nonsegregated setting. Although *Brown v. Board of Education* was decided in 1954, it took until the early 1970s for litigation specifically addressing the concerns of children with disabilities to occur. Between 1971 and 1975, at least forty-six "right to education" cases were decided in twenty-eight states; together they helped determine that "the right of a handicapped child to participate in a publicly supported educational program was no longer to be questioned." These cases addressed not only the right of children with disabilities to attend public school—a practice routinely ignored by school districts unwilling or unable to accept them—but also helped establish the principle that these children had the right to be taught in settings alongside their "normal" classmates.[21]

Of all these cases, four garnered the most attention and hence are considered the most influential in establishing the right to a public education in as normal an environment as possible. Two of these, *Pennsylvania Association for Retarded Children v. Commonwealth of Pennsylvania* (1971) and *Mills v. Board of Education of the District of Columbia* (1972), challenged the practice of excluding disabled children from

public schools. *PARC v. Pennsylvania* involved a class action suit on
behalf of fourteen different families who argued that their children,
identified as mentally retarded, were not receiving the free public education to which they were entitled. These families challenged the Pennsylvania law absolving school districts of responsibility for
"uneducable" or "untrainable" children. The case was settled by a con-
sent agreement, where the state of Pennsylvania acknowledged its
responsibility to an appropriate education in a public school at no
expense to the family. The *Mills* case similarly was a class action suit,
brought on behalf of seven children in the District of Columbia; these
children exhibited various disabilities, including brain damage, hyperactivity, epilepsy, mental retardation, and orthopedic impairment. This
case was brought before a federal court and resulted in a decision in
favor of the plaintiffs, stipulating that the District of Columbia schools
had to provide all children—regardless of the severity of disability—
with a free, appropriate education. The court responded to the district's
plea that such a policy would be prohibitively expensive by ordering the
district to nevertheless factor the needs of disabled students in equi-
tably in determining and distributing budgets.[22]

Two other decisions from California directly affected the processes
of identifying and labeling exceptional children: *Diana v. State Board of
Education* (1970) and *Larry P. v. Riles* (1972). The *Diana* case involved
nine children of Hispanic origin who had been placed in special education classes as a result of their poor performance on standardized intelligence tests. The *Larry P.* case focused on a single African-American
child but examined the same issue: placement procedures involving
standardized tests and other allegedly culturally or linguistically biased
methods of identification of disability. In both these cases, the courts
found that the processes districts used for identifying mentally retarded children were indeed biased and discriminatory, either due to the
child's lack of language skills in English or the cultural bias alleged to
be inherent in intelligence tests. The courts noted the overrepresenta-
tion of minorities in special education and charged the schools to
address this concern by changing identification procedures and providing any necessary compensatory education. These decisions called close

attention to special education's processes in identifying and ultimately segregating such children on the rationalization of disability and sought to protect the rights of minority students who might otherwise and unnecessarily be placed in segregated special education programs.[23]

Meanwhile, the various states had moved ahead of the federal government in rewriting special education law. Fueled, according to one study, by "widespread publicity and political activism on behalf of concerned parents and professionals," state legislatures moved to adopt legislation requiring that public school districts accept and accommodate disabled children rather than turn so many away. As of 1972, more than 70 percent of the states had enacted such legislation; by 1975, every state but two had some provision requiring districts to provide a publicly supported education for "at least the majority of their handicapped children." Many of these anticipated both the spirit and the language of the federal law passed in 1975.[24]

While federal legislation had assisted in the development and funding of an organized and influential structure of special education, and had addressed a number of issues related to disability—most notably Section 504 of the Vocational Rehabilitation Act of 1973, which protected the civil rights of the disabled—PL 94-142 was the most sweeping and comprehensive federal legislation to date. Injecting itself directly into public school policy through the protection of the rights of disabled children, PL 94-142 mandated "a free and appropriate education in the least restrictive environment" for all children identified as disabled. Children could no longer be excluded from public education solely on the basis of their handicap; they were entitled to identification, diagnosis, and classification procedures that were free of bias and that used multiple sources of information; they were assured the right to the Least Restrictive Environment, an instructional setting that was as close to that established for their regular education peers as feasible; they were granted the right to receive an education that was appropriate for their needs and abilities, as stipulated in an "individualized education program"; and they were guaranteed due process of law in all aspects of implementing those rights. The law did not use the terms *integration, mainstreaming,* or *inclusion;* it did, however, challenge every school district in the country to render its schools significantly more accommodating and accepting of children with special needs, doing so in integrated settings to a much greater extent than ever before. [25]

Looking to the Future: The Meaning of Mainstreaming

The passage of PL 94-142 signaled a new era in special education, one in which integration—to use the then-current term, *mainstreaming*—served as the operative paradigm. By no means were all special educators completely supportive of this shift from special education's traditional reliance on segregated programs. Some argued that the harsh critiques of the efficacy of special classes also failed to show conclusively any harmful effects of such classes, that in fact studies did show their benefits, especially in developing self-competence and social skills. The absence of rigorous, reliable studies of any sort should not be taken as a sign that special classes needed to go, it was argued; on the contrary, it suggested that much more extensive research was needed before jettisoning such a long-held, widely supported practice. Others stated plainly that special classes had never been properly implemented or supported and therefore their condemnation was premature and unfair, similar to attacking a "straw man." Still others maintained that Dunn's article, taken by many to be a clarion call for the abolition of segregated instruction, had been grossly misinterpreted and misused in the course of the debate, that in fact Dunn acknowledged the need for separate classes for certain groups of exceptional children. To many, the segregation/integration debate had become polarized, to everyone's detriment, and the jump to the "bandwagon" of integration—to see it as the one true way for special education—was overly rushed and ill-advised. Edwin Martin, an otherwise staunch advocate of what had become known by 1974 as the mainstreaming movement, admitted:

> I am concerned . . . about the pell-mell, and I fear naïve, mad dash to mainstream children, based on our hopes of better things for them. I fear we are failing to develop our approach to mainstreaming with a full recognition of the barriers which must be overcome.[26]

Nevertheless by 1976, the shift toward mainstreaming and more thorough integration of special education with regular education was undeniable. In 1973, the CEC approved a policy statement regarding the "Organization and Administration of Special Education." This official statement sanctioned the concept of a free public education for all children and endorsed a closer linkage of special education and regular education to enhance and influence the ideas and practices of each upon the other. It formally adopted Deno's "cascade of services," emphasizing the importance of the regular classroom in the education of most disabled children, noting that "under suitable conditions, education within the mainstream can provide the optimal opportunity for many exceptional children." The CEC statement still advocated separate budgets for special education and continued delineation of separate responsibilities for special and regular education and appeared cautious about the move to mainstreaming; even so, it was a significant shift of position from its earlier emphasis on building a strong and influential separate structure for special education, the position Lilly had criticized in 1970.[27]

The shift from "integration" to "mainstreaming" as the accepted terminology for efforts to integrate children with special needs more fully and authentically into regular school settings took place slowly. Unlike learning disabilities, another widely used term in special education that was essentially born and baptized the day Samuel Kirk used it in his conference paper in 1963, *mainstreaming* seemed to emerge out of informal discussions, conference papers, and other vehicles for its use rather than from a single definitive statement. The word was rarely used if at all in the professional literature into the early 1970s; the first book to use it in the title appears to have been Keith Beery's *Models for Mainstreaming*, published in 1972. Nonetheless, the term was being widely employed in scholarly articles and conference paper topics by 1974.

Given its collective, ephemeral origin, it is not surprising that determining a universally accepted definition of the concept proved problematic. "For better or for worse," stated one position paper in 1976,

we have entered the era called 'mainstreaming' in special education. This is evident in the space or time given to the concept and its imple-

mentation in nearly every periodical or conference in special education. But our entry into the new era has its confusion and its uncer-
tainties, as is evident in the attempt to find a consensus definition of
the concept.

The authors of this paper observed that two basic definition "camps"
existed: one that merely stressed its desegregating and delabeling
intent, and the other that typically featured "some steps in which a
child is assisted in a regular education program." Thus the ideological
as well as pedagogical elements and ramifications of mainstreaming
were apparent in the variety of definitions used. Jane Mercer offered a
vague definition as simply a "continuum of special education services,"
with one end of the continuum being children succeeding with no special assistance in the classroom. By contrast, Jack Birch's definition
included fourteen descriptors for authentic mainstreaming practices.
Perhaps the most widely cited definition was that offered by Kaufman
et al. in their 1975 article, "Mainstreaming: Toward an Explication of
the Construct," which defined *mainstreaming* as

> . . . the temporal, instructional, and social integration of eligible excep-
> tional children with normal peers based on an ongoing, individually
> determined, educational planning and programming process requiring
> requires clarification of responsibility among regular and special edu-
> cation administrative, instructional, and supportive personnel.

To Kaufman et al., a proper definition of mainstreaming emphasized
the intention to integrate special education students, to plan and adapt
their individualized instruction carefully, and to coordinate the work of
all educational professionals for the benefit of the child.[28]

Regardless of the specifics of any formal definition, the concept of
mainstreaming was both exciting and troubling to those concerned
about the future of special education. Supporters as well as skeptics of
mainstreaming recognized its likely profound impact on the structure,
operation, and financing of public schools and sought to caution all
interested parties about potential challenges. MacMillan, Jones, and
Meyers, for example, sought to distinguish the apparent nobility of the

principle from the complications of its implementation—as they put it, "belief is not enough" to make mainstreaming work. They also expressed concern about the readiness of regular education to adapt to the mainstreaming approach, the attitudes harbored and preparation experienced by regular education teachers, and the divergent perspectives of administrators, teachers, and child advocates. Noting problems and frustrations that arose in some programs in California, they argued that "if mainstreaming is not a fad . . . then regular class teachers are going to have to have some background on, at least, the mildly handicapped learner." They concluded their article by noting that "the enthusiasm over mainstreaming [possibly] stems from the belief that it is morally right. In the present article the authors have attempted to explore some of the potential problems of mainstreaming. It is hoped that solutions, in the form of hard work and challenges, can be found now to avoid a future of frustrations." Edwin Martin condemned the powerful effects that segregated institutions of all sorts had on human beings, asserting that "on this basis alone, the human concern for human beings, we must attempt to have handicapped children, in sight, in mind, and in settings where they will receive the fullest measure of our educational resources. If we also believe their actual achievement in educational terms will also prosper—so much the better." Even so, Martin expressed wariness about the future of mainstreaming. In a moving and highly instructive statement, he said:

> There is a mythical quality to our approach to mainstreaming. It has faddish properties, and my concern is that we do not deceive ourselves because we so earnestly seek to rectify the ills of segregation. We must seek the truth and we must tolerate and welcome the pain that such a careful search will bring to us. It will not be easy in developing mainstreaming, but we cannot sweep the problems under the rug.

Over the next several years, that effort would yield a remarkable store of ideas and practices that would reshape special education while reaffirming the essentials of a debate that had existed for generations.[29]

5

1977–1985: Refining the Concept of Integration

> At its root, mainstreaming is a moral issue. It raises age-old questions: How do we want to live with each other? On what basis should we choose to give priority to one value over another? How far does the majority want to go in accommodating to the needs of the minority? .... To the extent that we put discussion of mainstreaming in the context of education and schools, we are likely to find ourselves mired in controversies centering on law, procedures, administration, and funding. These are legitimate controversies because they deal with practical, day-to-day matters that affect the lives of everyone. But the level of difficulty we encounter in dealing with these matters ultimately will be determined by the clarity with which the moral issue is formulated. This clarity will not "solve" the practical problems but, at the very least, it will make us more aware of two things: (a) so called practical matters or problems always reflect moral issues, and (b) differences in moral stance have very practical consequences.
>
> —*Seymour Sarason & John Doris, 1978*[1]

ADJUSTING TO the mandates of PL 94-142 as well as to the implications and possibilities of mainstreaming proved to be a tremendous challenge in developing and implementing special education in the public schools of the United States during the late 1970s and into the 1980s. The implementation of this sweeping and complicated federal law proceeded slowly and fitfully as high hopes and a strong sense of promise faced off with considerable obstacles and significant resistance, while the conceptual and practical aspects of mainstreaming underwent extensive scrutiny as scholars, administrators, teachers, parents, and certainly students attempted to realize its objectives and spirit in classrooms across the country. These initial adjustments to the new realities of and expectations for special education were directed at the immediate needs and concerns of schools and families. Nevertheless, they also stimulated continued debate in the field as well as even stronger calls for the radical, fundamental reform of both special and regular education—calls that would, in turn, energize defense and support of more traditional approaches to the education of children identified as disabled.

Issues of Definition

The search for a universally accepted definition of mainstreaming continued over the next decade without success. Not only did mainstreaming have multiple definitions, but the term *least restrictive environment* found in PL 94-142, a phrase which formed the cornerstone of the mandate to bring exceptional children into regular classrooms whenever possible, experienced the same fate. Consequently, debates about mainstreaming's or the law's efficacy, viability, or propriety foundered as discussants often did not share a common understanding of the spirit, the character, or the practice of the term or the legislation.

In 1975, the Council for Exceptional Children (CEC) offered its vision of what mainstreaming was—and was not. To the CEC, mainstreaming meant "providing the most appropriate education for each child in the least restrictive setting . . . looking at the educational needs of children instead of clinical or diagnostic labels . . . looking for and creating alternatives that will help general educators serve children with learning or adjustment problems in the regular setting. . . . [and] uniting the skills of general education and special education so all children may have equal educational opportunity." It was not, according to the CEC, "wholesale return of all exceptional children in special classes to regular classes." Nor was it keeping such children in the regular setting without providing them with "the support services they need," or "ignoring" those children whose needs require a separate setting, or merely a less expensive way to deal with exceptional children.[2]

Other proposed definitions expressed themes similar to those found in the CEC definition as well as in that provided by Kaufman and colleagues, as noted in the previous chapter. For example, James Paul, Ann Turnbull, and William Cruickshank considered mainstreaming to be "an educational slogan" that was "an attempt to focus on the strengths and learning potential of children in contrast to the historical preoccupation . . . with the deficits of children." To them, mainstreaming was a systemic initiative that "challenges the entire educational ecology. . . . Protecting the child's right to the best education program that can be provided while protecting him or her from stigma or unnecessary restraint is a mission that is as complex as it is necessary." The definition provided by David Johnson and Roger Johnson of the University of Minnesota reflected major elements of PL 94-142 and stressed the socialization purpose of integration through mainstreaming:

> The provision of an appropriate educational opportunity for all handicapped students in the least restrictive alternative, based on individualized education programs, with procedural safeguards and parent involvement, and *aimed at providing handicapped students with access to and constructive interaction with nonhandicapped peers* (emphasis in the original).

Others viewed the term more simply; for example, as "the growing and often legislatively mandated practice of integrating exceptional children into the 'regular' classroom." And to some, Jack Birch's definition of mainstreaming as "enrolling and teaching exceptional children in regular classes for the majority of the school day under the charge of the regular class teacher" most closely represented their perception.[3]

To other special educators, however, these views of mainstreaming were overly limited and cautious. Rejecting the notion of mainstreaming as something that should involve only some exceptional children for only part of the time, Margaret Wang, who would become one of the leading figures in the call for full inclusion of exceptional students, saw mainstreaming as "an integration of regular and exceptional children in a school setting where all children share the same resources and opportunities for learning on a full-time basis. . . . Mainstreaming in this context is seen as a way of eventually eliminating the need for remedial programs and tracking systems for exceptional students." Gunnar Dybwad, the venerable advocate of more integrative practices for the mentally retarded in all aspects of society, dismissed most definitions of mainstreaming as too narrow, saying that mainstreaming should more closely align itself with normalization and take into account the economic, social, and vocational aspects of life as well. The range of definitions confounded those who attempted to understand the authentic principles and practices of main-streaming. Robert Bogdan of Syracuse

Margaret Wang

University, who undertook perhaps the first extensive qualitative study of mainstreaming, noted, "As we entered schools to start our observations, the clear concepts of 'mainstreaming' and 'disability' turned into mirages. They blurred when we tried to use them to order the murky world we were in."[4]

Similar struggles of definition existed with the terms *least restrictive alternative* or *least restrictive environment,* a cornerstone concept of PL 94-142 whose meaning and subsequent implementation nonetheless proved difficult to establish in a uniform fashion. As Harvey N. Switzky and Ted Miller of Northern Illinois University observed, "while the notion of the least restrictive alternative frequently appears in professional literature and in recent legislation . . . it is doubtful that this concept raises a single connotation or promotes a unified course of action for service providers. . . . the concept of the least restrictive alternative is only partially defined and thus only partially understood." Part of the problem was that the term was not defined specifically in the law; another aspect was that the concept implied—if not required—a certain amount of fluidity in image and structure as well as case-by-case implementation. "What must be recognized and is at the heart of applying the least restrictive alternative to education," wrote one analyst, "is that different children have different educational strengths and weaknesses which dictate the need for different education programs." If placement in a regular classroom meant that a child would not have access to the services, materials, or techniques she deserved under her Individualized Education Plan, then the regular classroom would not be the least restrictive alternative, or the *appropriate* setting, even if it might be the ideal *preferred* setting. Deaf children who rely on sign language for communication, a child with a chronic health condition requiring certain medical equipment, or a student whose behavioral abilities led to unmanageable disruption of the learning environment thus would most likely have more segregated settings as their least restrictive environment—assuming the schools could demonstrate that they had done all they reasonably could to accommodate the child in the regular class as the law required. Disagreement as to what constituted reasonable accommodation or necessary services rendered identification of the truly least restrictive environment problematic for many students in special education. Thus, while both *mainstreaming* and *least restrictive alternative* (or environment) connoted a generalized understanding of a more integrative approach to special education, the terms continued to mean different things to different people, complicating both research and practice.[5]

Even so, most of these definitions shared certain characteristics. Clearly the emphasis was on the purposeful effort to have more children with disabilities spend more time in regular classrooms, where their instruction would be individualized appropriately and supported by technology and specially trained personnel. Of particular note were the added expectations that the regular classroom teacher assume greater authority and responsibility for the education of exceptional children and that socialization was an important, perhaps even primary, purpose of mainstreaming. "The net effect of mainstreaming, if it is successful, will be to get students together," wrote Paul et al., while Johnson and Johnson asserted that "by far the most important resource [in mainstreaming] is interaction with nonhandicapped peers who provide entry into the normal life experiences of members of our society. . . ." These definitions typically pointed to both the administrative and pedagogical aspects of mainstreaming, underscoring the importance of planning, training, communication, and shared vision. The end result, it was hoped, would be better and more appropriate education for all children and a breaking down of barriers between special and regular education.[6]

Issues of Controversy and Uncertainty

The debate over mainstreaming was by no means limited to matters of definition. As had always been the case, the idea of greater integration of children with disabilities drew criticism from a number of commentators with a variety of perspectives. Ronald Childs, director of the Newell C. Kephart Child Study Clinic, saw mainstreaming as a direct threat to the traditional vocational and functional curriculum for children with mental retardation, a "drastic change" in curriculum that was ill-advised and inappropriate. Childs believed an increase in academic study, which he saw as an inherent outcome of mainstreaming, would frustrate students and fail to prepare them for their life after school. Frank Gresham of Louisiana State University argued that mainstreaming was "based in part upon three faulty assumptions": that mere physical placement of disabled children "will result in an increase in social interaction" with their nondisabled peers; that it will cause "increased social acceptance" of the disabled by the nondisabled; and that mainstreamed exceptional children "will model or imitate the behavior of their nonhandicapped peers as a result of increased exposure." He deemed such beliefs as "misguided" because mainstreaming did not allow for preparation or provisions to make such outcomes possible. Switzky and Miller reiterated the concern that the clash between the principle and the practice was too severe, with implementation typically failing to achieve the goal represented in the principle or even be able to anticipate what it might need to do to accomplish it.[7]

In their comprehensive review of some of the conditions and assumptions affecting the implementation of mainstreaming, Seymour Sarason and John Doris identified several key points of opposition. To begin with, they noted, historically any movement to achieve greater integration of children with disabilities had been "spearheaded by a dedicated minority" and had "at every step of the way . . . encountered opposition, especially from personnel in schools, institutions, and state agencies who saw how drastic the proposed changes would be for them." The same held true for the mainstreaming initiative, which at least indirectly challenged the motives of the opposition and called for fundamental reworking of the ways schools did business—two factors that would naturally generate strong resistance. Mainstreaming also threatened the deeply ingrained and generally comfortable divisions between special education and regular education, not just in schools but in the training programs at colleges and universities; this separation was not only familiar—and hence comfortable—but the isolation it generated contributed to suspicion and miscommunication that could dramatically impede discourse and reform.[8]

Sarason and Doris also called attention to skepticism and resistance among the public and within the schools themselves; as an example, they cite a magazine article that reported on the consequences of Massachusetts's mainstreaming law, passed a few years earlier in 1972. The article was entitled "Schooling for Kids No One Wants" and noted "it could prove as controversial as busing," at the time a highly charged issue in the state. They also referred to a newspaper article from that same year describing PL 94-142, which focused on the resistance to the law among teachers and their unions and implied that special education students were getting more than their deserved share of the public education budget. Of even greater concern, they observed, was the remarkable lack of preparedness most districts exhibited in addressing the requirements stipulated by PL 94-142. To Sarason and Doris, this public and professional resistance, combined with the schools' general state of unreadiness to respond to the demands of the mainstreaming law, demonstrated that mainstreaming's proponents had failed to convince important stakeholders of its merit or viability. Edward Zigler and Susan Muenchow of Yale University shared that caution by calling attention to mainstreaming's rapid ascension without proper support:

> Mainstreaming can have many positive effects on handicapped children, but this policy will be an empty slogan, with many negative effects, if not accompanied by adequate teacher training and support services. Furthermore, mainstreaming must not be presented as a

panacea for handicap. . . . Much more work is needed to determine not just which children, with which handicaps, can benefit from main-streaming, but also what the environmental nutrients are that promote full development.[9]

While the debates over the definitions, merits, and drawbacks of main-streaming continued, those involved in implementing mainstreaming in schools and in getting teachers ready for it were active on multiple fronts. Professional literature in education—not just those publications limited to special education—responded to the realities of PL 94-142 by increasing dramatically the number of articles and even whole issues dedicated to the purposes and practices of mainstreaming. For example, the journal *Teacher* announced in its June 1977 issue that it would feature an article on mainstreaming in every issue on "the handicapped child in the regular classroom." Other periodicals in education, psychology, and of course special education—scholarly journals as well as practice-oriented journals for regular classroom teachers—published mainstreaming-related articles on a regular basis. Meanwhile, textbooks used in special education courses in colleges and universities by the late 1970s typically included at least some discussion of main-streaming, outlining what it involved and offering suggestions on how to implement it. While some of the literature was critical of main-streaming, most accepted it on philosophical and practical terms and concentrated on getting teachers and administrators ready for it. And despite methodological obstacles, many of which dated from the early efficacy studies and later examinations of academic achievement and socialization processes of special vs. regular class placement, researchers turned to mainstreaming to determine its effectiveness and find ways to help make it work—or even find alternatives to it.[10]

Approaches to Mainstreaming Under PL 94-142

Traditionally, special education had delivered the great majority of its specialized instruction to specially labeled children in settings separated from the regular classroom, using teachers who—at least theoretically—had received specialized training for the task. The passage of PL 94-142 was a seismic event for school districts and states across the

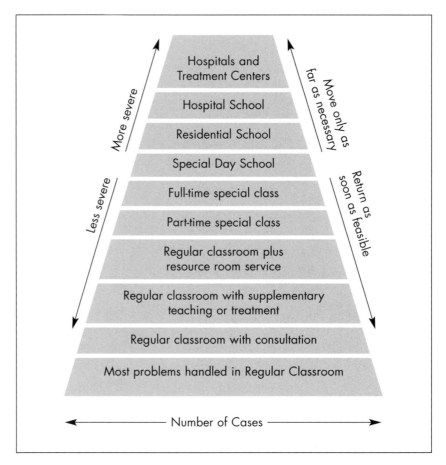

Figure 5. Reynolds's pyramid illustrating special education programs. From Maynard C. Reynolds, "A Framework for Considering Some Issues in Special Education," *Exceptional Children* 28 (March 1962): 368. Copyright 1962 by the Council for Exceptional Children. Reprinted with permission.

country: Its demands for all students to be served appropriately in some way, in a "least restrictive environment," with an "individualized education plan," by public schools at no cost to families presented monumental challenges in staffing, funding, curriculum development, and other logistical concerns. As a result, administrators turned to familiar approaches in order to render their task as painless and efficient as possible. The "cascade of services"—the pyramid-like schematic repre-

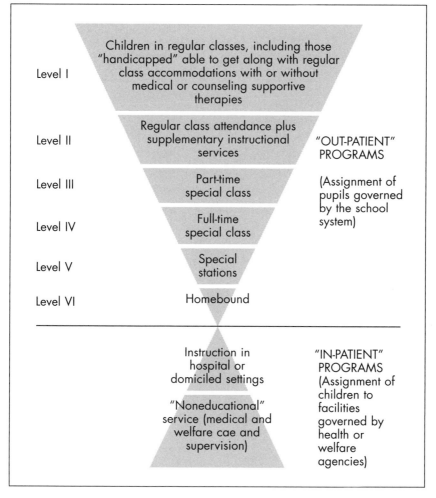

Level I — Children in regular classes, including those "handicapped" able to get along with regular class accommodations with or without medical or counseling supportive therapies

Level II — Regular class attendance plus supplementary instructional services

Level III — Part-time special class

Level IV — Full-time special class

Level V — Special stations

Level VI — Homebound

"OUT-PATIENT" PROGRAMS

(Assignment of pupils governed by the school system)

Instruction in hospital or domiciled settings

"Noneducational" service (medical and welfare cae and supervision)

"IN-PATIENT" PROGRAMS (Assignment of children to facilities governed by health or welfare agencies)

Figure 6. Deno's inverted "cascade system of special education service" pyramid. From Evelyn Deno, "Special Education as Developmental Capital," *Exceptional Children* 37 (November 1970): 235. Copyright 1970 by the Council for Exceptional Children. Reprinted with permission.

sentation of the range of special education services first proposed by Maynard Reynolds in 1962 and inverted by Evelyn Deno in 1970—provided a manageable and relatively comfortable model for designing special education programs in local districts and school buildings. This representation solidified in the minds of many the need for various segregated settings (resource rooms, special classes, special schools) that would serve as the "least restrictive environment" for those exceptional children whose presence in the regular classroom was deemed too problematic, and its inclusion in many if not most of the era's standard special education texts reinforced its influence.

PL 94-142 also strengthened the importance of categories of disability and the need for definitive diagnosis and labeling of individual special needs students. In practice, funding under the law was largely dependent on ascertaining the specific numbers of students falling under each category or label, which encouraged this process that Jane Mercer and many others had openly challenged. These categories, in turn, contributed to "a myth of differentness" and "fragmented service delivery," each of which created multiple "'boxes' within the 'box' of special education" and made extremely difficult the implementation of truly integrative programs. In addition, PL 94-142 did not address training practices for special education teachers. As a result, teachers continued to be divided in the training between "teachers" and "special education teachers"; the latter group was prepared to work in specialized, typically segregated settings, with little consultation or sharing of "special" knowledge with the regular teaching staff. The continued separatist approach in teacher training at colleges and universities prepared thousands of school personnel to conceive of special education as a truly separate entity, one that did not and need not involve intensive collaboration or even cooperation with regular classroom teachers in regular classrooms. All these factors helped maintain a climate of separation, where even the "least restrictive environment" was often seen as a segregated setting for much, and often all, of the school day.[11]

Statistics from the mid-1980s demonstrated both the dramatic increase in the number of students receiving special education services through the public schools as well as the continued reliance on segregated settings for the delivery of those services. Between 1976–77 and 1985–86, the total number of children in special education in the fifty states, the District of Columbia, and Puerto Rico rose from 3,703,033 to 4,361,312, an increase of almost 18 percent. Of those children in educational settings between the ages of 3 and 21, 26.69 percent were enrolled in regular classes; 41.63 percent received instruction in both regular classes and resource rooms; 23.77 percent spent their entire school day in a separate class; and the balance were in a separate public school facility, a residential facility, or were taught at home or in a hospital. In other words, almost three-fourths of special education students still spent at least some of their time in segregated settings during the 1985–1986 school year. The report containing the data did explain that "significant variation in placement patterns existed among the various handicapping conditions. For example, while most learning disabled and speech or language impaired students were serviced in regular classes or resource rooms, over 50 percent of mentally retarded students were placed in separate classes." Clearly, students receiving special education services were being mainstreamed or integrated to a much greater extent than they were prior to PL 94-142. Nevertheless, the kind of full-scale integration advocated by proponents of more thorough integration was still a long way off.[12]

Critique of PL 94-142

Passage of PL 94-142 certainly constituted a monumental event in American public education. After its enactment in 1975, the law was widely hailed by legal and governmental organizations, advocacy groups, disability rights advocates, and educators as a much-needed and long-overdue acknowledgement of the right of children with disabilities to a free public education in as normal a setting as possible. By all accounts, the effect of the law on public schools in general and special education in particular in its first five years was profound. There existed near universal agreement that the intentions of the law were well-founded, yet there also existed by the early 1980s a body of critique and caution related to the practical aspects of its implementation. While some educators such as Margaret Wang felt the law did not push hard enough for integration, others took a more critical view of the law and its alleged potential effects on public schooling.

Critics of the legislation grounded their objections in two major arguments: that the law perpetuated an antiquated approach to policies, methods, and services in special education, and that the federal law placed too many intrusive, unrealistic, and unsupported legal, fiscal, and educational demands to address the law's requirements on teachers and schools. The former body of critique strengthened in the early 1980s and was reflected in the work of those dedicated to breaking down the many walls between special education and regular education that, they argued, prevented the more authentic and complete integration of students with disabilities in regular classrooms. PL 94-142, they claimed, perpetuated those barriers through its emphasis on using rigid classification categories and employing funding practices that rewarded the development and maintenance of segregated settings. The latter avenue of criticism found some popularity among administrators, teachers, and other professionals who questioned the law's reach and worried about the public schools' ability to meet the mandates for resources, staff training, teacher expertise, equipment and technology, and in-classroom services that they thought the law mandated. Few expressed their opposition in the harsh and vivid terms of one critic, who claimed that "if the road to hell is paved with good intentions, PL 94-142 certainly represents enough of a brick to cover half the distance. It is to education what Three Mile Island is to the use of nuclear energy." Nevertheless, the law's complexity, scope, and its arguably severely underfunded mandates for services that placed enormous financial and administrative pressures on local districts deeply troubled authorities who professed a desire to improve special education but were hardly sure PL 94-142 provided the best means for doing so.[13]

Making Mainstreaming Work: ALEM as a Case Study

By the early 1980s, mainstreaming had become a central concern of school professionals and others engaged in shaping the social, cultural, and educational lives of persons with disabilities. In the realm of education, the realities of PL 94-142—its sweeping scope, its mandates for a free and appropriate education in the least restrictive environment for all children, and its emphasis on individualized instruction as embodied in the required Individualized Education Plan (IEP) for exceptional students—drove school officials to seek ways to accommodate the law as much as possible yet still address the economic and administrative demands it generated. Much of this activity took place on a local level, either through the district office or, as had been the case with the models developed during the 1970s, at the school building level. In addition, research continued on the efficacy of various approaches to reforming the education of students with disabilities, especially with regard to children identified as mildly mentally retarded (EMR). Nevertheless, in terms of shaping the debate over the theory and practice of mainstreaming—even to the point of eventually challenging the importance of alternative instructional settings and disability categories solidified by PL 94-142—the Adaptive Learning Environments Model (ALEM), proposed by Margaret Wang and her colleagues, proved to be the most notable—and certainly among the most controversial.[14]

The ALEM had its roots in a pilot individualized instruction program developed during the mid-1970s at the Learning Research and Development Center (LRDC) at the University of Pittsburgh. In 1980, Margaret Wang, who had been involved with the LRDC, published an article in *The Elementary School Journal,* linking this kind of approach with mainstreaming. She argued that the model—referred to in this article as the Adaptive Learning Environments Program (ALEP)—held great potential for effectively mainstreaming children with disabilities in regular classrooms to a much greater extent than had been accomplished elsewhere. Noting the "pressing need for effective mainstreaming of exceptional children" in light of the mandates of PL 94-142, other court decisions, and organized efforts by advocates for children with disabilities, Wang praised the ALEP as a major step toward developing "well-researched and implementable educational programs" that would satisfy such needs.[15]

Wang stated that traditional special education emphasized the child's disability or deficit or "problem": that deficit was identified and the child labeled. The child was then considered the province of "special education," meaning only those specifically trained as special educators should or could be responsible for planning and implementing that child's instruction, typically in a segregated setting. ALEP, she maintained, rejected this "problem"-centered approach in favor of a more "constructive" one that sought "to increase the capability of the usual classroom learning environment for meeting individual needs," thus shifting the "problem" from the student to the instructional setting. This shift allowed each child's "uniqueness" to be celebrated and addressed by modifying the classroom in ways that would support all learners, including those identified as disabled. Wang argued that decades of research had failed to show either special classes or traditional regular classrooms as being clearly favorable to the instruction of children with disabilities, and recent research had failed to show that mainstreaming, which essentially had been grafted on to these traditional approaches, was beneficial to either exceptional children or their nondisabled peers. She attributed these unimpressive results in large part to the "shared-time" model of mainstreaming most popular at the time, where exceptional children were frequently withdrawn from the regular classroom for instruction in resource rooms or other segregated settings, making it most difficult for disabled children "to be full participants in the social and intellectual life of the regular class." The ALEP approach, she asserted, "may very well have different and more dramatic effects than the shared-time models" because it drastically reduced the separation of the two groups of children and, in fact, essentially merged the two groups into one.[16]

Wang then outlined how "recent technological and pedagogical developments in individualized instruction" made such an approach to mainstreaming more feasible. She asserted that several individualized instruction programs had proven successful, and in the process, more effective means of assessing individual capabilities and more appropriate curricular materials had been developed. Key to such success was the effort to describe individual differences not in terms of categories of disabilities but rather "in terms directly relevant to instruction." Echoing concerns about the general uselessness of disability-based labels for determining appropriate instruction, Wang did not identify what these more appropriate terms were but argued that by using them, "exceptional children can begin to relate to others as members of a heterogeneous world rather than an exceptional one." Ultimately, under ALEP, "when adequate instructional resources, both human and material, are combined within a well-designed system for planning instruction and scheduling access to available schooling resources, the learning needs of both exceptional and regular children can probably be met within the same classroom."[17]

ALEP featured eight identified characteristics that Wang claimed were essential to effective mainstreaming. These included early identification of learning problems; delabeling the exceptional child; individualized instruction; teaching of self-management skills; a comprehensive organizational and resource support system; multi-age grouping; team teaching; and family involvement. ALEP was designed to employ each of these to the maximum extent feasible through five specific components: "a prescriptive learning component made up of a series of highly structured and hierarchically organized curricula for academic skills development"; an "exploratory learning component that includes a variety of learning options" that would be "flexible" in order to be able to "adapt to the constraints of classroom physical space and other instructional and learning supports"; a "classroom management system designed specifically to teach students self-management skills"; a "family involvement program that attempts to reinforce the integration of school and home experiences"; and "a multi-age and team-teaching organization" that could "use the talents, time, and interests of the teachers and the students to maximize student learning."[18]

By 1984, Wang and colleagues Stephen Peverly and Robert Randolph had transformed the ALEP into the ALEM and described it in an article in the journal *Remedial and Special Education*. The core features remained the same, but the details had evolved as a result of several years of experience and experimentation. Targeted students specifically included students identified as moderately disabled, remaining true to the model's fundamental beliefs yet extending efforts to fully integrate exceptional children beyond the traditional emphasis on those with mild disabilities. Core assumptions had also been redefined somewhat but still featured ALEP's basic suppositions. ALEM sought to establish "environments in regular classes where special needs students are integrated socially and academically with their general education peers." It operated on the principle that "all students . . . learn in different ways as individuals and require varying amounts of instruction and time to learn. Thus, educational programs that recognize the 'special' needs of each student . . . are a direct application of the principle of appropriate educational services in the least restrictive environment." Under ALEM, it was argued, "all students are more likely to experience learning success" because "the focus is on educational intervention rather than placement." With "individual differences . . . [being] viewed as the norm rather than the exception . . . all students, but particularly those requiring special education services, are less likely to develop perceptions of themselves as exceptions or to be stigmatized because of their special needs."[19]

Making ALEM work also required specific approaches to classroom organization, instruction, and management. Under the assumption that "all learning involves both external and internal adaptation," ALEM made individual adjustments to both the "modes and forms in which new task content is present to the learner," who then engaged in "internal adaptation" to accommodate the learning. The goal was not only appropriate individualization of material and content, but more importantly the effort to "foster students' ability to effectively assume self-responsibility for making necessary adaptations" in all aspects of their own learning. ALEM's approach to effective mainstreaming also "requires the establishment of functional linkages and integrated services among classroom instructional staff and specialized professionals" specifically trained in special or compensatory education. The role of the special education teacher included consultation of the regular class teachers as well as frequent instruction of special education students in the regular classroom. As in other mainstreaming models, general education teachers would assume responsibility for primary instruction of all students, including those identified as disabled.[20]

Wang and her associates combined these descriptive narratives with formal educational research into the effectiveness of the ALEP/ALEM models. Examining a wide range of topics—from classroom processes to selected student achievement outcomes to attitudes of students regarding disability—Wang et al. attempted "to investigate the feasibility and effectiveness of the ALEM as a full-time mainstreaming program for moderately handicapped students in a large urban school system." Their hypothesis stated that "under the ALEM, instructional provisions could be effectively adapted to the needs of most students," and that successful implementation would "facilitate positive academic and attitudinal outcomes for both general education students and mainstreamed special education students." Overall, they argued, their investigation supported their hypotheses: "not only was it possible to establish and maintain implementation of the ALEM across schools with different demographic characteristics, but also that program implementation led to predicted changes in classroom processes over time. These changes, in turn, seemed to result in "certain intended outcomes," especially unexpectedly significant gains in reading and math for both the regular education and special education students. Their positive findings reinforced similar positive findings related to the smaller-scale implementation of the ALEP model several years earlier. "These findings," they argued, "have particular significance for educational practice. The implication for further operationalization of the least restrictive environment mandate of the Education for All Handicapped Children Act (Public Law 94-142) are especially noteworthy." The authors claimed that the achievements of ALEM stood above those of other mainstreaming models built around more traditional (i.e., separate) approaches to mainstreaming, which did not maximize opportunities for instruction in a truly least restrictive environment. While noting that adaptive, individualized instruction has been used in segregated settings such as self-contained classes and resource rooms, the investigators differentiated ALEM as an approach that allowed a "high degree of implementation of such practice by general education teachers in regular classroom settings."[21]

Another widely publicized approach grounded in individualized instruction and offered as a means of educating children identified as disabled was the Team Assisted Individualization program (TAI) developed by Robert Slavin and colleagues. TAI featured a strong cooperative learning component, where heterogeneous groups of children were identified as high, average, and low achievers, "academically handicapped students," and "students of any ethnic groups in the class represented in the proportion they make up of the entire class." Teams consisted of four or five members and were reassigned every four weeks. In the teams, students would work on specific instructional materials and skills, using group study and tutoring to facilitate the learning of each child. The approach also used frequent testing and positive reinforcement techniques; teachers would introduce topics and facilitate as necessary, but significant responsibility for teaching and study lay with the students themselves. A study of two experimental "treatments" showed that when used for a full 24-week pilot period, significant gains were reported for both mildly academically handicapped students and their nonhandicapped peers compared with control groups. TAI also stressed the importance of social interaction and peer acceptance—a key purpose of the cooperative learning/heterogeneous grouping employed in the program—and reported the results of gains in that area as "quite positive." The study determined that when mildly academically handicapped students work in small groups with non-handicapped classmates, they are better accepted than are students who do not work in such groups. The study concluded that both the teaming and the significant individualization of instruction contributed to the success of the program. The authors consequently argued that TAI could be a useful model for delivering special education within the regular classroom on a consistent basis and declared, "if . . . the implications of the TAI research summarized here are correct, a major rethinking of special education and mainstreaming may be necessary."[22]

Over the years ALEM, TAI, or models quite similar to or derived from them were implemented in various schools nationwide. By 1984, Wang and her colleagues claimed that the model or its various iterations were being "implemented in a considerable number of public and private schools, either as a general education program or as a special program in conjunction with a variety of school improvement efforts." They noted that thanks to funding from various federal sources, "components of the program [were] in use in over 150 school districts across 28 states." Eventually ALEM was joined by other experimental programs that had different names but took similar approaches adapted to local needs and conditions. These included the Integrated Classroom Model of the Isssaquah, Washington school district; Project MERGE (Maximizing Educational Remediation in General Education), based in Olympia, Washington; similar pilot efforts in cities such as Minneapolis, Syracuse, and Indianapolis; and state education department efforts in such states as Delaware, Iowa, and Pennsylvania. While these specific models were faithfully implemented in but a relatively small number of schools due to their financial, training, and programmatic demands, their basic principles eventually helped define the core concept of more complete inclusion of special education students in the regular classroom.[23]

Voices of the Disabled and Their Advocates: On Mainstreaming

The changes in and challenges to special education brought on by PL 94-142 were not lost on persons and families with disabilities or their advocates. As encouraging as well as discouraging reports about the viability and advisability of integrative models for special education emerged, and as school districts became more experienced with mainstreaming efforts and their implications for school practice, mainstreaming's impact on the lives of persons directly involved with special education attracted greater attention and concern. As Sarason and Doris had noted, special education could not avoid the need to address mainstreaming's ethical and practical manifestations. By the mid-1980s, debate over the relative importance of these aspects in determining special education policy and practice occurred with greater frequency and intensity, and began to draw increasing attention from the disabled community and those who claimed to speak for them.

Voices from and on behalf of the disabled had been gathering strength for decades, starting with the era of honest confessions about and confrontations of disability in the 1950s. By the mid-1970s, the statements and positions of disability advocates had acquired a more urgent and assertive tone, as exemplified by the heightened attention to and increasingly firm language of groups such as the CEC and NARC, lawyers arguing for the causes of the disabled in courts, and writers promoting normalization and recognition of basic human rights. These broad-based and proactive efforts reflected the growing force and influence throughout the country and the world of what has been generically called the Disability Rights Movement.

As a social and political movement, Disability Rights gained significant strength during the 1970s and 1980s, learning from and assimilating many of the tactics, symbols, premises, and language of the civil rights, anti-Vietnam War, and other movements. Drawing on this "new politicized perspective on disability issues," leaders in the movement concluded "that real reform could be assured only by the development of a broad-based coalition of disabled people throughout the United States who demanded both fundamental national policy reforms and community based support services that would permit them to break the tradition of dependency and institutionalization and live as part of

the social and economic community." One early leader of the movement, Judith Heumann, founded Disabled in Action in 1970 as a conse-
quence of her struggles with discriminatory practices while seeking a
teaching position as person who used a wheelchair. Local efforts across
the nation, especially those advocating independent living, coalesced to
a great degree during the late 1970s and 1980s; by 1990, nearly thirty
advocacy organizations were involved in lobbying for the passage of the
landmark Americans with Disabilities Act.

As a movement, however, Disability Rights has struggled with some
of its own history and the nature of disability itself. Its origins in local
efforts and its widespread grounding of advocacy in specific categories
of disability have contributed to its somewhat "splintered" nature, with
efforts often focusing on limited definitions of populations and on
occasion leading to conflicting goals and demands. This has also held
true in the world of education. While the Education for All Handicapped Children Act has been described as one of the legislative "pil-
lars" of the Disability Rights movement, various advocacy groups have
taken different, if not polar opposite, positions on the practices of
mainstreaming, inclusion, and full inclusion. Nevertheless, the concepts of self-determination—"Nothing About Us Without Us," as one
definitive slogan states—and the ethical and equitable treatment of citizens with disabilities have cut across categories and priorities and
raised the profile of disability in social and political arenas. More than
specific positions on issues, the arousal of strong public advocacy for
the disability community, broadly defined, has lifted the consciousness
of and applied palpable and consistent pressure on those establishing
educational policy and practice for students with disabilities.[24]

By the late 1970s, the writings of those within the disabled community had clearly moved from confessionals and testimonials to personal political statements and direct discussion of important issues, not
just in terms of lives and communities but also in terms of education
and schools. Through personal statements, research, and formal commentary, parents of the disabled as well as advocates for the disabled
revealed a not-unexpected ambivalence about the relative value of PL
94-142 and the movement toward mainstreaming. While generally sup-

porting the law's intent, serious concern and difference were expressed over the realities of mainstreaming in schools and what it meant for their children; their concerns were more personal than structural.

Of particular concern, especially to parents, was the emotional environment in the classroom—whether segregated or integrated—and the extent to which their child felt comfortable and accepted. A study of parental attitudes toward mainstreamed and segregated settings for young children indicated the diversity of opinion on this issue. One parent supported her child's presence in a mainstreamed setting, even though it had its problems:

> You need to learn to deal with this world the way it's designed to run right now, which is toward the nonhandicapped. You cannot live in a sheltered environment, whether it be your own home, or a private school for the handicapped, and then all of a sudden become of age and be thrown out into the world and never learn to deal with it. She's got to learn to deal with some of the cruelties the other children are going to come up with. She's going to have to learn to take care of herself in situations where there is not someone there to protect her.

Alternatively, other parents were quite wary of the exposed nature of an integrated setting. "He's pretty young to be the only one different," said one. Another noted the extent to which she would feel uncomfortable: "The children [in the mainstream classroom] would be capable of doing things that he wouldn't do—he would feel left out. I don't guess that he would know the difference, but I guess I think it's more for myself—I think to myself I wish he could do like the other kids—and that sort of makes me feel sad." As another parent stated bluntly, "Children rarely overlook difference, and they can be very nasty to each other. If mainstreaming were easy, the special class would not have been invented in the first place."[25]

Most parents and advocates, however, expressed a cautiously optimistic faith that integration and mainstreaming would benefit their children in the long term. Wrote one parent in a concise yet truly representative statement,

I believe that exposure and integration will in the long run improve attitudes toward the disabled, just as they have for other minority groups. If schools supplement the mandated changes with imaginative educational programs that help able-bodied children to understand disabilities and cope with their own responses to the unfamiliar, they will avert a good deal of transitional pain.

Certainly differences in beliefs about mainstreaming continued to exist. While the parent of a blind child extolled the virtues of mainstreaming in a 1979 book, parents of deaf children expressed great skepticism about the value of integration (as will be discussed in a later chapter). Other evidence suggests that some parents of children with disabilities even found children with certain kinds of disability (notably mental retardation and autism) to be much less acceptable as members of a mainstreamed class. Concerns about the quality of experience in a mainstreamed classroom—whether it truly provided the least restrictive environment for their child's particular educational and social needs—continued as schools worked to satisfy the expectations of PL 94-142.

What was becoming more universally accepted was the need for children with disabilities, their parents, and their advocates to step up their activities in affirming and ensuring the rights accorded by PL 94-142. The basic right to a "free and appropriate education in the least restrictive environment" was guaranteed by law, but guaranteeing it in reality took much work and persistence. A regional director for a county advocacy group, Kathryn Gorham, wrote that although it was acknowledged that mentally retarded children had a right to a free education, that right was not being respected in the real world. "We are told again to inform our legislators of the need. Why must we tell them *again*?" While noting the exhausting trials of being parents of children with disabilities, Gorham stated,

The new parent today faces a world which is fortunately improved in many ways. The fact that his child has a legal right to education and training does not surprise this parent, and he *expects* programs to be provided. . . . He is not asking for services as if they were charity nor is he left with no option other than the institutions if the few existing public or private special classes refuse his children. . . . Some things have not changed, however, and will not unless we make them.

From 1975 into the mid-1980s, the world of special education did change much, but Gorham's recognition that constant, public, at times politicized advocacy was absolutely necessary to make sure the law was implemented and to make known the views of members of the disabled community anticipated the activities of the next fifteen years. During the 1980s, the voices of persons with disabilities, and of those who spoke on their behalf, increased in frequency and deepened in tenor, even as issues of integration became more and more fundamental to all discourse related to the advancement and future of special education.[26]

6

1985–1992: Integration, Mainstreaming, and the Regular Education Initiative

I N 1984, Susan and William Stainback published what would become one of the seminal statements in the debate concerning integration in special education. Their article, "A Rationale for the Merger of Special and Regular Education," appeared in the October 1984 issue of *Exceptional Children.* Briefly, the Stainbacks presented a case, built upon practical, experiential, and ethical grounds, for abandoning altogether a separate structure for special education. Noting that special education scholars Maynard Reynolds and Jack Birch had described the history of special education as one of "progressive inclusion," the Stainbacks declared, "At this point in the progressive inclusion trend, it is time to stop developing criteria for who does or does not belong in the mainstream and instead turn the spotlight to increasing the capabilities of the regular school environment, the mainstream, to meet the needs of *all* students." [1]

"A Rationale for the Merger of Special and Regular Education" was but one of a series of articles and books published during the mid-1980s that, much as Dunn's article had in 1968, propelled special education into intense controversy and discussion about its very nature and purpose. Drawing on a range of educational, political, and ethical justifications, proponents for more radical approaches to achieving virtually full integration of students with disabilities in regular classrooms argued that the time was long past due to vest full rights and privileges—including, but not limited to, full-time participation in the

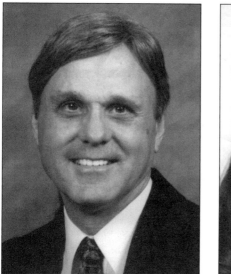

William and Susan Stainback

regular classroom—in all students with disabilities. Such proposals naturally generated substantial critique, with critics and skeptics questioning and challenging the logical, ethical, and practical merits of wholesale special education reform. During the late 1980s and early 1990s, the central feature of this debate moved from the term *mainstreaming* to the *Regular Education Initiative* (REI), a sweeping proposal for fundamental school reform regarding the education of children with disabilities, which originated as a two-part initiative proposed by Margaret Wang, Maynard Reynolds, and Herbert Walberg and received significant support from the federal government through the Reagan administration. Yet couched in the controversy over the REI framework were fundamental issues concerning all that special education had experienced and had to offer—past, present, and future. The debate over the REI was really a debate over the soul of special education, one that would lead to the discussions over the issue of inclusion that dominate discourse in the field today.[2]

The Stainbacks' 1984 proposal for the "merger of special and regular education" proved to be a pivotal concept in the debate over the segregation, integration, and mainstreaming of children with disabilities in regular classrooms. Their article helped establish them as key advocates for fundamental reform of special education along more inclusive lines, not only in terms of classroom practice but also in the multifaceted provision of all special education services in public schools. Even so, the Stainbacks and Margaret Wang were by no means alone in their strong, highly visible advocacy of fundamental changes in the education of children with disabilities. Joining them during this key decade of educational reform were others who had helped shape such discussions for many years (e.g., Maynard Reynolds and Jack Birch) or who had begun to make their voices known in the early and mid-1980s (Robert Bogdan, Douglas Biklen, Dorothy Lipsky, Alan Gartner, Madeleine Will, and Thomas Skrtic, to name a few). Their research, commentary, and practice in favor of more complete integration of special education students, providers, and services naturally engendered disagreement and controversy from others (such as James Kauffman, Douglas and Lynn Fuchs, and Laurence Lieberman) who became equally well-known and widely cited for their continued thorough critique of that view as well as for their determined defense of more traditional values, assumptions, and practices of special education. While much of this complex debate was grounded in the context of the REI, it also moved well beyond the specifics of that concept, encompassing the practical, legal, and ethical issues that discourse related to segregation and integration in the field had always addressed.

Rejecting the "Dual System"

The rationale offered by the Stainbacks for merging special and regular education focused on one central argument: that the traditional dualistic approach, where special educators were responsible for the education of students formally identified as disabled and regular educators taught everyone else, had become cumbersome, inefficient, and unnecessary. To begin with, seeing students as two distinct groups—normal and exceptional—was simplistic and counterproductive. Students in fact "differ along continuums of intellectual, physical, and psychological characteristics"; even those whose differences are seen as "extreme" are still part of that single continuum, and "the designation of arbitrary cutoffs does not make students any more different between the special and regular groups than within these groups." Since "all students are unique individuals," and the abilities and characteristics of children are as subtle as they are complex, the convenient division of education into two major groups, with an assumed clear line between the two, was unrealistic and of little help to the school. Every student, they argued, deserved a "special" or individualized education, adapted to her or his abilities and talents.[3]

This false dichotomy between two supposedly distinct groups of students extended in practice to a dualistic delivery system of individualized services and instructional methods. The traditional assumption that only students in special education required an individualized instructional program and mysterious, specialized methods of delivering that program was to the Stainbacks "educationally discriminatory. . . . there is nothing to warrant that individualized programming should be a privilege provided only to 'exceptional' students. Tailor-made instructional programs should be provided for all students, whether considered bright, handicapped, minority, or average." Nor were there "two discrete sets of instructional methods—one set for use with 'special' students and another set for use with 'regular' students." The Stainbacks cited research that they claimed indicated that "the longstanding assumption that there are two methodologies or psychologies of learning—one for 'special' people and one for 'regular' people—is beginning to erode." (The argument that there was little that was truly special about special education—at least as carried out in the special classes of the 1950s, 1960s, and 1970s—in fact had existed for decades.) Since all learners were unique, programming and instruction could not nor should not be separated into two mutually exclusive approaches to teaching, as typically had been the assumption under the dual system.[4]

The negative consequences of perpetuating a dual system of special and regular education pervaded schools and classrooms in other significant ways, according to the Stainbacks. Determining eligibility for special education required categorization and labeling of children, an often stigmatizing and unreliable process that had little to do with determining appropriate instruction. Worse, the requirement that a student be categorized in order to receive special instructional services put regular education students at a disadvantage. "The only reason for eligibility criteria is if some people are entitled to assistance and others are not," they wrote. "However, in education, *all* students are (or should be) entitled to assistance if they need it. . . . To do otherwise is to blatantly discriminate against some students." These category restrictions also limited curricular options by inhibiting cross-fertilization of course or subject offerings between special and regular education. Eliminating categorization and the dual system would allow all students to take advantage of all the methods, practices, and resources—both "special" and "regular"—which would become available under a combined system. In essence, the categorization requirement of special education required a student be labeled as "deviant" before being able to receive appropriate instruction, while those not so labeled—many of whom struggled significantly in school—would be denied services that could help them. The Stainbacks argued that merging the systems would reduce the "inefficiency" inherent in the dual system approach as well as make the goal of improving the academic and social achievements of all children more attainable.[5]

The Stainbacks predicted other significant benefits arising from a merger of the two systems. Professional relationships and communication between special education teachers and regular education teachers, which suffered under pressures of time, territory, and responsibility under the dual system, could improve considerably under a system that values both equally. "Artificial barriers" would break down in a merged system that supported all teachers and provided an environment and climate much more conducive to cooperation, coexistence, and shared rather than competing advocacy. Termination of the process of identifying and classifying children for special education services would free time and money for teachers and support personnel, which then could be used to provide more effective individualized instruction for all students. Joining special and regular education would, they believed, allow more authentic and educationally responsive perceptions of individual differences among students. And expecting regular education to make the necessary adjustments to each child was far preferable than shunting children who cannot adjust to the rigid expectations of current regular education practices off to special education. Noting the contradiction of trying to mainstream or integrate exceptional children within a traditional dualistic, separated structure of special and regular education, the Stainbacks argued that mainstreaming and the mandates of PL 94-142 are important steps for exceptional children, but that

> It is now time in the historical evolution of special education to consider merging with regular education. This move could help ensure that all students not only receive an appropriate education, but that they receive it as an inherent right and not as a 'special' provision. . . .
>
> A dual system of education can serve to legitimize exclusion of some students from regular education, reduce opportunity for equal participation by other students, and sanction other forms of discrimination. . . . Thus, it is important to explore, suggest, and attempt change.[6]

The Stainbacks' rationale for merging special and regular education revealed how the debate over the segregation or integration of children with disabilities had become part of a much larger discourse about the quality of schooling and the need for educational reform. While several issues that had emerged during debates of the past remained—efficacy of instruction, value of socialization, concerns over the effects of labeling, the impact of the presence of children with disabilities on their nondisabled peers, the quality of teacher training—others took the debate to a new level. By the mid-1980s, mainstreaming factored into more generalized debates about how well the rights of persons with disabilities were being protected and advanced, how good a job American schools were doing of educating children, and how schools could be made to operate more economically, efficiently, and fairly in order to enhance educational equity and quality. Other advocates of more effective, extensive, and authentic integration of students with disabilities addressed these issues in their writings and research, continuing as well as extending the debate. These advocates typically called for fundamental restructuring that would transform a cautious, selective vision of mainstreaming into an educational world that left all forms of instructional segregation based on disability behind.

This vision gained greater articulation with the publication of Alan

Gartner and Dorothy Lipsky's "Beyond Special Education: Toward a Quality System for All Students" in the November 1987 issue of the *Harvard Educational Review*. In this sweeping review of the status of special education, Gartner and Lipsky, colleagues at the City University of New York, provided their interpretation of the impact and repercussions of PL 94-142, examined the current status of attitudes toward disability in the United States, identified factors in general education that they claimed promoted the exclusion of exceptional children, and offered their vision of what public schools and the education of all children— including those with disabilities—might look like in an educational world "beyond special education."[7]

For Gartner and Lipsky, PL 94-142 held mixed blessings at best. Its importance and value lay primarily in its establishment of the undeniable right of all students, regardless of the nature or severity of their disability or disabilities, to receive an appropriate education at public expense in the public school system. Given the commonplace exclusion from public schools of so many of these children prior to 1975, this was crucially important. Nevertheless, they argued, the law had produced a number of unfortunate outcomes. Its reliance on a cumbersome and highly suspect system of identification and categorization of students needing special education services through a lengthy referral and assessment process led to a negativistic emphasis on students' "problems" and questionable practices in placing students in certain categories. In particular, the category of "learning disabled" was prone to confusion, uncertainty, and abuse; this was significant given that it involved such a large percentage of students identified as disabled (close to 50 percent at the time). The law also encouraged placement for most children in segregated settings for at least part of the day, settings that were geared more to the realities of funding practices than to specific, distinct needs of students assigned to the various categories. Such practices often encouraged local districts to place students in more restrictive rather than less restrictive environments. As a result, claimed the authors, the percentage of children being served in segregated rather than integrated settings was essentially unchanged ten years after the law took effect. Their research also indicated that local districts too frequently purposely limited mainstreaming opportunities for students due to insufficient pupil preparation, teacher resistance, and lack of supportive resources. In their opinion, PL 94-142 had done little to realize authentic integration, or improve the quality of education, for students with disabilities.[8]

Gartner and Lipsky also addressed the issue of public attitudes toward disability, especially as they played out in schools. While persons with disabilities often disdained the notion that disability is a tragic, universally limiting condition worthy of pity, society nonetheless saw most of the disabled population that way, typically stigmatizing disabled individuals as necessarily dependent, if not helpless, and as "not quite human." Although the disability rights movement had tried to educate the public about the power and potential of persons with disabilities, such individuals still faced enormous social barriers that were far more external than internal in nature; that is, imposed by society rather than by the disabling condition. Such attitudes carried over to school policy and practice, where "an all-or-nothing concept of disability requires proof of total incapacity in order to gain entitlement to various benefit programs." Media depictions of persons with disabilities as "either the heroic individual or pathetic cripple, rather than as a human being with a multiplicity of qualities," compromised efforts to provide equitable treatment for exceptional students by lowering expectations and standards for functional capability and academic performance. "Having denied individuals with disabilities autonomy and decision-making authority," they wrote, "we then excuse their behavior, ascribing it to the disability." The ultimate outcome has been "a 'deal' between special and general education," sanctioned by special and general educators alike:

> The former asserts a particular body of expertise and unique understanding of 'special' students, thus laying claim both to professional obligation and student benefit. The latter, because of the lack of skills and resources or prejudice, is often happy to hand over 'these' students to a welcoming special education system.

In the 1980s climate of demands for greater achievement or "excellence" of students in schools, educators accepted this "deal" because "the pressure to 'succeed' with high test scores, and with the very large class sizes that make individual attention extremely difficult . . . teachers will seek uniformity of students rather than diversity." This pervasive condition runs directly counter to efforts to integrate or mainstream exceptional students into regular classrooms.[9]

For Gartner and Lipsky, the solution to this situation was as simple as it was sweeping: "It is not special education but the total educational system that must change." The system's focus on questionable categories, complex regulations, available funding, and exclusion of low-achieving students from the regular classroom, the authors stated, make the current structure of special education unmanageable and ethically untenable. To replace it, Gartner and Lipsky suggested "a merged or unitary system." They openly acknowledged that adopting such a system

> requires a 'paradigm shift,' a fundamental change in the way we think about differences among people, in the ways we choose to organize schools for their education, and in how we view the purpose of that education. It rejects the bimodal division of handicapped and non-handicapped students, and recognizes that individuals vary—that single-characteristic definitions fail to capture the complexity of people. Moreover, it rejects the belief, common to all human services work that incorporates a medical or deviancy model, that the problem lies in the individual and the resolution lies in one or another treatment modality. The unitary system, in contrast, requires adaptations in society and education, not solely in the individual.[10]

Their vision for such a system involved "effective practices in classrooms and schools that would characterize education for all students." Gartner and Lipsky stressed the importance of looking to school effectiveness research in designing inclusive classrooms and schools. They called for appropriate supports for all students both in the classroom and throughout the school, ranging from "multidimensional" assessment to research-based instructional practices and early intervention and transitional programs. They also reiterated the call for more extensive curriculum adaptations and individualized education "that would allow both general and special education students to take more difficult courses." This unitary system would not only involve the full integration of mild and moderately handicapped students at the building level but would also bring students with more severe disabilities into an integrated setting, relying not just on methods being developed in pilot programs but on "an attitude change" toward all students with disabilities as well. Their article offered only general guidelines for developing this merged system; instead, they focused on the moral imperative of such an approach. "The ultimate rationale for quality education of students in an integrated setting," they wrote, "is based not only on law or pedagogy, but also on values. What kinds of people are we? What kind of society do we wish to develop? What values do we honor? . . . To change the outcome, we need to develop another set of values." Quoting Ronald Edmonds, they close by saying, "'We already know more than we need in order to do this. Whether we do it must finally depend on how we feel about the fact that we haven't done it so far.'"[11]

While most such calls for the fundamental restructuring of special education originated from scholars in higher education, they also came from the federal government. Madeleine Will, Assistant Secretary for the Office of Special Education and Rehabilitative Services in the U.S. Department of Education, granted the Reagan administration's blessing for restructuring special education much along the lines suggested by the Stainbacks, Wang, and Gartner and Lipsky. Criticizing the pervasive "language of separation, of fragmentation, of removal" that characterized schools in general, Will detailed the multiple ways in which schools labeled and differentiated among children. This process, she declared, excludes many children who need help because they "do not fit into compartmentalized special programs." She lamented too the consequent stigmatization of labeling and the practice of waiting for a formal recognition of failure before seeking ways to address children's needs. The current system in effect lowered expectations for large numbers of children and inhibited effective partnerships among teachers, administrators, and parents. These practices not only were unfair to the children but also significantly interfered with the president's desire to achieve excellence for all children in schools. Will stated that the need to improve educational outcomes and "to more efficiently use resources

to accommodate students who are failing to learn through convention-
al education methods" had become urgent.[12]

Will's concerns were political and social as well as pedagogical. She
acknowledged the mandate for excellence in education arising from the
A Nation at Risk report, published in 1983, and observed that the federal government had a responsibility to help coordinate special education
programs, especially with the extension of government responsibility
for children from birth to age twenty-one. She reiterated the often-
voiced concerns about poor communication between special and regular education and about the continuing, significant obstacles to more
complete integration of the disabled in schools and in society. In Will's
view, schools needed to respect the abilities and potential of exceptional students to lead effective, independent lives. While recognizing the
effects of traditional practices and limited resources, Will maintained
that overcoming barriers and meeting needs was "a question of will and
character, both of which I think Americans have in ample supply."[13]

Also having a significant impact on Will's beliefs and advocacy was
her son Jon, who was born with Down syndrome. According to Will,
her desire for Jon to lead an independent, fulfilling life as an active, contributing member of society meant that "I wanted him to become an
adult who would know himself well enough to understand his own
needs and assume responsibility to the greatest extent possible for his
own happiness." In order to do so, an "emphasis on making and maintaining friends would grow more pronounced in the adolescent years,"
because "what matters to most people are their families and loved ones
and the qualities of those relationships. This fundamental human need
should be reflected throughout every phase of education." For Will, an
inclusion approach was most certainly the best way to accomplish such
fundamental goals for all children with disabilities.[14]

Will's suggestion was to engage in a "shared responsibility" among
all school professionals for the education of all students, especially at
the building level. Collaboration was essential in order to create schools
that would eliminate the barriers between special education and regular education, but equally important was the power of individual
schools to experiment with alternative approaches to special education.
She advocated better identification early on in a child's schooling and

Madeleine Will with her son Jon

the use of individualized instruction grounded in a curriculum-based needs assessment for each child rather than relying on categories or labels. *"This means,"* she stated, *"special programs and regular education programs must be allowed to collectively contribute skills and resources to carry out individualized education plans based on individualized education needs"* (emphasis in the original). Doing so, she asserted, would allow for more effective instruction without the stigma of the label and consequent social obstacles for the student. Will too encouraged using research on effective schools and practices to help undertake carefully designed "experimental trials" in schools. Under an atmosphere of trust, implementation of such collaborative efforts geared toward improving the education of all students "will mean the creation of a more powerful, more responsive education system, one with enhanced component parts." Ultimately, Will envisioned, these efforts would "mean the nurturing of a shared commitment to the future of all children with special learning needs."[15]

Another early and staunch advocate of complete integration was Douglas Biklen of Syracuse University. Biklen's *Achieving the Complete*

School: Strategies for Effective Mainstreaming, published in 1985 and written in consultation with several other authors, offered specific advice to principals, teachers, district administrators, and parents on how to plan and implement mainstreaming. More distinctively, it focused to a large degree on what he saw as the ethical and moral imperatives of integration in school and society of persons with disabilities. Biklen and his colleagues acknowledged the challenge mainstreaming posed to schools: "it is a new phenomenon. It challenges old ways of doing things. It raises eyebrows, even hackles. It tends to become a lightning rod for people's emotions about schools in general." He told of how the constantly asked question "Is mainstreaming a good idea?" is "a bit like asking, 'Is Tuesday a good idea?' Both are wrong questions. It's not so much whether mainstreaming and Tuesdays are good ideas as what we make of them." To Biklen, "the question of whether or not to promote mainstreaming is not essentially a question for science. It is a moral question. It is a goal, indeed a value, we decide to pursue or reject on the basis of what we want our society to look like."[16]

In one of the book's most remarkable passages, Biklen compared the debate over whether or not "science" could show that mainstreaming was ineffective, or that segregationist approaches might work in certain situations, with a hypothetical debate over whether "scientific evidence" existed that supported bringing an end to slavery. He explained that plausible economic and social arguments could have been made to support slavery's continuation, and that little "evidence" existed at the time of the Emancipation Proclamation that ending slavery would have practical benefits. Nevertheless, he argued, no scientific evidence of any sort could justify an immoral practice such as slavery. Similarly, he maintained, discussions regarding the "scientific evidence" for segregation or against integration in schools was irrelevant; like slavery, or the use of abusive conditioning techniques, segregation of students along any lines was wrong and could not be supported under any circumstances. "For some things," he summarized, "we need no evidence. The practice itself is simply not acceptable." Biklen's work helped establish the presumed moral imperative of full integration, a feature that remains central to the positions of those advocating full inclusion.[17]

The Regular Education Initiative

This collective body of commentary formed the nucleus of what became known as the Regular Education Initiative (REI). The REI emerged in the late 1980s as the symbol, exemplar, and lightning rod of the movement to bring about more complete integration of students with disabilities into the mainstream through a fundamental restructuring of the nature and process of delivering special education services. The origins of the REI are generally attributed to Will's call for "a shared responsibility" (published as the article in *Exceptional Children* but delivered originally as a keynote address at a conference in December 1985) and to Margaret Wang and colleagues' "two-part initiative" (stemming from work dating to the early 1980s). Although the REI was more a generalized vision than a concrete plan with specific elements, it did contain several features acknowledged by most commentators as key to understanding its nature and scope—features which served as focal points for sustained and often sharp debate.

Neither Will nor Wang used the term *regular education initiative* in their presentations. Will's concept of a "shared responsibility," a "partnership," and a "collaboration" captured an essential element of the REI: a much more seamless and cooperative relationship between regular education and special education, with the latter becoming much less visible (or important) as a distinct, separate program. Reynolds, Wang, and Walberg suggested a "two-part initiative" that would ultimately lead to a more equitable and effective approach to educating all students, including those with special needs. The first part called for "the joining of demonstrably effective practices from special, compensatory, and general education to establish a general education system that is more inclusive and that better serves all students, particularly those who require greater-than-usual educational support." The second part of the initiative, drawing largely from Will's suggestions, called "for the federal government to collaborate with a number of states and local school districts in encouraging and supporting experimental trials of integrated forms of education for students who are currently segregated for service in separate special, remedial, and compensatory education programs." This aspect, according to Reynolds, Wang, and

Walberg, may necessitate a "waiver of performance," meaning schools or districts that experimented with such an approach would not have to follow certain rules or regulations or lose categorical funding losses in order to facilitate experimentation. Schools and districts in exchange would be required to provide data on school performance resulting from the experimentation. Thus, REI called for a federally initiated, sweeping consolidation of all programs specifically targeted for potential or actual low achievers in schools, including students identified as disabled, and a pooling of talent and resources to realize effective instruction for such students in regular classrooms. Under such a program, the formal classification and labeling of exceptional children would be abandoned, with determinations about appropriate instruction to be made on a case-by-case basis for *all* students. Thus the ultimate outcome of the initiative would be "full access to a restructured mainstream."[18]

In an attempt to summarize and explicate the basic assumptions of the REI, Joseph Jenkins, Constance Pious, and Mark Jewell of the University of Washington expressed some concern about its use as a focus of debate. To them, the REI was "an impressionistic sketch, drawing in broad strokes both the nature of the problems requiring attention and possible solutions. It is not an architectural blueprint. . . . [T]he REI could eventually be expressed in many ways, incorporating combinations and permutations of the best that the field has to offer. . . . But we are a long way from even laying the foundations for this effort." Nevertheless, Jenkins et al. determined some key assumptions of the initiative. First, support programs for all low-achieving students need to be coordinated at the school level, with the principal being authorized to distribute resources as she or he saw fit. Second, the responsibility for educating children with learning problems—including designing, providing, and managing instruction as well as organizing individualized assistance from specialists—should be returned to the regular classroom teachers. Specialists working with exceptional children would typically work alongside regular classroom teachers in regular classes, with much less reliance on working in resource or pull-out settings. No longer would special education belong primarily to teachers trained as special educators. Third, REI proponents seem to call for greater integration of students traditionally left out of even mainstreamed class-rooms, but the extent to which students with severe mental, physical, or behavioral disabilities would be included in regular classrooms was left open. Some proponents specifically excluded such students because regular classroom teachers may not have had the training, or did not have the support services available, to include such children successful-ly; others suggested all students belong in the regular class on a regular basis. "Disagreement among REI proponents about the inclusion of students with severe disabilities," Jenkins et al. asserted, "points out the ambiguities in both the intent and nature of this initiative." As it stood, the ultimate determination would apparently be based on the realities of the specific site: "Removal from the regular classroom would occur only when children could not be helped by the classroom teacher and a cadre of support personnel."[19]

Critique of Mainstreaming and the REI

Not surprisingly, this complex, ambitious movement toward more thorough integration of students with disabilities and a more collabo-rative and interconnected relationship between special education and regular education did not go unchallenged. While few scholars, practi-tioners, or other professionals criticized the spirit of PL 94-142 or efforts to create more opportunities for children with mild disabilities to interact with their nondisabled peers, many other aspects of the call for significant increases in regular class placement of exceptional chil-dren in particular, and for special education reform in general, encoun-tered earnest and extensive critique. In fact, debate became quite intense when addressing the advisability of expanding mainstreaming opportunities for students with moderate, severe, or multiple disabili-ties, the quality and reliability of research on the various pilot main-streaming projects—particularly the Adaptive Learning Environments Model (ALEM)—and on the wisdom of dismantling the traditional structures for delivering special education services in schools. Most major elements of this critique were raised in examinations of the Stainbacks' 1984 article advocating the merger of special and regular education; of ALEM as an effective model for mainstreaming; and in more generalized commentary on the practical and ethical dimensions of the REI.

Even with the advent of more assertive calls for greater integration of all students with disabilities, the idea of including students with severe, multiple, and other low-incidence disabilities in regular class-rooms on a more permanent basis struggled to gain acceptance. The ambiguity of the REI's stance on the practice underscored the ambiva-lence many experienced about the issue. Its primary focus was on advancing the inclusion of students identified as mildly labeled, espe-cially those with mild mental retardation, learning disabilities, or other disorders requiring less intense intervention. The ALEM did move toward including students with moderate as well as mild disabilities in its programs, but Team Assisted Individualization and other pilot pro-grams more often focused on the latter, since these represented the vast majority of exceptional children. In their interpretation of the REI, Jenkins, Pious, and Jewell surmised

> that with sufficient personnel and material resources, it would be pos-sible to deliver an appropriate instructional program in the regular classroom to any students, no matter what their curriculum goals, no matter how severe their handicap, with the possible exception of stu-dents who are given to extreme violence and aggression. But that in our view is not the intent of the REI. It would not be fair to regular class-room teachers (or their students) to hold them responsible for teach-ing all possible skills, for example, basic discriminations, mobility, self-care, community living, sign language, speech reading, and Braille reading. Students requiring these services would be placed in special classes. The line needs to be drawn somewhere to protect teachers from unrealistic demands and to assure parents of normally achieving stu-dents that their children will prosper.[20]

A representative example of the development of this effort was Martha Snell's analysis of the segregating effect PL 94-142 had on the education of students with severe disabilities and her proposal for including them more effectively in the regular classroom. Snell examined the efforts of the previous two decades and concluded that not only was successful full integration possible, it was educationally and ethically necessary. Snell maintained that schools needed to counter the segregationist effects of PL 94-142 by taking purposeful, proactive steps to include in regular classes all children regardless of the nature or severity of their disability. She noted the accepted "continuum of alternative placements" as well as "widespread ignorance about the education of people with severe disabilities" had led to continued segregation of such children into separate classes, schools, or other facilities. But she also pointed out that court decisions during the 1980s consistently established the right of all children to be in a truly least restrictive environment, which has been made so through the incorporation of the latest advances in teaching strategies, technology, and other resources.[21]

In April 1985, *Exceptional Children* published two critiques of the Stainbacks' "A Rationale for the Merger of Special and Regular Education" as well as the Stainbacks' rejoinder to these. John Mesinger of the University of Virginia disagreed with several of the Stainbacks' assumptions. First, Mesinger did not believe that American education held a tenet that the school program "should fit the needs of the student"; in fact, he stated, history and research show the opposite, and their view, he said, is "a distinctly minority viewpoint," and to use that as a basis for creating a student-centered merger of special and regular education is presumptuous at best. Mesinger also claimed that the proposed merger would require "far more specialized personnel than we now have," even at a time when schools and districts were struggling mightily to find qualified special educators and other specialists. While the Stainbacks suggested that states could fund more research and training to ease the shortage, Mesinger expressed strong skepticism that they would do so. He also described a series of concerns regarding the willingness and ability of regular education teachers to assume the responsibilities inherent in a merged system where they are deemed the person responsible for an exceptional child's education. "Excellent teachers are leaving and fewer talented people are entering the profession," he wrote, also noting that only some teachers possess the qualities necessary to "teach groups of differing ranges and intensity of diversity." In addition, even "special education preservice training programs have not always produced a good product," implying that even the "specialists" may have trouble managing the widely diverse classrooms inherent in a merged system. Finally, he noted, special education came about and continued because regular education had been unwilling and/or unable to accommodate children with disabilities, and continued to do so: "Agreeing with them on this statement about the nature of the beast, I do not believe it is time to place our handicapped children in the cage with it." Given the state of public education as described, Mesinger concluded that "the Stainbacks' proposal seems premature by years."[22]

In his commentary, Laurence Lieberman, a special education consultant, questioned the Stainbacks' assumption that the notion of "handicap" could be so easily dismissed by relying solely on a "continuum of services." While acknowledging that continuum, Lieberman could not likewise deny that the extremes of that continuum generated real disabilities. Not only in school but also in real life, he argued, those differences did in fact disable children, and that disability did have a negative impact on the child's life in and beyond school. Therefore, to propose a merger that minimized, downplayed, or denied the effects of disability would diminish the ability of special educators "to meet the needs of real handicapped children." Lieberman also doubted the willingness of regular classroom teachers to make all adjustments necessary for such a merger; "we cannot drag regular educators kicking and screaming into a merger with special education," he argued. "The daily evidence on mainstreaming attitudes is too overwhelming." When would they change? "How about a few millennia?" He was particularly concerned about the absence of input from regular educators into developing such a proposal. To him, the Stainbacks' initiative was unilateral—and doomed: "We have thrown a wedding and neglected to invite the bride. If this is an invitation to holy matrimony, it was clearly written by the groom, for the groom, and the groom's family."[23]

Lieberman questioned as "the height of optimism and even naiveté" the Stainbacks' assumption that a merger would result in a general education system that allows the child to dictate the curriculum. He challenged their belief that segregated instruction would nearly disappear: "Just hypothetically accept merger. Nothing changes. Students who are not successful in a particular class will be pulled out and taught by others, duality or merger notwithstanding." And he disputed their argument that labeling and categories were inherently wrong: While acknowledging drawbacks, Lieberman stated "that a child categorized by special education has a significantly better chance of being treated as an individual than if he or she remains noncategorized within the overall framework of regular education." To jettison these traditional structures and protections of special education would jeopardize the education of all disabled children. Although praising the Stainbacks for their "completely honest, courageous perspective . . . [that] is unquestionably fair, just, and humanistic," he dismissed the proposal as unrealistic in light of special education's entrenched history and necessary services. "Merging regular and special education into one unified system will never result in the attainment of these worthy goals," he declared. "It can only occur with each party maintaining a strong sense of individual identity, while creating an ideal interface between the two."[24]

In their rejoinder, the Stainbacks essentially expressed a strong optimism and a more assertive call to action to confront these critiques and realize the possibilities of an authentic merger. Mesinger and Lieberman, they argued, underestimated the talent and willingness of both special and regular educators to initiate and sustain the planning and implementation necessary to help a merger succeed. Instead of being held hostage by an "us vs. them" past, they suggested, both special and regular educators needed to abandon relatively petty issues of control, territory, and self-preservation and look to an exciting future of collaboration and professional development. They reaffirmed their belief that labels serve no educational purpose and denied that disability could weigh down children to the extent their critics suggested. Claiming that segregated instruction has "never been shown to be of any major instructional value," the Stainbacks insisted that the opportunity existed to move forward:

> If we believe that an integrated, unified system of education is right and desirable, we should not let present-day realities keep us from working *toward the goal.* We fully realize that based on present-day

realities, there are likely to be many obstacles, battles, wars, and blood-baths along the way and it is likely to take a very long time. But the central question is: Should we give up on our ideals and goals because present-day reality dictates that they will be difficult to achieve?

For the Stainbacks, clearly the answer was no.[25]

Emerging Themes of the REI Critiques

By the late 1980s, critique of the REI itself focused on several recurring themes. Some of these addressed the REI in particular, considering its qualities as a concrete proposal; others encompassed broader issues that had been and continued to be central features of the debate about the nature and extent of efforts to more fully integrate students with disabilities into regular classrooms. Themes included the alleged ambiguity and inconsistency of REI proponents in defining and characterizing the initiative; the REI's rejection of traditional practices of categorization and labeling of students for special education services; concerns regarding the effects that more extensive integration of exceptional children in regular classrooms would have on academic achievement, socialization, and teacher activities and effectiveness; the actual nature of the current relationship between special and regular education; the suspect nature of research validating integrative programs crucial to the REI's success; and interpretations of the benefits and drawbacks of special education throughout its existence. Finally, an intriguing interpretation of REI as a thinly veiled attempt to pursue a conservative political agenda for public education merits some discussion.

REI critics expressed considerable reservation about the REI's nebulous character, noting that it lacked a consistent, universally accepted definition and that certain important elements remained poorly defined even after years of discussion. Was it merely a "partnership," as Madeleine Will suggested, or was it a true "merger" that would lead to the dissolution of a "special education" and the establishment of a "unitary system," as suggested by the Stainbacks and by Gartner and Lipsky? Did REI champion the full integration of all students, regardless of disability, or did it sanction segregated settings for students with severe disabilities or those who engage in dangerous classroom behaviors? One task force listed more than 250 questions that required attention before implementing REI, according to Jenkins et al. Lieberman asserted that "within a short period of time, the meaning of REI is becoming murky. . . . people are using the term *REI* and not knowing that their own sense of what it means is different from that of others. This is true even among special educators themselves." The absence of specificity even for aspects generally agreed upon also drew criticism.[26]

The decades-old debate about the relative merits and drawbacks of categorizing and labeling students for special education services became a central feature of discourse over the REI. Proponents decried the practice, once again citing the stigma associated with labels, the absence of educational or pedagogical value attached to such labels, and the "waste" of time and money used in the process. However, REI opponents maintained their defense of categorization and labeling. Kauffman, Gerber, and Simmel argued that disability labels, especially the generic "handicapped" and more specific "mentally retarded" were "reasonable and ultimately beneficial as they are applied to *some* individuals" and that labeling "indicating the need for special education is, in fact, appropriate for most (though certainly not all) students now receiving special education services." The process, required by PL 94-142, also helped protect special education resources in times of cutbacks and provided a vehicle for parents of disabled children to claim appropriate services for their child. Attacking the notion of "rights without labels," Kauffman noted that without the labels or other identifying designations, society may well ignore the needs of such individuals; citing Judith Singer, he observed, "taking away their label will not make their problem disappear." Besides, it was argued, the stigmatizing effects of labeling were not as negative or serious as REI proponents proclaimed.[27]

Opponents of REI were especially critical of the REI's assumptions about what would and should take place in the regular classroom once almost every student was mainstreamed into it. They saw the major issue as one of just how a regular class teacher, now responsible for the educational achievement of children with disabilities as well as of those without, would balance the competing goals of excellence versus equity. Excellence called for a classroom and a school to improve academic achievement, to approach excellence in all academic endeavors. Equity required teachers to provide every student with the attention she or he needs, meaning that those students who struggle will get most of the attention, presumably at the expense of the average and above-average students, thus diluting efforts to achieve excellence across the board. Kauffman, Gerber, and Simmel framed this as trying to both "maximize mean performance of the group" and "minimize the variance in performance of the group," a goal they deemed unattainable, since the goals were virtually mutually exclusive given the practical realities of classrooms. Such difficult circumstances would place enormous and unfair expectations on all teachers, especially the regular education teacher who was, in the end, responsible for student achievement in her or his classroom. Ultimately, they argued, "we see handicapped students being set up for a fall." As Kauffman observed, "Teachers cannot avoid this dilemma, which would be made more painful by the inclusion of more difficult-to-teach students in regular classrooms."[28]

The problem of how best to plan and implement instruction for students with and without disabilities in a fully integrated regular classroom pointed to what several critics saw as a glaring flaw in the REI: the failure to solicit input, hear the voices, or consider the intellectual and temperamental competencies of regular classroom teachers, almost all of whom had poor training in special education or, more likely, no training at all. William Davis charged that the REI development and debate had taken place almost entirely in the rarified air of higher education, divorced from the realities of the public schools and the concerns of other major stakeholders: parents, local districts, students, even scholars in other disciplines. Laurence Lieberman had mockingly suggested that the REI be known as SEIFRE (Special Education Initiative for Regular Educators), commenting that despite its name, the movement came from those most disaffected with special education. Echoing Lieberman's metaphor of a wedding without the bride, Davis admonished REI proponents for their exclusivity and challenged them to pay much greater heed to the training, aptitudes, working conditions, and attitudes of regular educators. He noted how regular class teachers felt "overburdened and unfairly criticized" in discussions of the need for educational reform and in particular "viewed increased special education mandates as being especially intrusive and unrealistic." Jenkins, Pious, and Jewell gave detailed attention to the implications of REI for regular classroom practice, emphasizing the complex nature of instruction and behavior management in such a classroom that placed such heavy responsibilities on teachers and administrators who, at least at the time, were insufficiently trained, prepared, or inclined to accept it. They observed that REI would not magically solve issues of territory, power, or status between special and regular educators and conjectured that there existed a strong possibility that a true "partnership" would continue unrealized. Others openly questioned not only the willingness but also the ability of significant numbers of regular classroom teachers to do what needed to be done to make integrated classrooms successful, given their typical lack of training, experience, or empathy in working with exceptional children. [29]

Other key stakeholders ignored by REI advocates, insisted Davis, were the students who were to be included in regular classrooms and expected to succeed academically and socially. "The widespread absence of *consumers* themselves in the REI debate," he charged, "if not surprising, is particularly disturbing." Davis reminded his readers that students had been routinely denied a voice in setting special education policy and practice throughout its history in virtually every arena, and that this situation demanded fundamental reform. "I am not referring to token involvement on the part of consumers [such as] in the Individual Education Program process," he explained, "where seldom does any real discourse occur. Typically, professionals talk and clients (students and parents) listen." Instead, Davis called for

> the real, meaningful involvement of consumers in the REI debate, especially those students at the secondary level. I strongly suspect that students frequently feel "jerked around" by the educational system. They become either benefactors or victims, in varying degree, of philosophical debate, litigation, and legislative mandates that are subsequently transformed into educational policies and practices . . . .Yet how often are students really listened to or their opinions truly valued? . . . Very simply, I am urging that students not be denied access to the REI

debate . . . . Should this not occur with significantly greater frequency, not only will opportunities for valuable input for the shaping of the debate be lost but also many students, both handicapped and non-handicapped, will continue to labor under totally invalid assumptions about what *others* are trying to do with, for, and to *them* (emphasis in the original).[30]

In a response to Davis's plea to hear from public school professionals about their views of the REI, Maryann Byrnes of the Sudbury, Massachusetts, public schools, noted the progress made for children with disabilities under traditional approaches to special education. She also offered cautionary statements about the difficulties inherent in special and regular educators building and maintaining effective partnerships, doubts about the ability of schools to provide necessary supports to teachers in the classroom, and concerns that REI would be forced upon local school districts before other possibilities or alternatives had been sufficiently explored. She concluded that "the REI is not ready for implementation. Much more dialogue needs to occur, with a broader group of participants. . . . we should remember that, just as no two children are exactly the same, no one method will work equally well for everyone." To their critics, proponents of REI and the extensive integration of most children with disabilities into the regular classroom had failed to either listen to regular classroom teachers or consider their readiness for it.[31]

Besides, some critics proclaimed, the research base supporting the potential for more integrative approaches was thin at best, and special education was not as troubled or sinister as some advocates for greater integration and the abolition of a "dualistic" system believed. Continuing the long line of discussion over the quality of research on special education practices and outcomes, Douglas and Lynn Fuchs argued that the ALEM, identified by many as an exemplar of an integrated public school program, had not earned its acclaim as a successful program. The Fuchs charged that evaluations of ALEM that showed it to be successful were flawed for a variety of reasons and thus yielded unreliable and questionable results, and that the positive interpretations of much of the data did not hold up under closer analysis. Kauffman claimed that the entire research base supporting the REI "reflected a

Douglas and Lynn S. Fuchs

cavalier attitude toward experimentation and research," not only by promoting alternative, REI-grounded programs but also by criticizing special education's past activities. Careful examination, skeptics argued, showed that the "schism" or "dualistic system" between special and regular education was not nearly as pronounced as advertised. Most students with disabilities, it was pointed out, do participate at least part of the day in integrated settings; sufficient cooperation between special education and regular education had led to significant accomplishments for millions of exceptional children; and PL 94-142 had been quite successful in bringing children with disabilities into viable school programs and in ensuring a steadily increasing supply of funding and other resources to assure their free and appropriate education in the least restrictive environment. There was, critics argued, little need to jettison a system that demonstrated far greater success than failure.[32]

One other line of critique moved the debate from beyond the world of education and into the political arena. James Kauffman, in an article published in 1989 in *The Journal of Special Education*, charged that the REI was in fact an outcome, indeed a cornerstone, of efforts by the Reagan administration to dismantle programs intended for disadvantaged populations in schools and apply "trickle-down" economic theory to public education. Noting the wholesale rejection by REI advocates of long-standing "segregationist" assumptions and practices in special education, Kauffman maintained that the "new, 'integrated' model in which all students are special" dovetailed nicely with the administration's efforts "to reduce federal expenditures for social programs" and its belief that "the general improvement of education is the best strategy for educating handicapped students—a trickle-down theory of educational benefit—is consistent with the Reagan-Bush administration's education policy and political strategy." Kauffman reminded readers that Madeleine Will, a key advocate of the push for more complete integration of exceptional children in schools, was "a Reagan political appointee" whose work wielded a strong influence over that of other REI proponents. Kauffman interpreted the REI to be a manifestation of the conservative agenda: to deny necessary services to those in need, to reduce expenditures by abolishing expensive endeavors such as special education, and to favor students from more privileged backgrounds over those whose backgrounds put them at a great disadvantage. He acknowledged the irony of so many educators who likely considered themselves politically liberal but nonetheless maintained that those who support REI were in fact supporting the Reagan agenda.[33]

Naturally this drew heated denials; Lori Goetz and Wayne Sailor asserted that Kauffman's position was "emotionally charged" and "simply does not hold water." The inclusion of students with disabilities would lead to a "trickle-up" effect, one where all students benefit. Goetz and Sailor clearly resented Kauffman's assumption that REI is designed "to free up more money to further benefit the high achieving children of the wealthier classes" and that "presumed liberals like ourselves are hapless dupes in this process, pursuing our well-intentioned agenda for progressive inclusion within a more egalitarian society at the unwitting expense of needy children with disabilities." Such an exchange, combined with another heated debate through scholarly journals between the Fuchs and Wang and Walberg—one that incorporated (or perhaps degenerated into) more personal and emotional considerations—typified the status of the debate over integration by the early 1990s.[34]

Voices: Assessing the Value of Integration in Special Education

While the debate intensified within the sphere of professional educators and scholars, others directly involved in special education—the children with disabilities, their families, and their advocates—also weighed in on the concept and practice of main-

James M. Kauffman

streaming and more complete integration of students with disabilities in the schools. Increasingly, the comments of students, parents, and caregivers found their way into various public forums as evidence in support of greater inclusion or as voices expressing skepticism and concern.

As had been the case in the initial landmark court decisions concerning special education in the 1970s, parents continued to play a significant role in advancing the cause of greater integration on the legal front. In one high-profile example, a strong and vocal cohort of parents combined forces with the Disability Rights Education and Defense Fund to bring about the desegregation of students with disabilities in the Richmond, California, public schools in the early 1980s. A letter to the California State Commission on Special Education from a group of parents of children assigned to a segregated special education school in the district argued that "segregated education is but another form of institutionalization which we view as extremely detrimental to the growth and development of disabled and nondisabled children alike." Through a strong parental alliance that produced not only letters but formal complaints and local political action, the Richmond district closed the segregated school and took significant, numerous steps to ensure a smooth and rapid transition to more authentic and complete integration of students with disabilities through increased appropriations and staff development. Inservice training for the district's teachers was a crucial feature of the plan, and its apparent successful implementation helped parents feel more positive and secure about the decision to integrate their children in the schools. Another outcome was the formation of Parents and Advocates for Special Education in the district, an organization that claimed membership from a considerably broad segment of the city's population. Not all parents in the district agreed with the approach or policy adopted by these parent advocates: a representative of another group of parents of children attending a different district-based segregated special education school argued that "integration is not the answer for most of our children. While a few might benefit, the majority would not," the group said, asserting that their segregated school provided "a safe atmosphere for the children." Even so, the district exemplified that power and voice that parents and organizations can exercise to achieve certain ends in special education policy and practice.[35]

The voices of parents and children also played key roles for certain agencies presenting the cause of integration. Among the most visible was the Massachusetts Advocacy Center's report *Out of the Mainstream*, published in May 1987 as a fervent attempt to explain the value of integration in special education to a still skeptical public. The document highlighted the commentary and praise of parents and students expressing their support and gratitude for efforts to advance the cause of integration for themselves and their peers. One former student noted that segregated school experiences leave students "completely unprepared for the real world . . . . Believe me, a segregated environment just will not do as preparation for an integrated life." Another recalled her segregated school setting: "We were isolated. Symbolically—and appropriate to the prevailing attitudes—the 'handicapped and retarded' classrooms were tucked away in the corner of the school basement. . . . [T]he only contact we had with the 'normal' children was visual. We stared at each other. . . . We were internalizing the 'yech' message—plus a couple of others." The report contrasted such poignant reflections with statements celebrating the value of integration. One parent of a child with autism praised her child's presence in a regular classroom by observing,

My child can talk. And, that's one reason why he can. It's because of the other children. The typical children kept coming up to him and talking to him and demanding that he talk. They knew how to get an answer from him, and they wouldn't let him get away with a single-syllable response. Now I ask you, what teacher or teachers could do that for my son, much less for a whole class of kids with autism?

The report also identified areas where schools and other authorities were failing to advise parents of their rights under the law and the schools' responsibilities in providing more integrated settings and services. It attempted to identify areas where parents needed to increase their awareness, visibility, and advocacy on behalf of their children, claiming that, in fact, schools were either ignoring or dishonoring the rights of the disabled in schools.[36]

In fact, parents often expressed concern if not outright frustration with their encounters with school officials—before and after PL 94-142—especially regarding placement issues. Parents' perceptions of hostility toward their children, as well as resistance to the hard work needed to realize effective integration on the part of teachers and administrators, caused many parents to react harshly to the perceived intransigence and patronizing attitudes of school representatives. Such views typically went unexpressed—at least publicly—but other parents were pushed to prepare detailed critiques of schools' reluctance to pursue more complete integration, often within the contexts of formal hearings and lawsuits. For example, parents were instrumental in initiating and sustaining the complex legal maneuvering involved in *Daniel R. R. v. State Board of Education*, a 1989 court case that led to mixed results in the courts but resulted in greater integration opportunities for the child in question.[37]

However, parents were not of a single voice on the potential and reality of a more integrated special education. One parent noted the sea change in what parents of children with disabilities were advised before PL 94-142 and after:

Before PL-94-142 became law, we parents were told that our handicapped children were more comfortable, safer, and better educated in special classes. After the law passed, parents heard the phrase that special ed kids were going to have to function in a general ed world. As our children grew older, we realized the latter is true, that integration is truly all-encompassing. . . . When disabled children carry out socially accepted tasks in regular environments, they are preparing for a general ed world.

Even so, this same parent affirmed the ambivalence felt by many others toward mainstreaming or integration: "Parents of both disabled and nondisabled children are concerned about educational mainstreaming. . . . In many situations, opposition to mainstreaming has come from parents of disabled children, who . . . wonder if schools are ready to integrate special needs children. These fears are justified." Another parent, who prepared a guide to the world of special education for other parents, stressed the positive social effects of integration on all children and noted that creative and positive steps toward more integration can enliven a school's environment and atmosphere. However, the parent also acknowledged that segregated settings were valuable to some children if designed and used properly and were truly geared toward the child's effective education. Another parent described how her child failed when placed in a poorly prepared regular classroom. "In special ed," wrote the parent, "the students can be kept with their peers while being allowed to function at a level at which they can function. . . . The child can and does learn." But when her daughter was placed in the regular class, "she started stuttering so badly she couldn't communicate with us at all. . . . We felt that [her physician] was being proven right. He had warned against placing her in a situation where she couldn't succeed." Such expressions of optimism and dismay characterized parental voice during the post-PL 94-142 era, where the nature, planning, and execution of more integrated approaches varied widely—as did the needs and preferences of the children and families involved.[38]

National organizations and associations of and for groups of persons with disabilities also reflected such ambivalence. For example, in its 1990 position statement on education, The Arc (formerly the National Association for Retarded Citizens) stated that schools should value all students, that sound preparation for life beyond school requires an education alongside a diverse group of peers, that "each student with a disability belongs in an age-appropriate classroom with peers who are not disabled," and that each student merits individualized instruction. The document noted several practical benefits of integration of students with disabilities but also said that it "does not need to be justified on this basis, for it is really a matter of human dignity and human rights." Their 1992 report card on the state of integration gave failing grades to forty-two states, and "C"s to only two (Massachusetts and Vermont). Their hope was that the report would "stimulate action toward the goal of full inclusion in the nation's public schools for all children with mental retardation and other disabilities." In contrast, the Council for Children with Behavioral Disorders (CCBD) expressed doubts about the viability of the REI for children with behavioral disorders especially. "Advocates of the REI," stated the Council's *Position Statement on the Regular Education Initiative,* "frequently fail to recognize the magnitude and difficulty of the task of accommodating all students appropriately in general education. . . . Implementation of the REI will reinforce the view that students' offensive behavior is *their* problem . . . rather than . . . a school-owned problem requiring combined efforts of professionals from several disciplines." Accordingly the CCBD expressed "a reaffirmation of the need for an array of service options" that would guarantee carefully considered and designed segregated settings when necessary and appropriate. Segregated settings, it argued, need not automatically be considered failures, nor integrated settings automatically assumed successes; rather, "improving the quality of pull-out programs may be a feasible strategy for improving the school experience of behaviorally disordered students."[39]

By the early 1990s, the themes surrounding the merits and drawbacks of greater integration, mainstreaming, or (by then) inclusion were well established; what changed was the heatedness and tone of the discussion. During the 1990s, discourse regarding integration, mainstreaming, and inclusion moved toward greater resentment, bitterness, and polarization, indicating not only the critical importance of the issue but also that the inevitable clash between the practical and moral or ethical aspects of the debate had intensified dramatically. During the next decade, *inclusion* would become one of the most controversial and divisive issues facing public education.

7

Resistance to Integration: Giftedness and Deafness

ERHAPS THE most powerful legacy of the *Brown v. Board of Education* decision in 1954 was the widespread acceptance in national legal and educational policy of the ethical necessity of authentic, meaningful integration whenever and wherever possible. The abuse of civil and human rights caused by the forced segregation of various social groups has haunted the country throughout its history. Certainly the view of segregation as inherently and universally unjustified permeates the literature supporting the movement toward complete integration of students with disabilities in the regular classrooms of the public schools. Nevertheless, the view of segregation as indefensible is not shared by all. Two particular groups of advocates for children considered exceptional—the gifted and the deaf—have publicly and forcefully argued that for many, if not most or even all, of the children in these two categories of exceptionality, segregated classes and schools may well be not only justifiable but preferable. The views of advocates for these groups have by no means been universally agreed to or accepted—even within each group—but the constancy and urgency of those who maintain that segregated settings for these children are appropriate and certainly constitute the least restrictive environment stand out in the inclusion debate as noteworthy and provocative assertions.

Gifted Education and the Question of Integration

The question of how best to provide for children whose intellectual and creative abilities far surpass those of most other students has concerned educators since the beginning conceptualizations of universal public education in this country. Thomas Jefferson's notion of "raking" the brightest children from the "rubbish" of the general population and W. E. B. DuBois's advocacy for establishing higher education programs for the "talented tenth" of the African American population provide interesting and provocative comparisons with Horace Mann's and John Dewey's belief in egalitarian approaches that resist separating such learners from their peers in the name of democracy and equality.

Historians have framed this contrast as a debate between "excellence" and "equity," applying it not only to issues related to gifted education but also to curriculum planning for public education in general. The debate continued during the 1950s, when criticism of the alleged "soft" pedagogy and anti-intellectualism of progressivism gained strength and the launch of Sputnik startled not only educators but Congress into paying closer attention to rigorous academic training of America's most talented students. From the late 1950s into the late 1960s, a renewed emphasis on science and mathematics education (especially for academically talented students), on better understanding of how students learn, and on developing creativity in children directed national attention to the education of a strictly defined intellectual "elite" and to core values of gifted education. With increasing concern over the struggles minority, disadvantaged, and disabled children were experiencing in schools, however, resources were for several years redirected to help such children gain greater opportunity in schools, especially from the late 1960s through early 1970s. Once again, however, the pendulum shifted toward the development of excellence as educators became alarmed at falling test scores and the public reacted to the "rising tide of mediocrity" in schools as proclaimed in the 1983 report *A Nation At Risk*. The nation continues to struggle with achieving an appropriate balance of developing talent and achieving equity, which, as noted in a previous chapter, complicated proposals for integrating children with disabilities more thoroughly in regular classrooms. Consequently, there has been a constant rise and fall of both attention and resources being directed to the development of programs targeting the relatively small number of students identified as superior in academic and creative talent.[1]

Public schools had begun by the early 1900s not only to purposefully identify the most "intelligent" students but also to establish specialized programs to nurture their abilities and render school instruction more efficient. As of the mid-1920s, school districts across the country were using mental testing, especially the Stanford-Binet test developed by Lewis Terman, to stratify the intellectual abilities of all students and to identify either extreme of the continuum. In addition to the special classes for children identified as mentally retarded, a number of school systems introduced programs for students identified as gifted. Boston, for example, developed "rapid advancement" classes for gifted children during the 1910s, with enrollment reaching almost 200 by 1918. The classes were discontinued in 1924 but reestablished several years later, with 282 students enrolled in them as of 1930. Soon "Terman classes" or other programs for gifted students were features of larger school districts nationwide.[2]

Discussions about the proper nature of and setting for gifted education revolved around two basic questions: Should the content provide an *accelerated* program, an *enriched* program, or both; and should it take place in heterogeneous or homogenous settings, that is, within the regular classroom or in a specialized, even segregated setting? From the 1910s, school districts employed various combinations of responses to these basic questions. Stephen Daurio's review of the literature related to gifted education shows that educators used both acceleration and enrichment in developing specialized programs and classes in both public and private schools. Boston's "rapid advancement" classes obviously focused on acceleration; that is, moving selected children through the standard curriculum at a more rapid rate in order to save money, as well as avoid boredom and possible consequent rebellious behavior on the part of an underchallenged student. Other schools and districts relied on acceleration as well; most of the "Terman classes" relied primarily if not exclusively on acceleration—especially those developed relatively early, like Boston's—and focused on trying to get students to finish their school programs at least a year early as well as encouraging many students to enter college at a younger age. However, considerable concern over the potential "socioemotional maladjustment" of children moving too quickly up the school ladder or being grouped with considerably older children dogged the acceleration approach and likely limited its use.[3]

Educational enrichment offered opportunities for greater variety and flexibility in gifted education and was also used widely. *Lateral* enrichment was typically seen as "nonaccelerative," involving opportunities for gifted student to expand their study of topics appropriate to their chronological age-grade levels. It consisted of "irrelevant academic enrichment," meaning that it was meant to "enrich educational lives of some group of intellectually talented students" but "pays no attention to the specific nature of their talents." Or enrichment might be "relevant," meaning that the subject matter "fits the specific educational needs" of each superior student; this represented a more individualized approach to enriching gifted curriculum. In either case, the idea was to expand a student's encounters with subject matter that, at its core, is age- and grade-appropriate and also allows students to explore topics and ideas of personal interest in greater depth and with more intensive analysis. Enrichment programs became especially popular during the 1940s, a decade that saw the development of separate programs and classes and even "library corners" reserved for the extra work of gifted children.[4]

A large body of literature described programs throughout the country that relied on an enrichment framework; these included private schools and programs, special programs within public schools, special segregated classes, and even special time carved out of a regular class during the course of the day. Districts such as New York City took a keen interest in such programs, as did the state of California and cities such as Pittsburgh and Cleveland. Cleveland's Major Work Program, for example, received significant attention during the 1950s as an enrichment-based program that offered opportunities from elementary through high school and relied extensively on separate classes designed for children with a measured IQ of 125 or more. The special classes featured greater student responsibility and independence and teachers who served more as facilitators than deliverers of information. Creators of the program expressed a strong conviction that enrichment was the appropriate approach for educating gifted students.[5]

Gifted education from the 1910s through the 1970s exhibited no strong preference either for segregated special classes or programs or for special projects or activities within the framework of the regular classroom program. Romaine Mackie's data from 1963 showed that of 214,671 students identified as gifted in the public schools, 49,624 were in a special class full-time, 89,510 spend at least part of their day in regular classes, and 75,537 were "not reported by program." To the Council for Exceptional Children (CEC), the location of gifted education was not as important as its existence and content. In a 1973 policy statement, the CEC stated that "if the advanced capacity of the gifted is taken seriously, the usual school arrangements must be altered." It went on to say that

> No single administrative plan or educational provision is totally appropriate for the gifted. . . . the task is one of accommodation to the needs of the individual. New arrangements and new provisions must be utilized, including freedom to pursue interests which might not fit the prescribed curriculum. . . . These kinds of arrangements must go on in all educational settings and procedures for the gifted, whether in the regular classroom or in highly specialized situations.

Because giftedness was not a category of exceptionality authorized under special education law in PL 94-142, districts have been able to determine how—or whether—to organize, structure, and deliver education for students identified as gifted and talented. There continues to exist a wide variety of programs and approaches to integration for gifted education throughout the country; these can include ability grouping in a regular class, separate tracks or special classes of particular grades for gifted children, public school magnet programs, and private schools.[6]

The debate over whether gifted students should be placed in segregated settings continues as well. While some argue that such students belong in the regular classroom, learning with and assisting in teaching their "non-gifted" peers, others maintain that effective gifted education demands separate instructional settings. One of the strongest advocates for keeping gifted students in the regular classroom, Mara Sapon-Shevin, challenges several assumptions she attributes to those who argue for segregated programs, averring that all students exhibit gifts in a multitude of ways and that "gifted education" is nothing more than a sound, individualized educational program that all students deserve. She identifies what she considers negative academic, social, and emotional consequences of isolating gifted children from their peers and laments the elitist nature of segregated gifted education that she maintains perpetuates the advantages of the privileged. According to Sapon-Shevin, segregating gifted students has unfortunate effects on parents, families, teachers, schools, and society. Framing her arguments within those supporting generalized inclusion of all exceptional children, she advocates keeping the gifted child in the regular classroom, where all children are entitled to an individualized education appropriate to their needs and interests and where all children can benefit from its diversity and opportunity. Supporting such thoughts, Thomas McDaniel argues that "gifted students should, to the maximum degree possible, be taught in the regular classroom," although he acknowledges that much work must be done to make that regular classroom suitable for the instruction of gifted (and all other) children. To that end, June Maker's edited volume, among many others, consists of practical suggestions on a number of levels for making the regular classroom more accommodating to gifted students.[7]

However, many other educators strongly disagree with this perspective and argue instead for separate programs. Barbara Clark, a longtime advocate of specialized education for the gifted, observed that there are indeed students whose gifts and talents clearly distinguish them from most of their age-mates and that nurturing those qualities requires a sophisticated, comprehensive program, tailored to their abilities, which requires careful planning as well as specialized activities, resources, strategies, and other services. She argues that "if these needs are not met . . . these learners will not maintain their ability—they will lose their ability. . . . Programs that do not provide for this group of learners do a disservice not only to these students but to all of society, as they waste our finest minds." Clark states that a wide array of programmatic options must be offered to gifted students and that it would be impossible to ensure these only in regular classrooms. "In a perfect world," she writes, "the ideal classroom could exist that would make this range of programs unnecessary, however, with the barriers now commonly found in regular education classrooms we must provide alternatives."[8]

Seconding Clark's arguments, Aimee Howley, Craig B. Howley, and Edwina Pendarvis bluntly stated, "Normalization and its prime placement stratagem, mainstreaming, are *not* principles that maximize the potential of the gifted" (emphasis in the original). Claiming that the gifted do not suffer the isolation and stigmatization that the disabled typically experience, they maintain that separation is a definite benefit for gifted students. Segregated programs, they claim, guarantee the smaller class size, appropriate pacing and distribution of time accorded various activities, and more appropriate use of a teacher's time and skills than do regular classrooms. According to Howley, Howley, and Pendarvis, placement of gifted students in regular classes limits or even denies them opportunities to develop their academic and/or creative abilities. Rather than maximizing the gifted child's potential, an inclusive setting "amounts to a diminution of potential. . . . Moreover, because of the enduring and perhaps inevitable practices of the regular classroom, full-time placement in the regular classroom is usually the least appropriate alternative for gifted students." The authors also challenge the notion that segregated gifted instruction is elitist because "cognitive aptitudes and skills are, on a personal level, irrelevant to the way in which social inequality is structured." They propose an extension of the continuum of alternative placements that would not only permit but also encourage special classes and schools for those children showing the most superior gifts and talents. Like other exceptionalities, giftedness has generated considerable debate as to the viability of the regular classroom to maximize instruction for all students as well as to the consequences that labeling and segregation can have on those labeled exceptional as well as those who are not.[9]

The Deaf Community and Its Challenge to Integration

The education of the deaf has the longest recorded history of any specialized approach to education, at least in the Western world. Until the early twentieth century, virtually all of that education took place in segregated settings. Residential institutions have housed most of these programs, serving mostly persons who are severely or profoundly deaf. In 1869, day schools for the deaf began operating when the Boston public schools opened a School for Deaf-Mutes; by turn of the century, such schools existed in several cities and states. During the early twentieth century, a considerable number of public school systems initiated either day schools or other settings, such as "lipreading" or "speechreading" classes for students with mild or moderate hearing loss.

As these different settings for educating deaf students emerged, a fundamental controversy over the most appropriate means for teaching deaf children and for communicating with other deaf persons as well as the hearing world took shape. The traditional medium of communication among deaf persons—sign language—had served the deaf community for hundreds of years yet precluded easy communication with most persons who could hear. By the 1860s, an alternative mode of communication—*oralism*—began to garner the attention of deaf as well as hearing persons. Oralism advocated the use of lipreading and oral speech training for deaf persons, with oralist advocates contending that such an approach would allow deaf persons to become more accepted and respected in the dominant world of the hearing. By the late 1800s, both manualism and oralism were being taught in institutions, but the day schools began and continued to serve as bastions of the oralist philosophy. With the support of prominent individuals such as Alexander Graham Bell and Helen Keller, and the endorsement of an international convention of teachers of the deaf held in Milan, Italy, in 1880, oralism gained ground as the preferred mode of communication and the principal focus of training and instruction in the day schools and public school classes. This occurred despite the protestations and efforts of traditional manualists such as Edward Miner Gallaudet.[10]

The manualism-oralism debate held key implications for the education for the deaf and for decisions about the integration or segregation of deaf students in public schools. Whereas manualism represented the sense of pride, self-assuredness, and unique identity the deaf community felt toward itself, oralism reflected the belief, so clearly articulated by Bell, that deafness was an inferior, damaging quality that restricted and stigmatized the lives of those who suffered from it. Manualism constituted a powerful mechanism for maintaining an independent deaf culture as well as a symbol of its integrity; oralism manifested the belief that deafness was a blight on American society that needed to be masked, overcome, and eventually extinguished. Hence, manualism served as a means of perpetuating a segregated (and proudly so) deaf community, and its use in residential institutions stood as a method to preserve that sense of community and maintain the richness of deaf culture. Oralism, on the other hand, offered an opportunity to break down barriers between the deaf and hearing worlds while providing deaf people with previously denied access to and prestige within the overwhelmingly dominant hearing community.

As programs developed in the public schools, they maintained their traditional, overwhelming focus on children who had at least some partial hearing. Children who were severely or profoundly deaf were typically placed in the school programs of residential institutions for the deaf; if not, their profound hearing loss relegated them to totally segregated special classes or schools within school districts. Of the 28,551 deaf and hard of hearing students in the public schools in 1963, 6,612 were classified as profoundly deaf, and only 960 of those participated to any extent at all in regular classrooms. As noted earlier, however, significant strides had been made in including children with mild or moderate hearing loss in regular classes at least to some extent, usually facilitated by teaching such students to read lips and to engage in basic oral speech with their hearing peers. Integrated programs also frequently relied on extra resources being made available to regular classroom teachers, including interpreters, speech therapists, assistive hearing devices, and occasional inservice training. Even so, most children who were congenitally and/or profoundly deaf were not able to master those skills—especially intelligible oral communication—that school officials deemed requisite for even part-time participation in regular classes.[11]

Over the next twenty years, the segregated nature of instruction for deaf students changed little. According to data from the 1984–1985 school year, 71,160 deaf or hard of hearing students were being educated—in public and private institutions, day and residential schools, various public school classes, hospitals, correctional facilities, and at home. Of these, 14,933 were enrolled in regular public school classes for the entire day. All other children with hearing impairments spent all or part of their day in segregated settings: 16,666 in resource rooms, 22,009 in a separate class, 5,135 in a separate public school facility, and the rest—over 11,000 students—in segregated private schools, residential institutions, or other facilities. Consequently, more than 80 percent of children with any sort of substantial hearing loss spent part of their day in a segregated resource room or all of their day in a fully segregated setting.[12]

Specialized speech and lipreading training, assistive technology, and the advent of total communication (combining manual and oral approaches) and bilingual/bimodal communication have rendered access to the regular classroom more possible for students with hearing impairments, and numerous attempts to design and implement programs that proactively integrate deaf students into regular classrooms have occurred. Yet integration has never been seen by many deaf education advocates as the optimum development for deaf students. In fact, efforts to mainstream deaf students, which have increased notably in the past two decades, disturb large segments of the deaf community and have attracted open and direct criticism. As is the case with giftedness, deafness is widely considered by many as an asset rather than a disability, one that can be and should be addressed with and enhanced by separate, unique programs that encourage the development of the full potential of the identified students and that the regular classroom to this point is considered unable to support.

Programs attempting to integrate deaf students more effectively in public schools typically follow two models: regional programs and coenrollment programs. Regional programs provide resource rooms for deaf and hard of hearing students, which support their learning environments yet still provide extensive contact with other children within the context of a regular public school classroom where most of the children can hear. Coenrollment programs place the hearing impaired child in a regular classroom for most or all of the school day, with an interpreter and a resource specialist occasionally providing support as needed—or whenever possible. Coenrollment programs tend not to bring together sizable numbers of hearing impaired students to the same setting; in many instances, contact with other hearing impaired children is limited at best, perhaps nonexistent. While regional programs continue to assign such students to segregated settings for at least part of the day, many deaf students prefer them to coenrollment programs, which more closely match the definition of mainstreaming or inclusion and often provide more intensive social integration with hearing students but severely limit contact with deaf peers.[13]

Although many deaf education advocates recognize the potential for successful social integration of hearing and hearing-impaired students in mainstreamed or inclusive settings, many others express serious reservations about the capability of such models to fully satisfy the unique educational, communication, social, and cultural needs of children who belong to the deaf community. Simply put, integrative programs for deaf students, it is argued, present considerable obstacles in terms of language development, academic achievement, class participation, peer interaction, and preservation of deaf culture and community.

In a detailed analysis of one public school program integrating deaf and hard of hearing students, Claire Ramsey drew attention to the complex role of language development for deaf children and the difficulties regular classrooms and teachers encounter in addressing that development. After the school made the decision to integrate deaf children, they failed to anticipate their unique needs or provide sufficient—and admittedly intensive—training and preparation for the regular education teachers. Moreover, even with the availability of interpreters and signers, deaf children struggled to develop sufficient language skills to achieve their potential in the integrated setting, and the typical unavailability of interpreter services outside formal academic instruction inhibited their effective socialization in the school. The differences between the deaf child's language—sign—and the dominant oral language of the classroom proved prohibitive to progress. Although perhaps well-intentioned, Ramsey argued that "the mere placement of deaf and hearing children in the same room is a waste of deaf children's developmental time and a thoughtless burden to place on them. At Aspen School [the focus of the study] no educational goals were achieved in the mainstream that could not have been achieved in the self-contained classroom more efficiently and more comprehensively."[14]

Other scholars have indicated the difficulties inherent in planning integrative programs for deaf students in schools that typically rely exclusively on a language and culture that are fundamentally foreign and highly problematic, socially as well as academically, to almost all deaf children. For example, Irene Leigh called attention to the deaf child's limited access to deaf culture and community in most regular classrooms and the importance of these very qualities to her or his social development. While not condemning inclusion, Leigh does note the need for such settings to become much more attuned to the social and emotional needs of deaf children and to create greater opportunities for interaction among significant numbers of deaf children. And in a largely philosophical analysis of the relationship between mainstreaming and deaf education, Jeffrey Nash argues that bringing hard of hearing or deaf students intentionally into public schools for mainstreaming purposes without sufficient suitable accommodations often makes for more isolating educational experiences than in traditional segregated programs. "Although deaf children are present in the regular school," he writes, "they actually have a much different set of experiences from regular students and, at least socially, are in their own school. . . . Deaf children with inappropriate social selves are tracked into special classes and deprived of the very expanded educational opportunities that mainstreaming's philosophy seeks to provide." By denying traditional extensive access to fellow deaf students in segregated deaf schools and placing them in educational environments which offer little academic, linguistic, or social support, mainstreaming proves more harmful than beneficial.[15]

This complex set of viewpoints regarding the complicated nature of deaf education in public school settings was underscored by those who had personally experienced it or were its close observers. Barbara Poitras Tucker wrote vividly of her schooling as a deaf person in a public school after her parents determined that sending her to a residential school would "make her Deaf, with a capital D." Tucker describes her struggles in settings that never could accommodate or accept her condition or their need to adapt to it, detailing occasions of alternating cruelty and kindness from her hearing classmates and teachers. Researchers examining the lives of deaf children observed that the low incidence of deaf persons affected schools' ability to develop and support appropriate educational programs for deaf or hard of hearing children, especially in more sparsely populated areas, thus forcing parents to make difficult choices of sending a child away to a residential school or making do with what public schools can offer. According to Marc Marschark's *Raising and Educating a Deaf Child* for parents and educators of deaf children, residential schools receive support as places that could provide the instructional, technological, and psychological support necessary for effective education of the deaf. The guide did note that "for some students, a mainstream classroom with appropriate academic support services can provide excellent educational opportunities." However, it also cautioned that "*mandatory* inclusion does not seem an appropriate response to either the needs of deaf children" or to the law's stipulation for a least restrictive environment, and commented that "some parents prefer that their children sink or swim in the public school full inclusion setting. In my view, sinking is not a viable alternative. . . . For now, one can only hope that innocent children will not get caught in the undertow of politics and run the risk of being overwhelmed." And deaf authors Carol Padden and Tom Humphries assert that "public schools are not likely to understand the need for a community of Deaf people. . . . the new social order of 'mainstreaming,' instead of introducing new worlds to deaf children, may well lead them to a new kind of isolation."[16]

Beyond such important practical repercussions of attempts to integrate deaf children in regular classrooms, concerns about the entire philosophy of integration as applied to the deaf community trouble advocates for the deaf. Given its emphasis on de-emphasizing issues and qualities of difference among students, a philosophy of integration runs counter to the deaf community's staunch defense of its own sense of unique identity and culture. Mainstreaming, proclaims Harlan Lane, forces an assimilationist worldview on deaf children, who are left to "drown in a mainstream" that neither respects their culture nor supports their unique linguistic, intellectual, and social traditions. According to Lane, mainstreaming flies in the face of the demonstrated effectiveness of segregated, deaf-oriented educational programs that have proven their value to generations of deaf children. He sees it as an obvious attempt to save money and denigrate deaf persons individually and the deaf community as a whole. Douglas Baynton captures the sense of dismay, if not outrage, many in the deaf community feel toward efforts to integrate deaf children in regular classes:

> The angriest objection to mainstreaming from deaf people is that in the name of liberating children from their supposed "isolation" in the deaf community, a true and potentially devastating isolation is risked. In the name of inclusion in "the" community, deaf children are frequently denied true inclusion in any community. For the sake of an abstraction known as the "mainstream," deaf children are denied the solid and tangible fellowship, culture, language, and heritage of the deaf community.

The practical and philosophical challenges to implementing integration for children identified as gifted and talented and those who are deaf or hard of hearing would by the last decade of the twentieth century led to widespread discussion of the issue, fueled by deeply held assumptions, beliefs, and resentments that would place integration—under the framework of inclusion—at the forefront of educational discourse and controversy.

8

1992–2004: The Promise, Limits, and Irony of Inclusion

TODAY, special education stands at a crossroads. After decades of efforts to create truly *special* education for children with disabilities, decades of internal and external critique of the scope, form, and substance of special education within public school systems, and decades of trial and error—intellectual as well as practical—in trying to shape special education in ways that would allow it to serve a wide range of stakeholders while trying to address goals and expectations that were so often mutually exclusive, special education arrived at a point where it was more visible and contentious than ever. Between 1990 and today, special education has continued to evolve as a result of legislative action, court decisions, practical experience, and exposure to some long-held but never outdated visions as well as concerns. As the debate moves into the new century, the perspectives that continue to resurface are fundamentally empirical, pedagogical, operational, ethical, ideological, and emotional in nature, all qualities that have been present in the discussions in varying degrees for decades. While there is no imminent end to the controversy over the proper extent to which children with disabilities should be integrated in regular classrooms, the beginning of a new century does provide an opportunity to consider what has brought the debate to this point and assess what we may have learned from it thus far.

Legislation and court decisions continued to validate and spur on

efforts to bring more and more children with even more involved disabilities into the regular classroom. In 1990, PL 94-142 was reauthorized
as the Individuals with Disabilities Education Act (IDEA). The reauthorization continued the emphasis on the need for regular classrooms
to engage in purposeful adaptation for students with disabilities, maintained the importance of the least restrictive environment, expanded
services to children with disabilities, and added conditions such as
autism and traumatic brain injury to the list of disability categories. In
1997, IDEA was again reauthorized, this time to protect the rights of
students whose disabilities result in "violent or dangerous" behavior
and to improve parent participation as well as school-parent relationships in special education. The 1997 IDEA also revamped funding in
order to ease the financial impact of special education on local districts
while also "account[ing] more accurately for poverty." It should be
noted, however, that this reauthorization also redefined the construct of
"free and appropriate education" to comply more fully with the *Rowley*
decision of 1982, in which the court determined that an *appropriate*
education did not require districts to provide the *best possible* education. Court decisions in civil lawsuits brought against schools by parties
representing disabled children more often than not found in favor of
the child, thus reinforcing the responsibilities of school districts to
ensure that the regular classroom could effectively serve as a child's least
restrictive environment. Such decisions, grounded in civil rights law,
provided continued impetus to those advocating for greater integration
and put schools on notice that limited resources, past expectations, or
the difficulties involved in making necessary changes or accommodations to the regular classroom were insufficient reasons to avoid doing
so. Legislation and court action for the most part underscored the
assumption that the regular classroom was essentially the default least
restrictive environment for all children, and that schools were expected
to do more to keep it that way.[1]

As the federal government, state legislatures, and court decisions
pressed for more complete and authentic integration of exceptional
children in regular classrooms with an eye toward the rights issues
involved, the debate about the educational implications and ramifications of that trend continued at full throttle. The complex and intense

controversy over the Regular Education Initiative (REI) maintained its high profile and attracted widespread interest and attention both within the profession and, increasingly, among the public. It was during the early 1990s within the context of such debates that *inclusion* began to emerge as the definitive term describing the range of efforts to serve many more students with disabilities than ever before in regular classrooms. As with the term *mainstreaming*, inclusion as a definitive term did not appear in the law and did not arise from a single event, document, or scholarly work. The term had been used in its current context seldom if at all prior to the late 1980s; but by the mid-1990s, it clearly had superseded mainstreaming both as a term and a concept in the discourse concerning the proper extent to which exceptional children should be educated alongside their normal peers in the regular classroom.

Differentiating among widely but inconsistently used terminology related to the integration movement had always existed and did not disappear with the increasing popularity of inclusion as a descriptor. To begin with, the terms *mainstreaming* and *inclusion* generated considerable confusion not just over what they meant in and of themselves but also their meanings in relation to each other. Many writers or speakers used the terms interchangeably or synonymously. Others, however, saw them as quite different. Mainstreaming often was seen as the practice of taking special education students and placing them only in academic and/or social settings in which they could succeed with no or limited adaptations. With inclusion, however, the regular classroom was expected to exert considerable effort to adapt its environment to the needs of the exceptional children enrolled, so that the child could only be removed after intense intervention attempts had taken place in the regular class—and had failed. According to Stinson and Foster, for example, mainstreaming relied heavily on resource rooms and other alternative placements for the exceptional child, whereas inclusion worked very hard to eliminate that kind of segregation. "Philosophically," they wrote, "the difference between mainstreaming and inclusion is that mainstreaming implies that the child will adapt to the regular classroom, whereas inclusion implies that the regular classroom will adapt to the child." This use of the term *mainstreaming* runs counter to its use in the 1970s and 1980s, where it was seen as a much more aggressive program of fundamental, intentional integration. Consequently, the current distinction between the two terms, which typically sees mainstreaming as a more archaic, passive, or compromised approach and inclusion as the more assertive, proactive, and defensible one, clearly shows how the bar has been raised regarding expectations for more complete integration.

These issues have resurfaced in further distinctions between and among *inclusion, progressive inclusion, uncompromising inclusion, ideological inclusion,* and *full inclusion.* Once again, the terms have been employed synonymously by various parties. To some, inclusion and full inclusion mean the same thing: the practice of 100 percent of students being educated within the regular classroom 100 percent of the time. Others use *inclusion* and *progressive inclusion* to refer to a purposeful effort to more fully include children with disabilities into all aspects of school life yet still retain a "continuum of services," that is, segregated options and settings for children whose least restrictive environment and Individualized Education Plan calls for such. Others equate *uncompromising, ideological,* and *full* inclusion with each other, carrying the implications those qualifiers convey. A sufficient number of organizations as well as widely read and respected scholars advocate a full inclusion approach, meaning that indeed whatever adaptations are necessary for any child can and should take place in a regular classroom (which then would become a very different place than that we've known in the past); therefore the distinction is relevant and important. In some ways, the inclusion-full inclusion distinction is analogous with the mainstreaming-inclusion distinction noted above: It reflects disagreement over the degree to which the regular classroom should change to ensure it is the least restrictive environment for a child with disabilities. Even so, full inclusion is clearly the logical extension of arguments advanced as early as the 1970s that any sort of segregation of students with disabilities was ineffective, illegal, and just plain wrong.[2]

The Case for Full Inclusion

The nature, content, and tone of the continued debate are apparent in a variety of documents and other sources, which have crowded the discussion of inclusion and explored the topic in great depth. Throughout the 1990s, a plethora of books, texts, articles, manuals, newsletters, and other publications appeared that examined the concept of inclusion, explained its importance and value, and provided ideas and suggestions as to how to help make it happen not only in the classroom but in the district as well. Some of these works are considered seminal documents in the development of inclusion as an idea: Biklen's *Schooling without Labels*; Lipsky and Gartner's *Beyond Separate Education: Quality Education for All*; Thomas Skrtic's *Behind Special Education*; Paul, Rosselli, and Evans' *Integrating School Restructuring and Special Education Reform*; Villa and Thousand's *Restructuring for Caring and Effective Education*; and Stainback, Stainback, and Forest's *Educating All Students in the Mainstream of Regular Education* are just some of the most notable efforts to advance both the philosophy and theoretical underpinnings of inclusion. Moreover, an almost overwhelming amount of material in textbooks and serial publications address the topic of inclusion, explain it to professionals and the public, describe successful inclusion programs, and offer insights and practical ideas on classroom implementation.[3]

The arguments found in the professional literature supporting an aggressive approach to including all students with disabilities in regular classes continued along the lines advanced in prior decades. For proponents, the move to inclusion was necessary for several reasons: Segregated settings have not been shown to be effective; segregation itself, under any circumstances, is stigmatizing, degrading, and emotionally devastating to a child; integration creates multiple, necessary, and effective opportunities for socializing and educating disabled students with their nondisabled peers and eliminating the ignorance and prejudice among children that separation has caused; schools have the ability and resources to be much more proactive and effective in accommodating children with disabilities in regular classrooms; greater integration of students creates better opportunities for special educators and regular educators to pool knowledge and resources and to break down artificial intellectual and professional barriers between them; special education is a cornerstone of efforts to bring about fundamental and effective change in the way schools operate; and integration is an ethical imperative in ensuring the inherent rights of all children and in maximizing opportunities to develop community among diverse groups of children.[4]

Joining the call for fully inclusive education were several organizations and government agencies that issued policy statements, reports, or other documents supporting such efforts. The Arc continued its strong support for IDEA and the move toward full inclusion in its laudatory report *20 Years of IDEA in America: A Celebration of the Impact of the Individuals with Disabilities Education Act.* The report quoted students, parents, teachers, and others involved in special education who offered glowing accounts of the benefits and successes inclusion brought to the world of students with disabilities. It included the voices of children and families from all over the country with a wide range of disabilities, all of whom asserted the importance of integrated education and the power that the law vested in families who very much needed it. The testimony ran from the scholarly to the emotional, but all stressed the value of commingling students with and without disabilities in natural classroom and social settings as preparation for a truly more inclusive society. Lana Green, the parent of a child with Down syndrome enrolled in a regular Indianapolis school classroom, offers a typical example:

> To me, mainstreaming didn't allow her to be a full member of the classroom. The teacher didn't take ownership, and the children didn't see her as part of the class. She was a visitor, and therefore the acceptance was less. . . . [In the inclusive classroom] she's been exposed to normal life situations. She's been able to learn life skills that she wouldn't have been able to learn in a self-contained situation. She's much farther along in terms of maturity and responsibility. . . . I feel so strongly about it. It's really to me a civil rights issue. It's just the right thing to do to make sure all kids indiscriminately have the right to learn.[5]

Another organization advocating widely for fully inclusive classrooms was the National Council on Disability (NCD). The NCD published several reports about IDEA and its impact on schools and on persons with disabilities. In a 1995 report, the NCD presented its case for truly inclusive school settings, and, like the Arc report, it included a series of statements by students and parents in support of its position. While acknowledging that inclusion did have its detractors, the NCD described the frustration that many parents had with districts that ignored and marginalized their children through special education policy and practice; criticized the intransigence of school personnel toward inclusion; outlined what they saw as the numerous positive outcomes of inclusive education; and reiterated the comparison of the segregation of students with disabilities to that of students of "African Americans a few decades ago." The NCD underscored the importance of effective staff development, home support, and careful planning to support successful inclusive programs. While acknowledging certain benefits of a "continuum of services," the NCD suggested that reliance on such a continuum has impeded movement toward more authentic integration because "it almost always involves segregation." Instead, the NCD suggested replacing the traditional continuum model with an "array" model that would offer "a wide variety of individually accessible, discrete support services that can be accessed freely from a regular educational environment," thus addressing the concerns of parents who rely on a continuum of services but also shifting the location of services altogether into the regular classroom. Other publications, such as those of the President's Committee on Mental Retardation and the Department of Education's annual reports to Congress on the implementation of IDEA, covered similar territory and came to similar conclusions.[6]

One characteristic of reports and advocacy statements supporting the move to full inclusion typically lacking in the professional literature was the use of parent and student voices in support of their position. All of the reports noted above included such statements; other examples were plentiful. Two such examples, published by the Institute on Disability at the University of New Hampshire, included a large number of comments from children with disabilities, their regular classroom peers, parents, and teachers, testifying to the widespread benefits of inclusion. Most again emphasized the power of having nondisabled role models for students with disabilities, the success that the higher expectations and more challenging and interesting activities in the regular classroom brought to students identified as disabled, and the eye-opening occurrences and behaviors that teachers experienced while teaching in inclusive classrooms that helped destroy their prior misconceptions about most students with disabilities and facilitated more effective collaboration with special education teachers, who became teachers of all children in the classroom. Other writings from parents, children, and families exposed the struggles that parents faced in fighting for the rights of their children against school bureaucracies and professionals who expressed thinly veiled disdain for inclusive practices and the children for whom they were intended. The use of such testimonials moved the debate beyond the often sterile and inaccessible realm of empirical research on the benefits of inclusion into the world of real humans and real feelings. As one parent stated, "Allison is living proof that with the proper supports and compliance by schools, children with special needs can succeed. What's important is the reputable fact that all children benefit from full participation of every student. There are important lessons to be learned early in life about the rights of all people." Parental sentiments also found their way into scholarly writing as researchers began to pay more attention to parents' attitudes and values regarding inclusion.[7]

The Case for Maintaining a "Continuum of Services"

Those who have doubts about inclusion have also managed to make their views known in substantive and noticeable fashion. The primary venues for such voices include articles in professional journals, the popular media of newspapers and magazines, conferences and conference proceedings, and policy statements of professional organizations. These sources offer commentary on inclusion ranging from brief calls of alarm to sophisticated and comprehensive analysis grounded in theory, practice, and empirical research. Opponents of inclusion have also made use of the popular press, expressing professional and personal opinion against inclusion on a regular basis in newspaper editorials and opinion pieces in general interest magazines. Such critics have struck a chord with parents, teachers, and administrators who continue to resist the movement and with the public, much of which remains skeptical and wary of bringing handicapped children into regular classrooms for a variety of reasons.

A series of publications appearing in the mid-1990s encapsulated the essence of the widespread concern about what many saw as a "rush to inclusion." Two of these appeared in *Exceptional Children*: James Kauffman's "How We Might Achieve the Radical Reform of Special Education," and Douglas and Lynn Fuchs' "Inclusive Schools Movement and the Radicalization of Special Education Reform." Both these seminal articles saw the advocacy of full inclusion as a highly politicized, emotionally charged push to effect dramatic change in schools with insufficient thought given to the practical aspects of institutional reform or the real needs of large numbers of children with disabilities. Other articles published in the professional literature that effectively summarized the more cautious approach to inclusion included Macmillan, Gresham, and Forness's "Full Inclusion: An Empirical Perspective" and Gerber's "Inclusion at the High-Water Mark? Some Thoughts on Zigmond and Baker's Case Studies of Inclusive Educational Programs." Each of these examined research related to inclusion and determined that the published claims of many full inclusion advocates could, in many cases, not be demonstrated or validated, and that the empirical base for many of those claims was weak at best. Other articles spoke more directly to teachers and the public in lay terms: A harshly critical article published in *Phi Delta Kappan* entitled "Thinking of Inclusion for All Special Needs Students? Better Think Again" and AFT President Albert Shanker's widely disseminated "Where We Stand on the Rush to Inclusion" both called attention to what they saw as alarming implications for implementing full inclusion in schools and among teachers who were not only ill-prepared but reasonably disposed not to accept the premise that all children regardless of ability belonged in the regular classroom. The *PDK* article put it bluntly: "to consider oneself an 'inclusionist' is to place a philosophy before the needs of children." Shanker alleged that

> The inclusion that is being advocated is the placement of all students
> with disabilities into general education classrooms *without regard to the*

nature or severity of the student's disabilities, without regard to their ability to behave and function appropriately in a regular classroom, without regard to the educational benefits they derive, and without regard to the impact that that inclusion has on the other students in the class (emphasis in the original).[8]

One compendium that sought to capture all that was ill-advised about the full inclusion movement was James Kauffman and Daniel Hallahan's *The Illusion of Full Inclusion: A Comprehensive Critique of a Current Special Education Bandwagon,* published in 1995. This edited volume contained a series of articles, essays, and position statements of organizations on the nature and value of full inclusion. Kauffman and Hallahan frame the book by stating in the preface that "special education is in danger of riding the bandwagon called 'full inclusion' to its own funeral. . . . This book is intended to show why full inclusion can provide only an illusion of support for all students, an illusion that is sure to produce disappointment, if not outrage, in its riders when the juggernaut crushes the students it was supposed to defend." Particularly representative positions are found in articles entitled "Swimming Against the Mainstream," "Inclusive Education: Right for <u>Some</u>," and "The Education of Deaf Children: Drowning in the Mainstream and the Sidestream." Other significant contents are an essay by Stanley Diamond who constructs the concept as "that Great God, Inclusion"; an essay by a mother and special educator who predicts that "if inclusion becomes a reality, the dropout rate for students with [learning disabilities] will soar to a nationally disgraceful figure" and an increase in substance abuse and suicide "that will wrap families in despair and grief"; and position statements from several organizations for and of the blind, the American Federation of Teachers, Children and Adults with Attention Deficit Disorders, the Consumer Action Network (on behalf of deaf persons), the Council of Administrators of Special Education, and the Council for Learning Disabilities, all of which call for maintaining a continuum of services that retains the possibility and viability of segregated instruction where necessary and appropriate. The book also includes the statement from TASH (The Association for Persons with Severe Handicaps), which calls for greater inclusion and for a revision of the continuum model to enable greater service provision in the regular classroom.[9]

Most critics of full inclusion do in fact agree that we should integrate and include students with disabilities as much as possible in regular classrooms, at least to the extent to which their presence in the regular classroom benefits all children. For them, however, there exist too many obstacles, too many extenuating circumstances, too much resistance from too many corners to demand that this must happen completely and happen very soon. Schools, it is argued, are not ready for it: The resistance to such wholesale reform is too strong, and school reforms of this magnitude are next to impossible to implement universally, especially when key stakeholders have not been party to developing proposed reforms or see no value in them.

Of greater importance are the practical implications of such a movement. Regular classroom teachers, it is argued, are not by any means sufficiently trained to accept the responsibility and lead role in planning and delivering instruction to children representing thirteen categories of disability at all levels of severity. Such extensive integration—and the virtual abandonment of resource rooms, self-contained classes, and other specialized settings—diminishes the effectiveness and professional standing of teachers specially trained in those areas. The result would be poor instruction for many students who are in a sense confined to a regular classroom that is unable to support their learning needs. The presence of children who, many argue, should not be in a regular classroom due to their particular medical or behavioral needs are of particular concern, with many arguing that such children would likely be a disruptive influence and limit the effectiveness of instruction—and of the teacher—for the rest of the children in the class. In addition, many such students benefit from segregated settings and in fact prefer them, with children who are deaf being a visible and instructive example. In short, schools are not ready, teachers are not ready, some students are not ready—and unless the nature of education or the preferences of certain groups of people radically change in fundamental, permanent ways, they will never be ready, and it is unfair and counterproductive to force on them something that simply will not work.

A Look to the Future

In their article "Disability, Schooling, and the Artifacts of Colonialism," published in *Teachers College Record*, Christopher Kliewer and Linda May Fitzgerald argue that "a huge segment of America's children construed as intellectually disabled continue to face harsh and delimiting educational segregation. . . ." They maintain that the majority of students identified as having moderate to severe mental disabilities "are presented daily with remedial training programs and fix-it teaching methodologies in environments that exist at the nethermost margins of the school. . . children are told . . . 'you are a broken version of what we wish you to be, and we will attempt to fix you to whatever degree possible in basement workshops out of the way of the general household.'" [10]

This powerful and damning statement, even if only partially accurate, dramatically reveals that after more than a century of special education practices and more than thirty years of calls to eliminate such conditions, the segregation of students with disabilities persists. In terms of maximizing our abilities to include most if not all exceptional children in regular classrooms, statements such as the above and the data from schools show that many believe there is still a long way to go. In addition, those core issues identified at the outset of this book—efficacy, efficiency and economy, territory, community, legality, power and identity, and axiology—continue to shape the nature of the debate. These categories are so interwoven as to be virtually indistinguishable, yet their presence is discernible throughout, and the rough framework they provide for considering elements of the inclusion debate can serve as a heuristic in order to give the debate some measure of clarity.

As this book has tried to show, many of the themes in the inclusion debate have been expressed, to some degree or another and in one form or another, for generations. Teachers in the mid-1800s were discussing the positive effects of disabled children learning with their "normal" peers as well as the problems the presence of disabled children created for teachers trying to teach and students trying to learn. Schools more than 100 years ago were discussing how effective or ineffective segregated settings were for certain student populations, especially those seen as mentally, physically, and behaviorally handicapped. Yet what has developed over the past twenty years or so is an increasing antagonism in the debate—a shift in tone from one of strict scholarly discussion to one where distance, skepticism, even overt discord between parties have become more frequent and more obvious. This is not to say that earlier debates were devoid of such matters, for they were not. Rather it is to say that clearly the meanings and the expected or experienced effects of inclusion—positive as well as negative—have become more immediate, more personal, and perhaps even more important to those engaged in the debate.

When seen as a "moral issue," as Sarason and Doris called it twenty-five years ago and a many others have defined it, the consequent heightening of tensions should not be surprising. In the late 1980s, Margaret Wang and Douglas and Lynn Fuchs had a testy exchange over the Fuchs's assessment of the Adaptive Learning Environments Model; charges of disingenuous statements, shoddy investigations, and accusations of "segregationism" arose out of what began as an apparent agreement to assist each other in evaluating the model's effectiveness. Kauffman's allegation that political conservatism was behind much of the REI injected politics into a debate considered scholarly and educational and riled several inclusion proponents. A considerable number of other instances exhibit a clear divisiveness over the issue that rarely if ever involves direct personal attack yet shows obvious signs of frustration and resentment with the opposing view. Much of the pro-inclusion literature presents itself as merely doing what is "right" and "ethical," prompting critics to resent the implication that challenging inclusion puts them on the other side of the fence. Naturally, labels for each "faction" have appeared: "inclusivists," "abolitionists," and "idealists" squaring off against "conservationists," "pragmatists," "realists," or "segregationists."

The degree of contention also manifests itself in much of the literature, even in the titles of pieces themselves. As noted earlier, Kauffman and Hallahan's compilation depicts inclusion as an "illusion" and a "bandwagon." Another author in the book refers to full inclusion as "mainstreaming with a vengeance." While such phrasing is not necessarily pejorative, the increasing polarization of factions in the debate is much more apparent. In reading the literature both for and against inclusion—and in particular, full inclusion—the tone and the language of the debate reflects a growing animosity and a sense that the "other" side doesn't truly understand or even try to understand, or intentionally misrepresents, "our" side. Such sensitivities have generated not only intense interest but a great deal of discomfort and uncertainty about who truly believes what.

Promising to complicate the direction and perhaps intensify the tone of the debate as we enter the new century is the landmark federal education law, the No Child Left Behind Act of 2001. While it is yet too early to discern exactly how this massive piece of legislation will affect special education in general and the debate over inclusion in particular, there are indications that several of its provisions will have a significant impact on the way administrators and other school authorities approach the idea of inclusive classrooms. Although the legislation does mandate that the directives of IDEA be incorporated into the preparations of the required state plans for school improvement, it is certainly possible that pressures to separate children with disabilities from their nondisabled peers will prove quite strong.

To begin with, students with disabilities are designated as their own specific population and student subgroup for assessment purposes, with their results "disaggregated" from those of the general student population. As such, schools would appear to be more likely to treat them as a separate group, organizing settings and programs designed to focus on that group alone. In addition, the law stipulates that even though alternate assessments are permissible for subgroups such as students with disabilities, Secretary of Education Rod Paige has stated that "because it is critical to ensure that students with disabilities are not excluded from State accountability systems, the final regulations provide that the same grade level academic content and achievement standards that apply to all public schools and public school students in the state will be applied to alternate assessments." In order to prepare students in special education for this task, it is likely schools will determine that separate, intensive, and individualized tutoring will be necessary. Given the intense pressures to "succeed" (in terms of achieving requisite passing levels on test scores) embedded in the legislation, it may well be that schools would be much less inclined to invest the time, effort, and resources necessary to initiate and maintain successful and authentic inclusive settings—especially when the touted benefits of such an approach emphasize ethical ideals and socialization practices over academic accomplishments. In addition, the near-overwhelming requirements of the law, rooted deeply in the drive to cause all students to achieve proficiency in content-based assessments, would seem to deflect, if not altogether derail, efforts to restructure schools for other, and in many ways contradictory, purposes. Such pressures and mutually exclusive goals will likely do little to reduce the suspicion, distrust, and dissatisfaction between those who advocate for full inclusion and those who see little value in pursuing that goal. [11]

Reflections and Possibilities

Since the beginning of special education, there has existed a continuous dialectic: Yes, we should do more to integrate children identified as disabled more effectively in regular education schools and classrooms, but no, we can't do too much, because our teachers don't have the training, our schools don't have the resources, and we don't have the knowledge, strategies, or wherewithal to accommodate more than a certain number of children with certain kinds of disabilities in those settings. Although the dialectic has persisted, the actual conditions have developed to the point where over time, we have been able to include more and more children, with more challenging or severe disabilities, into regular education settings for greater periods of time. From the almost universal segregation of the early 1960s to the extensive integration of exceptional children today under the policy, practice, and legal mandate of inclusion, our regular education classrooms have made definite strides toward being more integrated and more inclusive.

Most of this progress has been recorded with children who have mild disabilities. Representing almost 90 percent of the overall special education population, children identified as mildly disabled have been the foot soldiers in efforts to integrate regular classrooms, as their academic needs and classroom behavior supposedly demanded less in the way of classroom adaptations, classroom disruptions, or teacher time.

Students with mild learning disabilities, cognitive disability, emotional disturbance, attention deficit disorder, communication disorders, or even limited hearing or vision loss have been, since the 1940s, generally among those identified as students who could make it in the regular classroom without asking too much of the teachers or the "normal" students therein. In this sense, the thrust of an inclusion philosophy appeals to most educators, who share a belief that students who can be successful in the regular classroom belong there.

The conflict arises when considering the extent to which regular classrooms—their teachers, students, resources, operations—can or should change in order to accommodate those who require greater adaptations for their effective and constructive education. At a macrocosmic level, this is where the conflation of integrating special education students and their regular education peers with calls for radical, fundamental restructuring of not only special education but of the entire system of public education takes place. In order to successfully place, teach, and socialize *all* students in the regular classroom—the way its teachers are trained and work, the way its students understand and participate in its assumptions and activities, the way that certain resources are provided and operations conducted—must change in fundamental ways. Despite the clear disagreement among those who profess total agreement with or reserved support for integration, they do agree on this: The regular classroom requires fundamental reorganization for inclusion, let alone full inclusion, to work. How far are schools, teachers, parents, or students willing to go? How much are they willing to change? How much are they willing to invest in time, energy, resources, or money?

For advocates of inclusion who see this as an issue of ethics, rights, and possibilities, the fact that the answers to such questions are difficult or discouraging is no reason to abandon the goal. Several have noted that it will take time and require major effort, adjustment, even sacrifice, but to ask if we can do it is, as had been said, "to ask the wrong question." Instead, we should continue to press ahead on any and all fronts, with the idea that we keep going and don't give up in efforts to achieve the ultimate goal. While not all inclusion advocates agree that full inclusion—all children in regular classes all the time—must be achieved, their position is that we have no reason or excuse to surrender the effort. Children belong in the regular classroom, and they have a right to be there; it is our responsibility as educators to do whatever we can to make sure that occurs to the maximum extent possible. Better planning, improved training, more extensive and constructive collaboration, increased dedication to the value of education for all children—these are difficult, complex, exhausting goals to achieve, but doing so is by no means impossible. According to the pro-inclusion literature, a vast array of examples demonstrates that when the proper effort was undertaken, the success was unmistakable.

Nevertheless, the fact remains that our current systems of public schooling, teacher education, and school financing combine with continued ambivalent attitudes toward persons with disabilities to inhibit the idealized process described above. Traditions of rigid age-grade organization, of separate training programs for regular education and special education teachers, of suspicion and contempt toward the disabled, and the horrendous shortcomings of society's willingness and ability to finance the schools children deserve now—let alone the schools envisioned by those who would restructure special education—are powerful, undeniable obstacles to the implementation of an authentic inclusion ideal, certainly for a fully inclusive school system and even for one that is currently mandated by federal and state law. Much of the argument against current interpretations of inclusion echo those against mainstreaming and even initial integration efforts decades ago: We have no right or reason to mandate a practice that teachers, parents, and even students have arguably had little voice in developing; for which teachers, classrooms, schools, and even school systems are poorly prepared; and which at this point most likely would fail to provide a truly "appropriate education in the least restrictive environment." The literature from the 1990s arguing against "inclusion" constantly calls attention to these issues, and the resentment and resistance is palpable. To initiate, or force, the premature inclusion of a child into a poorly prepared, unsupportive setting can be a terrible mistake.

The other factor casting doubts on the possibilities of extending the reach of inclusion is the openly and clearly stated reluctance to consider an integrated setting the optimum one. Advocates for children who are deaf and for those who are gifted are among the most prominent voices of those who state that even a carefully planned, generously supported integrated setting may not be appropriate for such children. While advocates for the gifted generally claim that a truly inclusive setting that effectively accommodated all the needs of gifted children may be acceptable, those for the deaf, as noted earlier, see inclusion as a direct assault on the traditions and integrity of deaf culture and community, and many want no part of it. While it might be possible to structure an inclusive school in ways sufficient to meet most of a deaf child's linguistic, academic, and social needs, to many, the absence by definition of a close-knit, independent group of deaf children as peers renders an inclusive setting untenable. In any case, the question of whether schools have a right to direct children and parents into a setting where they have a *right* to be but *choose not* to be is a crucial one for those involved—especially given the near-universally accepted desire and ideal to effectively serve the individual needs of every child in school.

The Idea and Ideal of Inclusion

At the turn of the twenty-first century, the idea of inclusion attracts intense and conflicting interest and commentary from the world of American education as well as from the public. *Inclusion* has in a sense transcended the mere idea of integrating exceptional children with their nonexceptional peers in the regular classroom; rightly or wrongly, it had become a symbol of efforts to break down distinctions between special and regular education in fundamental and dramatic ways; to bring about difficult, profound changes in classrooms and schools; and to involve students who traditionally (and perhaps too comfortably) had been seen as needing special education, special help, and special services to address special needs—somewhere else. The extent to which the resistance to such a symbol is grounded in prejudicial attitudes towards disability, especially certain kinds, and/or is grounded in concerns regarding the ability of schools and teachers truly to meet the special needs of children identified as disabled as well as those of their "regular" students is highly debatable and certainly difficult to discern decisively from the published public record. At any rate, inclusion has indeed become a "buzzword," as one author put it, but it is a buzzword with a long history of attention, evolution, discussion, and adaptation.

At is core, *inclusion* embodies the right of every child to be educated in a common setting where her or his individual needs and those of all other children are addressed completely and effectively. The practice of shunting a child elsewhere solely to suit the prejudices or conveniences of others sadly has a long history, one that, according to some, has never gone away. But the history of special education also shows that specialized instruction in segregated settings did not occur only for those reasons, that in fact educators, parents, administrators, and other authoritative persons truly believed such segregation was necessary and beneficial for the child's proper education and socialization. Professional literature over generations has demonstrated the complex, multifaceted beliefs, attitudes, and sensibilities that brought about segregated instruction for exceptional children, and the motives and results behind them are as mixed as human diversity and experience would suggest.

The arguments, motives, and aspirations of those involved in current debates over inclusion are equally as complex. Sifting through these thoughts and ideas demonstrates that inclusion in its current interpretation and usage can be applied only so far. To a certain extent, inclusion must happen. The regular classroom can and should be the "default" least restrictive environment; this represents a dramatic shift from the days of mainstreaming and earlier, when a child with disabilities had to earn her way into regular classes and do most if not all of the adapting. Given current knowledge and skills, the vast majority of children requiring special education (or at least intensive individualized instruction) can be successfully accommodated in regular classes, and should be. While inclusion is not an easy process, schools and teacher training programs certainly have the ability to make this happen; and it is occurring with remarkable success across the country.

For those students for whom adaptations to the regular classroom involve much more, inclusion becomes a stickier issue. While it may be unfair to force a child into an unsupportive or resistive environment, the fact remains that she or he has a right to be in the least restrictive environment, and courts by and large have determined that schools typically need to do much more to make the regular classroom just that, so that such children can remain with their nondisabled peers. Schools need to engage in less manipulation of the system and in more genuine retooling of the regular classroom for students with moderate, severe, multiple, or low-incidence disabilities. Unfortunately, there are limits even to what the best-intentioned school can do; without sufficient support in terms of preparation, professional development, appropriate resources, or authentic professional and emotional investment, schools will not be able to do this, and they cannot create what they need out of thin air.

But what, then, to do with the children who have every right to be there, yet shouldn't be because of the school's shortcomings? And what of the children for whom an integrated, regular classroom setting is considered ill-advised and inappropriate by their advocates? One possibility: *Any* child who wishes to be educated in a regular class has the right to be there, and the school and district must engage in aggressive steps to make that a reality. Inclusion of all students thus becomes an absolute priority of public education. However, alternatives need to be made available for children who have a right to the regular classroom but prefer not to be there; their voices need to be heard. As with all public education students, these children could have the right to opt out of attending the regular class if they so choose, with private schooling being an option (although if parents withdraw their children voluntarily and the district can demonstrate that it has met the legal requirements for providing a free and appropriate education, parents must pay for the alternative themselves). This means that any child with a disability has the *right* to an education in the regular classroom, but does not bear a *responsibility* to attend. It becomes a matter of *choice*, with decisions regarding that choice vested in those who would choose to exercise it. Yet the difficulty with this scenario is twofold: What if the school were also required to support extensive public alternative *segregated* settings for those who wished (e.g., classes for the totally deaf); and what if individual or groups of children decide they don't wish to participate in the regular class for reasons other than the school's inability to address their disability, or choose to transfer from a "failing" school as identified by No Child Left Behind? Would nondisabled children have a right to segregated settings, removed from "undesirable" classmates? (Such questions are being addressed today in contexts other than disability; for example, school districts sponsoring classes segregated on the basis of gender, race, or curriculum.)

Under these circumstances, inclusion thus becomes more of an *ideal* than an *idea*, one to which schools should continually aspire but also one that remains unobtainable in the foreseeable future. Schools can and should continue to work toward the goal, but practical realities will also continue to frustrate and inhibit these efforts to such an extent that a truly universal "appropriate, least restrictive environment" located in the regular classroom may never come to pass. The irony is that integration, mainstreaming, and inclusion represent ideals to most but not all people, and that any program that assumes all children will succeed and be happy in an integrated setting—and indeed have a desire and a responsibility to be there—will force children into a setting they neither want nor benefit from, much as those thousands and thousands of children consigned to the school margins in segregated special education settings since the latter 1800s. Nonetheless for most children, in most cases, inclusion as an ideal, a process, and a goal represents their right to an education they need and deserve; that in itself justifies its continued attention and support.

Notes

Introduction

1. Maynard C. Reynolds, Margaret C. Wang, and Herbert J. Walberg, "The Necessary Restructuring of Special and Regular Education," *Exceptional Children* 53 (February 1987): 391.

Chapter 1

1. There exist several such histories, ranging from short summary paragraphs to extensive and detailed discussions. Some of the more extensive include Margret Winzer, *The History of Special Education: From Isolation to Integration* (Washington, D.C.: Gallaudet University Press, 1993), 6–73; Leo Kanner, *A History of the Care and Study of the Mentally Retarded* (Springfield, Ill.: Thomas, 1964); R. C. Scheerenberger, *A History of Mental Retardation* (Baltimore: Brookes, 1983), 3–87; Albert Deutsch, *The Mentally Ill in America: A History of Their Care and Treatment from Colonial Times,* 2d ed. (New York: Columbia University, 1949), 1–23; Philip L. Safford and Elizabeth J. Safford, *A History of Childhood and Disability* (New York: Teachers College Press, 1996), 1–54.

2. John Vickery Van Cleve and Barry A. Crouch, *A Place of Their Own: Creating the Deaf Community in America* (Washington, D.C.: Gallaudet University Press, 1989), 1–18; Harry Best, *Deafness and the Deaf in the United States: Considered Primarily in Relation to Those Sometimes More or Less Erroneously Known as "Deaf-Mutes"* (New York: Macmillian, 1943), 371–84; Winzer, *History of Special Education,* 31–37, 47–57.

3. Winzer, *History of Special Education,* 47–73; Kanner, *History of the Care, passim;* Scheerenberger, *History of Mental Retardation,* 31–50; Deutsch, *Mentally Ill in America,* 1–18.

4. Deutsch, *Mentally Ill in America,* 24–38; Winzer, *History of Special Education,* 85–86; Scheerenberger, *History of Mental Retardation,* 91–96.

5. Deutsch, *Mentally Ill in America,* 55–71; Scheerenberger, *History of Mental Retardation,*95–96.

6. Van Cleve and Crouch, *Place of Their Own,* 29–46; Harold Schwartz, *Samuel Gridley Howe: Social Reformer 1801–1876* (Cambridge, Mass.: Harvard University Press, 1956), 49–90, 137–47; Scheerenberger, *History of Mental Retardation,*101–4.

7. Schwartz, *Samuel Gridley Howe*; Winzer, *History of Special Education*,98–114; Van Cleve and Crouch, *Place of Their Own*,29–46; Ernest Freeberg, *The Education of Laura Bridgman: First Deaf and Blind Person to Learn Language* (Cambridge, Mass.: Harvard University Press, 2001); Howe, quoted in Anna M. Wallace, "History of the Walter E. Fernald State School" (n.d.: unpublished manuscript in author's possession), p. 10; quoted in J. E. Wallace Wallin, *The Education of Handicapped Children* (Boston: Houghton-Mifflin, 1924), 29 and Stanley P. Davies, *Social Control of the Mentally Deficient* (New York: Crowell, 1930), 40.

8. Douglas C. Baynton, *Forbidden Signs: American Culture and the Campaign against Sign Language* (Chicago: University of Chicago Press, 1996); James W. Trent, Jr., *Inventing the Feeble Mind: A History of Mental Retardation in the United States* (Berkeley: University of California Press, 1994); Scheerenberger, *History of Mental Retardation,* 109–35; Winzer, *History of Special Education,* 251–305.

9. Robert L. Osgood, "Undermining the Common School Ideal: Intermediate Schools and Ungraded Classes in Boston, 1838–1900," *History of Education Quarterly* 37 (winter 1997): 375–98; Robert L. Osgood, *For "Children Who Vary From the Normal Type": Special Education in Boston 1838–1930* (Washington, D.C.: Gallaudet University Press, 2000).

10. Osgood, *For "Children Who Vary,"* 67–76; Winzer, *History of Special Education,* 320–22.

11. Stephen Jay Gould, *The Mismeasure of Man* (New York: Norton, 1981), 158–71; H. H. Goddard, "Mental Tests and the Immigrant," *Journal of Delinquency* 2 (1917): 243–77; H. H. Goddard, *Feeblemindedness: Its Causes and Consequences* (New York: Macmillan, 1914); Trent, *Inventing the Feeble Mind* 155–69: Winzer, *History of Special Education,* 268–69; Scheerenberger, *History of Mental Retardation,* 139–45.

12. Osgood *For "Children Who Vary,"* 93–95; Scheerenberger, *History of Mental Retardation,* 139–40; Winzer, *History of Special Education,* 320–22; J. E. Wallace Wallin, *Education of Mentally Handicapped Children* (New York: Harper & Row, 1955), 17–19.

13. Wallin, *Education of Mentally Handicapped Children,* 19–20.

14. See for example Joseph A. Tropea, "Bureaucratic Order and Special Children: Urban Schools, 1890s–1940s," *History of Education Quarterly* 27 (spring 1987), 33; Barry M. Franklin, "Progressivism and Curriculum Differentiation: Special Classes in the Atlanta Public Schools, 1898–1923," *History of Education Quarterly* 29 (winter 1989), 585–93; Robert L. Osgood, "The Menace of the Feebleminded: George Bliss, Amos Butler, and the Indiana Committee on Mental Defectives," *Indiana Magazine of History* 97 (December 2001): 253–77; Seymour Sarason and John Doris, *Educational Handicap, Public Policy, and Social History* (New York: Free Press, 1979), 337–47.

15. J. E. Wallace Wallin, *The Education of Handicapped Children* (Boston: Houghton Mifflin, 1924), 92–93.

16. Wallin, *Education of Handicapped Children*, 94–97; see also Winzer, *History of Special Education*, 326–30.

17. Mary C. Greene, "Should the Scope of the Public-School System Be Broadened So As to Take in All Children Capable of Education? If So, How Should This Be Done?" *Addresses and Proceedings of the National Education Association*, (1903): 998; H. H. Goddard, in Meta Anderson, *Education of Defectives in Public Schools* (New York: World Book, 1917), ix–xvii; E. R. Johnstone, "The Functions of the Special Class," *Addresses and Proceedings of the National Education Association*, (1908): 1114–118; James T. Byers, "Provision for the Feeble-Minded," Indiana State Teachers Association, *Proceedings*, (1917): 169–70.

18. James Van Sickle, quoted in Seymour B. Sarason and John Doris, *Educational Handicap, Public Policy, and Social History: A Broadened Perspective on Mental Retardation* (New York: Free Press, 1979), 263; *33rd Annual Report of the Superintendent of the Boston Public Schools*, School Document no. 11 (Boston, 1914), 30; Katrina Myers, "Feeble-Mindedness in the Public Schools," *Indiana Bulletin* no. 100 (March 1915): 82; Boston Finance Commission, *Report on the Boston School System* (Boston, 1911), 93–94.

19. Tropea, "Bureaucratic Order," 32; Franklin, "Progressivism," *passim;* John G. Richardson, *Common, Delinquent, and Special: The Institutional Shape of Special Education* (New York: Falmer, 1999), 65; Marvin Lazerson, "The Origins of Special Education," in *Special Education Policies: Their History, Implementation, and Finance*, ed. Jay G. Chambers and William T. Hartman (Philadelphia: Temple University Press, 1983), 21.

20. Wallin, *Education of Handicapped Children*, 153–54; quoted in Osgood, *For "Children Who Vary,"* 74–76, 160.

Chapter 2

1. White House Conference on Child Health and Protection, *The Handicapped Child: Report of the Committee on Physically and Mentally Handicapped, William J. Ellis, LL.D., Chairman* (New York: Century, 1933).

2. Ibid., 63, 153–54, 395.

3. Stanley Powell Davies, *Social Control of the Mentally Deficient* (New York: Crowell, 1930), 299–302.

4. Cited in Osgood, *For "Children Who Vary,"* 29–30; Elise H. Martens, *State Legislation for Education of Exceptional Children*, Bulletin 1949, no. 2 (Washington, D.C.: Government Printing Office, 1949), 6–9.

5. Robert L. Osgood, "From 'Public Liabilities' to 'Public Assets': Special Education for Children with Mental Retardation in Indiana Public Schools, 1908–1931," *Indiana Magazine of History* 98 (September 2002): 224; Scheerenberger, *History of Mental Retardation*, 178–79, 200; Winzer, *History of Special Education*, 368–71; Wallin, *Education of Mentally Handicapped Children*, 19–21.

6. Martens, *State Legislation,* 23.

7. Ibid., 23–25.

8. Ibid., 52–57.

9. Sherman Dorn, "Public-Private Symbiosis in Nashville Special Education," *History of Education Quarterly* 42 (fall 2002), 372. Dorn notes that these efforts tended to blur apparent distinctions between public and private education in the United States. For a representative example of a state publication offering advice, see Jeanette Riker, "Who Is the Exceptional Child?" (Indianapolis, 1951). A representative example from the professional literature is Linnea Mae Anderson, "Do You Have a Mentally Handicapped Child in Your Classroom?", *North Dakota Teacher* (October 1956), in the ARC Files at the Archives and Library of the Coleman Institute for Cognitive Disabilities, University of Colorado.

10. Nelson B. Henry, ed. *The Forty-Ninth Yearbook of the National Society for the Study of Education: Part II: The Education of Exceptional Children* (Chicago: National Society for the Study of Education, 1950), vii, 1.

11. Ibid., 6–7, 12.

12. Romaine Mackie, *Special Education in the United States: Statistics 1948–1966* (New York: Teachers College Press, 1969), 36; Arthur S. Hill, "A Critical Glance at Special Education: It Is Time to Discard Platitudes and Speak in Realistic Terms!" *Exceptional Children* 22 (May 1956): 315.

13. Connecticut Special Education Association, *Development and Progress of Special Classes for Mentally Deficient Children in Connecticut* (New Haven, Conn., 1936), 94, 106–7; Alan Challman, "Mental Health in the Special Classes," *Journal of Exceptional Children* 8 (1941): 42–44.

14. "Segregation versus Non-Segregation of Exceptional Children," *Exceptional Children* 12 (May 1946): 235–40. See also Philip A. Cowen, "Education for Mentally Handicapped," *Phi Delta Kappan* 23 (1940): 71.

15. Cowen, "Education for Mentally Handicapped," 71; Katherine C. Coveny, "The Growth of Special Classes in the City of Boston," *Training School Bulletin* 39 (1942/1943): 57; "Segregation versus Non-Segregation," 235–38; Challman, "Mental Health," 45.

16. See, for example, Winifred Hathaway and Berthold Lowenfeld, "Teaching the Visually Handicapped," 137–39; Clarence D. O'Connor and Alice Streng, "Teaching the Acoustically Handicapped," 163–73; Lawrence J. Linck, Jayne Shover, and Eveline E. Jacobs, "Teaching the Orthopedically Handicapped and the Cardiopathic," 203–5, all in Nelson B. Henry, *The Forty-Ninth Yearbook of the National Society for the Study of Education: Part II: The Education of Exceptional Children* (Chicago: NSSE, 1950). For examples of similar comments from later in the decade, see Norris G. Haring, George Stern, and William M. Cruickshank, *Attitudes of Educators Toward Exceptional Children* (Westport, Conn.: Greenwood Press, 1958), 2–5, 187–98, 235–38. See also Lewis C. Martin, "Shall We Segregate Our Handicapped?", *Journal of Exceptional Children* 6 (March 1940): 224–25.

17. Anna M. Engel, "Our Goal Is Integration," in Illinois Commission for Handicapped Children, *The Handicapped Child in the Mainstream: Proceedings of the Tenth Governors Conference on Exceptional Children* (Chicago: Commission for Handicapped Children, 1953), 13; Maurice H. Fouracre, "What's Special About Special Education?" *Teachers College Record* 55 (1953): 144; F. E. Lord, "A Realistic Look at Special Classes—Extracts from the President's Address," *Exceptional Children* 22 (1956): 321–22.

18. Walter J. Cegelka and James L. Tyler, "The Efficacy of Special Class Placement for the Mentally Retarded in Proper Perspective," *Training School Bulletin* 67 (1970): 33–67; Edward A. Polloway, "The Integration of Mildly Retarded Students in the Schools: A Historical Review," *Remedial and Special Education* 5 (1984): 19–21; Howard L. Sparks and Leonard S. Blackman, "What Is Special about Special Education Revisited: the Mentally Retarded," *Exceptional Children* 31 (January 1965): 243–45.

19. "Segregation versus Non-Segregation," 239, 236; Maurice H. Fouracre, "What's Special?" 140–41, 144; G. Orville Johnson and Samuel A. Kirk, "Are Mentally-Handicapped Children Segregated in the Regular Grades?" *Exceptional Children* 17 (1950): 65–68, 87–88; Willie Kate Baldwin, "The Social Position of the Educable Mentally Retarded Child in the Regular Grades in the Public Schools," *Exceptional Children* 25 (November 1958): 106–8, 112.

20. "Segregation versus Non-Segregation," 235, 237–38; Arthur L. Rautman, "Special Class Placement," *Journal of Exceptional Children* 10 (1944): 99–100.

21. Hill, "A Critical Glance," 316.

22. Ibid., 317.

23. Henry, *The Forty-Ninth Yearbook*, 10; Riker, "Who Is the Exceptional Child?" 1; Samuel A. Kirk, "What Is Special about Special Education? The Child Who Is Mentally Handicapped," *Exceptional Children* 19 (1953): 138–39; F. E. Lord, "A Realistic Look at Special Classes: Extracts from the President's Address," *Exceptional Children* 22 (1956): 325; Haring, Stern, and Cruickshank, *Attitudes of Educators,* 3.

24. Martens, *State Legislation,* 14–22; Scheerenberger, *History of Mental Retardation,* 240–41.

25. Mackie, *Special Education,* 36–37; Trent, *Inventing the Feeble Mind,* 238.

26. Scheerenberger, *History of Mental Retardation,* 119; Winzer,*History of Special Education* 230, 334–336; Van Cleve and Crouch, *Place of Their Own,* 87–97; Frances A. Koestler,*The Unseen Minority: A Social History of Blindness in the United States* (New York: McKay, 1976), 13–24, 187–89.

27. President's Committee on Mental Retardation, *MR 76: Mental Retardation: Past and Present* (Washington, D.C.: GPO, 1977), 37–38; "A History of the National Association for Retarded Children, Inc.," http://www.thearc.org/history/anonymous.htm; Robert Segal, "The National Association for Retarded Citizens," http://www.thearc.org/history/segal.htm.

28. Scheerenberger, *History of Mental Retardation,* 214–15; Robert M. Buchanan,

Illusions of Equality: Deaf Americans in School and Factory (Washington, D.C.: Gallaudet University Press, 1999).

29. Trent, *Inventing the Feeble Mind,* 227–30; Scheerenberger, *History of Mental Retardation,* 197–200.

30. Scheerenberger, *History of Mental Retardation,* 240–44; Trent, *Inventing the Feeble Mind,* 225–43; President's Committee, *MR 76,* 40; Pearl S. Buck, *The Child Who Never Grew* (New York: J. Day, 1950); Dale Evans Rogers, *Angel Unaware* (Westwood, N.J.: Revell, 1953).

31. Henry Randolph Latimer, *The Conquest of Blindness: An Autobiographical Review of the Life and Work of Henry Randolph Latimer* (New York: American Foundation for the Blind, 1937), 182–89; Salvatore G. Di Michael, *Speaking for Mentally Retarded Children to America* (New York: National Association for Retarded Children, 1956); quoted in Dorn, "Public-Private Symbiosis," 384; Helmer R. Myklebust, *Your Deaf Child: A Guide for Parents* (Springfield, Ill.: Charles C. Thomas, 1950), 89–92.

32. John W. Tenny, "The Minority Status of the Handicapped," *Exceptional Children* 19 (1953): 260–64. For a thorough discussion of the relationship among disability, race, and class, see Douglas C. Baynton, "Disability and the Justification of Inequality in American History," in Paul K. Longmore and Lauri Umansky, eds., *The New Disability History: American Perspectives* (New York: NYU Press, 2001), 33–57. Tenny's comments anticipated much of the fundamental critique of the social status of the disabled in society put forth by disability rights advocates and others decades later. An especially provocative and eloquent examination of this status is Harlan Lane, *The Mask of Benevolence: Disabling the Deaf Community* (New York: Vintage, 1992).

33. Haring, Stern, and Cruickshank, *Attitudes of Educators,* 130–32.

Chapter 3

1. William Sloan, Presidential Address, American Association on Mental Deficiency, Portland, Ore., May 24, 1963. In ARC Files, Archives and Library of the Coleman Institute on Cognitive Disabilities, University of Colorado.

2. Edwin W. Martin, Jr., "Breakthrough for the Handicapped: Legislative History," *Exceptional Children* 34 (March 1968): 494–95.

3. President's Committee, *MR 76,* 52–53, 105–25.

4. Ibid., 105–25, 165; Martin, "Breakthrough," 495–501.

5. Trent, *Feeble Mind,* 266; Scheerenberger, *History of Mental Retardation,* 240–46; Mackie, *Special Education,* 37.

6. Trent, *Feeble Mind,* 250–66; Scheerenberger, *History of Mental Retardation,* 252; Burton Blatt and Fred Kaplan, *Christmas in Purgatory: A Photographic Essay on Mental Retardation* (Boston: Allyn and Bacon, 1966).

7. National Association for Retarded Children, "Give Thanks That Retarded Children Can Be Helped . . . By You: This Is Their Bill of Rights" (New York: author, August 1963), ARC Files, the Coleman Institute; National Association for Retarded

Children, "The Basic Aims of the National Association for Retarded Children and the Current Prime Objectives" (New York: author, January 1966), ARC Files, the Coleman Institute, 6–7.

8. An excellent, concise discussion of the emergence of learning disabilities as a category of disability from which this brief summary is drawn can be found in Barry Franklin, *From Backwardness to "At-Risk": Childhood Learning Difficulties and the Contradictions of School Reform* (Albany, N.Y.: SUNY Press, 1994), 49–77. See also Lester Mann, *On the Trail of Process: A Historical Perspective on Cognitive Process and Their Training* (New York: Grune and Stratton, 1979).

9. Franklin, *From Backwardness,* 49–77.

10. For example, see James J. Gallagher, "The Special Education Contract for Mildly Handicapped Children," *Exceptional Children* 38 (March 1972): 527–35; Florence Cristoplos and Paul Renz, "A Critical Examination of Special Education Programs," *The Journal of Special Education* 3 (1969): 371–79; Lloyd M. Dunn, "Special Education for the Mildly Retarded—Is Much of It Justifiable?" *Exceptional Children* 35 (September 1968): 5–22; Nikki Murdick, Barbara Gartin, and Terry Crabtree, *Special Education Law* (Upper Saddle River, N.J.: Merril, 2002), 55–74.

11. Seymour B. Sarason and Thomas Gladwin, "Psychological and Cultural Problems in Mental Subnormality: A Review of Research," *American Journal of Mental Deficiency* 62 (May 1958): 1293.

12. Burton Blatt, "Some Persistently Recurring Assumptions Concerning the Mentally Subnormal," *Training School Bulletin* 57 (1960): 48–53. See also Samuel Kirk, "Experiments in the Early Training of the Mentally Retarded," *American Journal of Mental Deficiency* 56 (1952): 692–700.

13. Mackie, *Special Education,* 36–40, 48.

14. Ibid., 44–45.

15. Ibid., 39, 5–6.

16. Ibid., 31–33, 44–45; Romaine Mackie, "Spotlighting Advances in Special Education," *Exceptional Children* 32 (October 1965): 77–81; see, for example, State of Virginia, *Services for Exceptional Children: A Guide for Program Improvement.* Richmond, Va.: Special Education Service, State Department of Education, Volume 45, No. 3, October 1962.

17. Maynard C. Reynolds, "A Framework for Considering Some Issues in Special Education," *Exceptional Children* 28 (March 1962): 367–70.

18. Ray H. Barsch, *The Parent of the Handicapped Child: The Study of Child-Rearing Practices* (Springfield, Ill.: Charles Thomas, 1968), 218–24.

19. Blatt, "Some Persistently Recurring Assumptions," 49–58.

20. A comprehensive summary of such studies dating from the 1930s through the late 1960s is found in Walter J. Cegelka and James L. Tyler, "The Efficacy of Special Class Placement for the Mentally Retarded in Proper Perspective," *Training School Bulletin* 67 (1970): 33–68. The references list to this article contains a comprehensive listing of efficacy studies carried out prior to 1970.

21. G. Orville Johnson, "Special Education for the Mentally Handicapped—A Paradox," *Exceptional Children* 29 (October 1962): 65–66.

22. Dunn, "Special Education for the Mildly Retarded—Is Much of It Justifiable?" 5.

23. Ibid., 7–8.

24. Ibid., 6–9.

25. Ibid., 8–11.

26. Ibid., 11–21.

Chapter 4

1. Lloyd M. Dunn, "Special Education for the Mildly Retarded—Is Much of It Justifiable?", *Exceptional Children* 35 (September 1968): 5–22.

2. Dunn, "Special Education," 5–8; Florence Christoplos and Paul Renz, "A Critical Examination of Special Education Programs," *Journal of Special Education* 3 (1969): 371–79; Arthur Kraft, "Down With (Most) Special Education Classes!" *Academic Therapy* 8 (Winter 1972–1973): 207–8. See also M. Stephen Lilly, "Special Education: A Teapot in a Tempest," *Exceptional Children* 37 (September 1970): 43–49 and Milton Budoff, "Providing Special Education Without Special Classes," *Journal of School Psychology* 10 (1972): 199–205.

3. James J. Gallagher, "The Special Education Contract for Mildly Handicapped Children," *Exceptional Children* 38 (March 1972): 527–31; Christoplos and Renz, "Critical Examination," 373; Jane R. Mercer, *Labeling the Mentally Retarded: Clinical and Social System Perspectives on Mental Retardation* (Berkeley: University of California Press, 1973).

4. Dunn, "Special Education," 6–9; President's Committee, *MR 76*, 143–47; President's Committee on Mental Retardation, *Report to the President: Mental Retardation: Century of Decision* (Washington, D.C.: GPO, 1976): 11–14.

5. Kraft, "Down With (Most)," 207; Evelyn Deno, "Special Education as Developmental Capital," *Exceptional Children* 37 (November 1970): 232, 236; Christoplos and Renz, "Critical Examination," 371–73; Lilly, "Special Education," 45–46.

6. Dunn, "Special Education," 5; G. Orville Johnson, "Special Education for the Inner City: A Challenge for the Future or Another Means for Cooling the Mark Out?" *The Journal of Special Education* 3 (1969): 245; Deno, "Developmental Capital," 231; Mary Engel, "The Tin Drum Revisited," *The Journal of Special Education* 3 (1969): 383; Christoplos and Renz, "Critical Examination," 372–73, 376.

7. Deno, "Developmental Capital," 229, 231; Lilly, "Special Education," 43; Dunn, "Special Education," 5.

8. Christoplos and Renz, "Critical Examination," 376–78; Richard P. Iano, "Shall We Disband Special Classes?" *The Journal of Special Education* 6 (1972): 167–77; M. Stephen Lilly, "A Training Based Model for Special Education," *Exceptional Children* 37 (Summer 1971): 745–46.

9. Deno, "Developmental Capital," 234–36; Lilly, "Special Education," 48.

10. Scheerenberger, *History of Mental Retardation*, 240–55; Trent, *Feeble Mind*, 266–67.

11. Bengt Nirje, "The Normalization Principle," in Robert J. Flynn and Kathleen E. Nitsch, eds., *Normalization, Social Integration, and Community Services* (Baltimore: University Park Press, 1980), 32–33.

12. Wolf Wolfensberger and Bengt Nirje, *The Principle of Normalization in Human Services* (Toronto: National Institute on Mental Retardation, 1972). See also Trent, *Feeble Mind*, 262–66.

13. Trent, *Feeble Mind*, 262–64; Scheerenberger, *History of Mental Retardation*, 250–52; President's Committee, *MR 76*, 50–53. For a clear explication of normalization and its relationship to deinstitutionalization, see R. C. Scheerenberger, *Deinstitutionalization and Institutional Reform* (Springfield, Ill.: Charles Thomas, 1976).

14. Dunn, "Special Education," 6; Lilly, "Special Education," 43; Budoff, "Without Special Classes," 201; Kraft, "Down With (Most)," 209.

15. Christoplos and Renz, "Critical Examination," 375–76.

16. National Association for Retarded Citizens, *Policy Statements on the Education of Mentally Retarded Children* (author: 1971), ARC Files, the Coleman Institute of Cognitive Disabilities, University of Colorado, 5–6.

17. Howard L. Sparks and Leonard S. Blackman, "What Is Special about Special Education Revisited: The Mentally Retarded," *Exceptional Children* 31 (January 1965): 242–43; Louis F. Brown, "The Special Class: Some Aspects for Special Educators to Ponder," *Education and Training of the Mentally Retarded* 3 (1968): 12–13.

18. Sr. M. Sheila, "When You Wish upon a Star: The Self-Fulfilling Prophecy and Special Education," *Education and Training of the Mentally Retarded* 3 (1968): 189–93; Kailas C. Panda and Nettie R. Bartel, "Teacher Perception of Exceptional Children," *The Journal of Special Education* 6 (1972): 261–66; Edward E. Gickling and John T. Theobald, "Mainstreaming: Affect or Effect," *The Journal of Special Education* 9 (1975): 317–28.

19. Jerry D. Chaffin, "Will the Real 'Mainstreaming' Program Please Stand Up! (or . . . Should Dunn Have Done It?)," *Focus on Exceptional Children* 6 (October 1974): 1, 5–17; Gilbert R. Guerin and Kathleen Szatlocky, "Integration Programs for the Mildly Retarded," *Exceptional Children* 41 (November 1974): 173; Robert H. Bradfield, Josephine Brown, Phyllis Kaplan, Edward Rickert, and Robert Stannard, "The Special Child in the Regular Classroom," *Exceptional Children* 39 (February 1973): 384–90.

20. Guerin and Szatlocky, "Integration Programs," 175–76; Robert H. Bruininks and John E. Rynders, "Alternatives to Special Class Placement for Educable Mentally Retarded Children," *Focus on Exceptional Children* 3 (September 1971): 7–10; Donald L. MacMillan, "Special Education for the Mildly Retarded: Servant or Savant," *Focus on Exceptional Children* 2 (February 1971): 10–11; Lu S. Christie, Hugh S. McKenzie, and Carol S. Burdett, "The Consulting Teacher Approach to

Special Education: Inservice Training for Regular Classroom Teachers," *Focus on Exceptional Children* 4 (October 1972): 1–10.

21. Jeffrey J. Zettel and Joseph Ballard, "The Education for All Handicapped Children Act of 1975: PL 94-142: Its History, Origins, and Concepts," *Journal of Education* 161 (summer 1979): 7–10.

22. Erwin L. Levine and Elizabeth M. Wexler, *PL 94-142: An Act of Congress* (New York: Macmillan, 1981), 38–41; Nikki Murdick, Barbara Gartin, and Terry Crabtree, *Special Education Law* (Upper Saddle River, N.J.: Merrill Prentice Hall, 2002), 12.

23. Murdick, Gartin, and Crabtree, *Special Education Law,* 13; Zettel and Ballard, "Education for All Handicapped Children," 12–14.

24. Zettel and Ballard, "Education for All Handicapped Children," 10–21.

25. Ibid., 12–21.

26. The "straw man" reference is from Susan B. Stainback and William C. Stainback, "A Defense of the Concept of the Special Class," *Education and Training of the Mentally Retarded* 10 (1975): 93; Edwin W. Martin, "Some Thoughts on Mainstreaming," *Exceptional Children* 41 (November 1974): 151. For other examples of critiques of mainstreaming and the special education critics, see also Gary M. Clark, "Mainstreaming for the Secondary Educable Mentally Retarded: Is It Defensible?" *Focus on Exceptional Children* 7 (April 1975): 1–5; James K. Myers, "The Efficacy of the Special Day School for EMR Pupils," *Mental Retardation* 14 (August 1976): 3–11; Donald L. MacMillan, Reginald L. Jones, and C. Edward Meyers, "Mainstreaming the Mildly Retarded: Some Questions, Cautions and Guidelines," *Mental Retardation* 14 (February 1976): 3–10.

27. "Two CEC Policy Statements Approved by Delegate Assembly: The Organization and Administration of Special Education," *Exceptional Children* 40 (September 1973): 70–73.

28. MacMillan, Jones, and Meyers, "Mainstreaming the Mildly Retarded," 3; Martin Kaufman, Jay Gottlieb, Judith A. Agard, and Maurine B. Kukic, "Mainstreaming: Toward an Explication of the Construct," *Focus on Exceptional Children* 7 (May 1975): 3–4.

29. MacMillan, Jones, and Meyers, "Mainstreaming the Mildly Retarded," 4–9; Martin, "Some Thoughts on Mainstreaming," 151, 153.

Chapter 5

1. Seymour Sarason and John Doris, "Mainstreaming: Dilemmas, Opposition, Opportunities," in Maynard C. Reynolds, ed., *Futures of Education for Exceptional Students: Emerging Structures* (Minneapolis: National Support Systems Project, 1978), 38–39.

2. Council for Exceptional Children, "What Is Mainstreaming?" *Exceptional Children* 42 (November 1975): 174.

3. James L. Paul, Ann P. Turnbull, and William M. Cruickshank, *Mainstreaming: A Practical Guide* (Syracuse, N.Y.: Syracuse University Press, 1977), 4; David W.

Johnson and Roger T. Johnson, "Integrating Handicapped Students into the Mainstream," *Exceptional Children* 47 (October 1980): 90; Kathleen Dunlop, "Mainstreaming: Valuing Diversity in Children," *Young Children* 32 (May 1977): 27; Jack Birch, quoted in Barbara Milbauer, "The Mainstreaming Puzzle," *Teacher* 94 (May/June 1977): 44. See also S. J. Meisels, "First Steps in Mainstreaming," *Early Childhood* 4 (1978): 1–2.

4. Margaret Wang, "Mainstreaming Exceptional Children: Some Instructional Design and Implementation Considerations," *The Elementary School Journal* 81 (March 1981): 196; Gunnar Dybwad, "Avoiding Misconceptions of Mainstreaming, the Least Restrictive Environment, and Normalization," *Exceptional Children* 47 (October 1980): 87; Robert Bogdan, "A Closer Look at Mainstreaming," *The Educational Forum* 47 (summer 1983): 426.

5. Harvey N. Switzky and Ted L. Miller, "The Least Restrictive Alternative," *Mental Retardation* 16 (February 1978): 52; Alan Abeson, "The Educational Least Restrictive Alternative," *Amicus* 2 (June 1977): 24.

6. Paul, Turnbull, and Cruickshank, *Mainstreaming,* viii; Johnson and Johnson, "Integrating Handicapped Students," 90.

7. Ronald E. Childs, "A Drastic Change in Curriculum for the Educable Mentally Retarded," *Mental Retardation* 17 (December 1979): 299–301; Ronald E. Childs, "Rebuttal," *Mental Retardation* 17 (December 1979): 306; Frank M. Gresham, "Misguided Mainstreaming," *Exceptional Children* 48 (February 1982): 422–423; Switzky and Miller, "Least Restrictive Alternative," 52–53. See also Thomas A. Burton and Alfred Hirschoren, "The Education of Severely and Profoundly Retarded Children: Are We Sacrificing the Child to the Concept?" *Exceptional Children* 45 (May 1979): 598–602.

8. Sarason and Doris, "Dilemmas," 7–10.

9. Ibid., 20–24, 33–37; Edward Zigler and Susan Muenchow, "Mainstreaming: The Proof Is in the Implementation," *American Psychologist* 34 (October 1979): 995. See also D. Milofsky, "Schooling for Kids No One Wants," *New York Times Magazine* (January 2, 1977): 24–25, 28, 33; Gene I. Maeroff, "Schools Forced to Pay More Attention to Disabled," *New York Times* (May 11, 1977): A20. For a comprehensive and skeptical review of mainstreaming that addresses most of these issues, see William M. Cruickshank, *Disputable Decisions in Special Education* (Ann Arbor, Mich.: University of Michigan Press, 1986), 117–21. See also Donald L. MacMillan and Laurence D. Becker, "Mainstreaming the Mildly Handicapped Learner," in Rebecca Dailey Kneedler and Sara G. Tarver, eds., *Changing Perspectives in Special Education* (Columbus, Ohio: Merrill, 1977): 221–24 for a cautionary view of the "unbridled optimism" of mainstreaming's proponents.

10. Milbauer, "Mainstreaming Puzzle," 44. For textbook coverage, see, for example, Frank M. Hewett and Steven R. Forness, *Education of Exceptional Learners,* 2d ed. (Boston: Allyn & Bacon, 1977); Lita Linzer Schwartz, *Exceptional Students in the Mainstream* (Belmont, Calif.: Wadsworth, 1984); S. Gray Garwood, *Educating Young*

Handicapped Children: A Developmental Approach (Germantown, Md.: Aspen, 1979); Bill R. Gearheart and Mel W. Weishan, *The Handicapped Student in the Regular Classroom,* 2d ed. (St. Louis: C.V. Mosby, 1980).

11. Quoted material is from Doug Fuchs and Lynn Fuchs, "Evaluation of the Adaptive Learning Environments Model," *Exceptional Children* 55 (October 1988): 115. See also Erwin L. Levine and Elizabeth M. Wexler, *PL 94-142: An Act of Congress* (New York: Macmillan, 1981); and Roberta Weiner and Maggie Hume, . . . *And Education for All: Public Policy for Handicapped Children* (Alexandria, Va.: Education Research Group, 1987).

12. June B. Jordan and Kathy Zantal-Wiener, eds., *1987 Special Education Yearbook* (Reston, Va.: Council for Exceptional Children, 1988), 10, 69, 81.

13. Stanley S. Herr, "Special Education Law and Children With Reading and Other Disabilities," *Journal of Law and Education* 23 (July 1999): 337–89; Levine and Wexler, *PL 94-142* ; Laurence E. Lynn, Jr., "The Emerging System for Educating Handicapped Children," *Policy Studies Review* 2 (January 1983): 21–58; Jeanne Silver Frankl, "A Response to Laurence E. Lynn, Jr.," *Policy Studies Review* 2 (January 1983): 59–63; McCay Vernon, "Education's 'Three Mile Island': PL 94-142," *Peabody Journal of Education* 59 (1981–1982), 29. See also Seymour Sarason and John Doris, *Educational Handicap, Public Policy, and Social History* (New York: Free Press, 1979), 362–79.

14. For representative examples of research on mainstreaming during this period, see Jay Gottlieb, ed., *Educating Mentally Retarded Persons in the Mainstream* (Baltimore: University Park Press, 1980); Louise Corman and Jay Gottlieb, "Mainstreaming Mentally Retarded Children: A Review of Research," in Norman R. Ellis, ed., *International Review of Research in Mental Retardation, Volume 9* (New York: Academic Press, 1978): 251–75; Phillip S. Strain and Mary Margaret Kerr, *Mainstreaming of Children in Schools: Research and Programmatic Issues* (New York: Academic Press, 1981); and Conrad Carlberg and Kenneth Kavale, "The Efficacy of Special Versus Regular Class Placement for Exceptional Children: A Meta-Analysis," *The Journal of Special Education* 14 (1980): 295–309.

15. Fuchs and Fuchs, "Adaptive Learning Environments," 115; Wang, "Exceptional Children," 196.

16. Wang, "Exceptional Children," 196–97.

17. Ibid., 197–98.

18. Ibid., 198–205.

19. Margaret Wang, Stephen Peverly, and Robert Randolph, "An Investigation of the Implementation and Effects of a Full-Time Mainstreaming Program," *Remedial and Special Education* 5 (November/December 1984): 21–22.

20. Ibid., 22.

21. Ibid., 23–30; Wang, "Exceptional Children," 205–18. See also Margaret C. Wang and Jack W. Birch, "Effective Special Education in Regular Classes," *Exceptional Children* 50 (February 1984): 391–98.

22. Robert E. Slavin, "Team Assisted Individualization: Cooperative Learning and Individualized Instruction `in the Mainstreamed Classroom," *Remedial and Special Education* 5 (November/December 1984): 33–42.

23. Wang and Birch, "Effective Special Education," 392; Dorothy Kerzner Lipsky and Alan Gartner, "School Administration and Financial Arrangements," in Susan Stainback, William Stainback and Marsha Forest, eds., *Educating All Students in the Mainstream of Regular Education* (Baltimore: Paul H. Brookes, 1992), 110–11.

24. Duane F. Stroman, *The Disability Rights Movement: From Deinstitutionalization to Self-Determination* (Lanham, Md.: University Press of America, 2003), 43–82; Jacqueline Vaughn Switzer, *Disabled Rights: American Disability Policy and the Fight for Equality* (Washington, D.C.: Georgetown University Press, 2003), 61–64, 70–80; Doris Zames Fleischer and Frieda Zames, *The Disability Rights Movement: From Charity to Confrontation* (Philadelphia: Temple University Press, 2001), 184–99; Sharon Barnartt and Richard Scotch, *Disability Protests: Contentious Politics 1970–1999* (Washington, D.C.: Gallaudet University Press, 2001), 20–25, 41–44.

25. Ann P. Turnbull and Pam Winton, "A Comparison of Specialized and Mainstreamed Preschools from the Perspectives of Parents of Handicapped Children," *Journal of Pediatric Psychology* 8 (1983): 63–65; Helen Featherstone, *A Difference in the Family: Life with a Disabled Child* (New York: Basic Books, 1980), 68.

26. Kathryn A. Gorham, "A Lost Generation of Parents," reproduced in Susan Hasazi, ed., *Maintaining Momentum: Implementing the Least Restrictive Environment Concept* (Reston, Va.: Council for Exceptional Children, 1980), 185, 188.

Chapter 6

1. William Stainback and Susan Stainback, "A Rationale for the Merger of Special and Regular Education," *Exceptional Children* 51 (October 1984): 110.

2. Margaret Wang, Maynard C. Reynolds, and Herbert J. Walberg, "Rethinking Special Education," *Educational Leadership* 44 (September 1986): 26–31; Maynard C. Reynolds, Margaret C. Wang, and Herbert J. Walberg, "The Necessary Restructuring of Special and Regular Education," *Exceptional Children* 53 (February 1987): 391–98.

3. William Stainback and Susan Stainback, "Rationale for the Merger," 102–3.

4. Ibid., 103–4.

5. Ibid., 104–6.

6. Ibid., 109–10.

7. Alan Gartner and Dorothy Kerzner Lipsky, "Beyond Special Education: Toward a Quality System for All Students," *Harvard Educational Review* 57 (November 1987): 367–95.

8. Gartner and Lipsky, "Beyond Special Education," 369–78.

9. Ibid., 379–83.

10. Ibid., 382, 388.

11. Ibid., 385–90.

12. Madeleine Will, "Educating Children with Learning Problems: A Shared Responsibility," *Exceptional Children* 52 (February 1986): 411–13.

13. Madeleine Will, "Let Us Pause and Reflect—But Not Too Long," *Exceptional Children* 51 (September 1984): 11–13.

14. Quoted in Ann Turnbull, Rud Turnbull, Marilyn Shenk, and Dorothy Leal, *Exceptional Lives: Special Education in Today's Schools* (2d ed.) (Upper Saddle River, N.J.: Merrill, 1999), 85. See also Madeleine Will, "The Question of Personal Autonomy," *Journal of Vocational Rehabilitation* 3 (1993): 9–10.

15. Will, "Educating Children with Learning Problems," 413–15.

16. Douglas Biklen (with Robert Bogdan, Dianne L. Ferguson, Stanford J. Searl, Jr., and Steven J. Taylor), *Achieving the Complete School: Strategies for Effective Mainstreaming* (New York: Teachers College Press, 1985), xi, 1, 3, 184.

17. Biklen, *Complete School*, 2–3.

18. Maynard C. Reynolds, Margaret C. Wang, and Herbert J. Walberg, "The Necessary Restructuring of Special and Regular Education," *Exceptional Children* 53 (February 1987): 394–95; Thomas Skrtic, quoted in William E. Davis, "The Regular Education Initiative Debate: Its Promises and Problems," *Exceptional Children* 55 (February 1989): 440.

19. Joseph R. Jenkins, Constance G. Pious, and Mark Jewell, "Special Education and the Regular Education Initiative: Basic Assumptions," *Exceptional Children* 56 (April 1990): 479–91.

20. Ibid., 485.

21. Martha E. Snell, "Schools Are for All Kids: The Importance of Integration for Students with Disabilities and Their Peers," in John Wills Lloyd, Nirbhay N. Singh, and Alan C. Repp, eds., *The Regular Education Initiative: Alternative Perspectives on Concepts, Issues, and Models* (Sycamore, Ill.: Sycamore, 1991): 133–48.

22. John F. Mesinger, "Commentary on 'A Rationale for the Merger of Special and Regular Education' or, Is It Now Time for the Lamb to Lie down with the Lion?" *Exceptional Children* 51 (April 1985): 510–12.

23. Laurence M. Lieberman, "Special Education and Regular Education: A Merger Made in Heaven?" *Exceptional Children* 51 (April 1985): 513–16.

24. Lieberman, "Special Education and Regular Education," 513–16.

25. Susan Stainback and William Stainback, "The Merger of Special and Regular Education: Can It Be Done? A Response to Lieberman and Mesinger," *Exceptional Children* 51 (April 1985): 517–21. Another example of exchanges of opinion can be found in Sheldon Braaten, James M. Kauffman, Barbara Braaten, Lewis Polsgrove, and C. Michael Nelson, "The Regular Education Initiative: Patent Medicine for Behavioral Disorders," *Exceptional Children* 55 (September 1988): 21–27 and Bob Algozzine, Larry Maheady, Katherine C. Sacca, Larry O'Shea, and Doris O'Shea, "Sometimes Patent Medcine Works: A Reply to Braaten, Kauffman, Braaten, Polsgrove, and Nelson," *Exceptional Children* 56 (April 1990): 552–57.

26. Jenkins, Pious, and Jewell, "Regular Education Initiative," 480; Laurence Lieberman, "REI Revisited . . . Again," *Exceptional Children* 56 (April 1990): 561; James M. Kauffman, "The Regular Education Initiative as Reagan-Bush Education

Policy: A Trickle-Down Theory of Education of the Hard-to-Teach," *Journal of Special Education* 23 (1989): 270–71.

27. James M. Kauffman, Michael M. Gerber, and Melvyn I. Semmel, "Arguable Assumptions Underlying the Regular Education Initiative," *Journal of Learning Disabilities* 21 (January 1988): 6–10; Kauffman, "Reagan-Bush Education Policy," 262–65.

28. Davis, "Regular Education Initiative Debate," 442; Kauffman, Gerber, and Semmel, "Arguable Assumptions," 9–10; Kauffman, "Reagan-Bush Education Policy," 266.

29. Davis, "Regular Education Initiative Debate," 441–42; Lieberman, "REI Revisited," 561; Jenkins, Pious, and Jewell, "Regular Education Initiative," 481–88. See also Robert D. Coates, "The Regular Education Initiative and Opinions of Regular Classroom Teachers," *Journal of Learning Disabilities* 22 (November 1989): 532–36.

30. Davis, "Regular Education Initiative Debate," 443–44.

31. Maryann Byrnes, "The Regular Education Initiative: A View From the Field," *Exceptional Children* 56 (January 1990): 345–49.

32. Douglas Fuchs and Lynn S. Fuchs, "Adaptive Learning Environments," 115–27; Kauffman, "Reagan-Bush Education Policy," 271–73; Lieberman, "Special Education and Regular Education," 515–16; Kauffman, Gerber, and Semmel, "Arguable Assumptions," 6–7; Lieberman, "REI Revisited," 562.

33. Kauffman, "Reagan-Bush Education Policy," 256–67, 273–75.

34. Lori Goetz and Wayne Sailor, "Much Ado About Babies, Murky Bathwater, and Trickle-Down Politics: A Reply to Kauffman," *Journal of Special Education* 24 (1990): 334–39.

35. Julia Landau, "The Richmond Case Study: Ending Segregated Education for Disabled Children," in Sheryl Dicker, ed., *Stepping Stones: Successful Advocacy for Children* (New York: Foundation for Child Development, 1990): 113–56.

36. Massachusetts Advocacy Center, *Out of the Mainstream: Education of Disabled Youth in Massachusetts* (Boston: author, 1987), 4–6, 33–35.

37. Reed Martin, *Extraordinary Children, Ordinary Lives: Stories Behind Special Education Case Law* (Champaign, Ill.: Research Press, 1991), 51–61. Examples of published parental perspectives and testimonials critical of the schools include Lori Granger and Bill Granger, *The Magic Feather: The Truth About "Special Education"* (New York: E. P. Dutton, 1986) and Joan Bennett, "Company, Halt," in H. R. Turnbull and Ann P. Turnbull, eds., *Parents Speak Out: Then & Now* (2d ed.) (Columbus, Ohio: Merrill, 1985), 159–73.

38. Nancy O. Wilson, *Optimizing Special Education: How Parents Can Make a Difference* (New York: Insight Books, 1992), 57, 64; Charles R. Callanan, *Since Owen: A Parent-to-Parent Guide for Care of the Disabled Child* (Baltimore: Johns Hopkins University Press, 1990), 290–304; Norene Pavlik, *One of Them* (Huntington, Ind.: Our Sunday Visitor, 1988), 103.

39. Sharon Davis, *Report Card to the Nation on Inclusion in Education of Students with Mental Retardation* (Arlington, Texas: The Arc, 1992), Arc Files, the Coleman Institute, University of Colorado, 1–4, 20; The Executive Committee of the Council for Children with Behavioral Disorders, "Position Statement on the Regular Education Initiative," *Behavioral Disorders* 14 (May 1989): 202–8. See also "The REI: A Statement by the Teacher Education Division, CEC, October 1986," *Journal of Learning Disabilities* 20 (May 1987): 289.

Chapter 7

1. A brief summary of these developments is provided in Thomas R. McDaniel, "Education and the Excellence-Equity Debate: Lessons from History," in C. June Maker, ed., *Critical Issues in Gifted Education: Programs for the Gifted in Regular Classrooms*, Vol. 3 (Austin, Texas: Pro-Ed, 1993), 6–17. For more general histories of some of these developments, see Herbert M. Kliebard, *The Struggle for the American Curriculum 1893–1958* (New York: Routledge, 1987); Lawrence A. Cremin, *The Transformation of the School: Progressivism in American Education 1876–1957* (New York: Vintage, 1964); and Richard Hofstadter, *Anti-Intellectualism in American Life* (New York: Vintage, 1962). For a key document exemplifying the focus and energy of these developments in the early 1960s, see Jerome Bruner, *The Process of Education* (Cambridge, Mass.: Harvard University Press, 1960).

2. Robert L. Osgood, *For "Children Who Vary from the Normal Type": Special Education in Boston 1838–1930* (Washington, D.C.: Gallaudet University Press, 2000), 52–55, 148–51; Winzer, *History of Special Education,* 353–55.

3. Stephen P. Daurio, "Educational Enrichment Versus Acceleration: A Review of the Literature," in William C. George, Sanford J. Cohn, and Julian C. Stanley, eds., *Educating the Gifted: Acceleration and Enrichment* (Baltimore: Johns Hopkins University Press, 1979), 23–27; Winzer, *History of Special Education,* 353–55.

4. Daurio, "Educational Enrichment," 17–24.

5. Ibid., 18–20; Walter B. Barbe and Dorothy N. Norris, "Special Classes for Gifted Children in Cleveland," *Exceptional Children* 21 (November 1954): 55–57, 71. See also Haring, Stern, and Cruickshank, *Attitudes of Educators,* 191–98.

6. Mackie, *Special Education,* 44–45; Council for Exceptional Children, "Two CEC Policy Statements Approved by Delegate Assembly," *Exceptional Children* 40 (September 1973): 74.

7. Mara Sapon-Shevin, "Including All Children and Their Gifts Within Regular Classrooms," in William Stainback and Susan Stainback, eds., *Controversial Issues Confronting Special Education: Divergent Perspectives* (Boston: Allyn & Bacon, 1992), 69–81; McDaniel, "Excellence-Equity Debate," 6; Maker, *Critical Issues* passim.

8. Barbara Clark, "The Need for a Range of Program Options for Gifted and Talented Students," in Stainback and Stainback, eds., *Controversial Issues,* 57–67.

9. Aimee Howley, Craig B. Howley, and Edwina D. Pendarvis, *Teaching Gifted*

Children: Principles and Strategies (Boston: Little, Brown, 1986), 69–91. For more on this debate, see, for example, James H. Borland, *Planning and Implementing Programs for the Gifted* (New York: Teachers College Press, 1989), 122–51; James H. Borland, ed., *Rethinking Gifted Education* (New York: Teachers College Press, 2003); and Bruce M. Shore, Dewey G. Cornell, Ann Robinson, and Virgil S. Ward, *Recommended Practices in Gifted Education: A Critical Analysis* (New York: Teachers College Press, 1991), 84–87. Shore et al.'s discussion includes a review of research on the issue.

10. For general histories of these developments, see, for example, Van Cleve and Crouch, *Place of Their Own* (Washington, D.C.: Gallaudet University Press, 1989); Harlan Lane, *When the Mind Hears: A History of the Deaf* (New York: Random House, 1984); Douglas Baynton, *Forbidden Signs;* and Richard Winefield, *Never the Twain Shall Meet: Bell, Gallaudet, and the Communication Debate* (Washington, D.C.: Gallaudet University Press, 1987).

11. Mackie, *Special Education,* 44–45. See also O'Connor and Streng, "Teaching the Acoustically Handicapped," 163–73; Haring, Stern, and Cruickshank, *Attitudes of Educators,* 227–38.

12. June B. Jordan and Kathy Zantal-Wiener, *1987 Special Education Yearbook* (Reston, Va.: Council for Exceptional Children, 1988), 86.

13. Michael S. Stinson and Susan Foster, "Socialization of Deaf Children and Youths in School," in Patricia Elizabeth Spencer, Carol J. Erting, and Marc Marschark, eds., *The Deaf Child in the Family and at School: Essays in Honor of Kathryn P. Meadow-Orlans* (Mahwah, N.J.: Erlbaum Associates, 2000), 195–97, 204–5.

14. Claire L. Ramsey, *Deaf Children in Public Schools: Placement, Context, and Consequences* (Washington, D.C.: Gallaudet University Press, 1997), 113.

15. Irene W. Leigh, "Inclusive Education and Personal Development," *Journal of Deaf Studies and Deaf Education* 4 (summer 1999): 236–48; Jeffrey E. Nash, "Shifting Stigma From Body to Self: Paradoxical Consequences of Mainstreaming," in Spencer, Erting, and Marschark, eds., *Deaf Child,* 223.

16. Barbara Poitras Tucker, *The Feel of Silence* (Philadelphia: Temple University Press, 1995), 22–63; Donald F. Moores and Thomas N. Kluwin, "Issues in School Placement," in Arthur N. Schildroth and Michael A. Karchner, eds., *Deaf Children in America* (San Diego: College-Hill Press, 1986), 120–22; Marc Marschark, *Raising and Educating a Deaf Child: A Comprehensive Guide to the Choices, Controversies, and Decisions Faced by Parents and Educators* (New York: Oxford University Press, 1997), 115–18; Carol Padden and Tom Humphries, *Deaf in America: Voices from a Culture* (Cambridge, Mass.: Harvard University Press, 1988), 116.

Chapter 8

1. "IDEA Sails Through Congress," *CEC Today* 3 (June 1997), quoted in Nikki Murdick, Barbara Gartin, and Terry Crabtree, *Special Education Law* (Upper Sad-

dle River, N.J.: Merrill Prentice Hall, 2002), 27–28. An informative and provocative collection of essays related to the current state of special education is Thomas Hehir and Thomas Latus, eds., *Special Education at Century's End: Evolution of Theory and Practice since 1970,* Reprint Series No. 23, *Harvard Educational Review* (Cambridge, Mass.: Harvard University, 1992).

2. J. David Smith and Alan Hilton, "The Preparation and Training of the Educational Community for the Inclusion of Students with Developmental Disabilities: The MRDD Position," *Education and Training in Mental Retardation and Developmental Disabilities* 32 (March 1997), 4–5; Dennis E. Mithaug, "The Alternative to Ideological Inclusion," in Stanley J. Vitello and Dennis E. Mitaug, eds., *Inclusive Schooling: National and International Perspectives* (Mahwah, N.J.: Erlbaum Associates, 1998), 6–8.

3. Douglas Biklen, *Schooling without Labels: Parents, Educators, and Inclusive Education* (Philadelphia: Temple University Press, 1992); Dorothy Kerzner Lipsky and Alan Gartner, *Beyond Separate Education: Quality Education for All* (Baltimore: Paul H. Brookes, 1989); Thomas M. Skrtic, *Behind Special Education: A Critical Analysis of Professional Culture and School Organization* (Denver: Love, 1991); James L. Paul, Hilda Rosselli, and Donnie Evans, *Integrating School Restructuring and Special Education Reform* (Ft. Worth, Texas: Harcourt Brace, 1995); Richard A. Villa and Jacqueline S. Thousand (eds.), *Restructuring for Caring and Effective Education: Piecing the Puzzle Togethe*r (2d ed.) (Baltimore: Paul H. Brookes, 2000); Susan Stainback, William Stainback, and Marsha Forest, eds., *Educating All Students in the Mainstream of Regular Education* (Baltimore: Paul H. Brookes, 1989).

4. Included among the most widely circulated articles capturing these main arguments are Dianne L. Ferguson, "The Real Challenge of Inclusion: Confessions of a 'Rabid Inclusionist,'" *Phi Delta Kappan* 77 (December 1995): 281–87; James McLeskey and Nancy L. Waldron, "Inclusive Elementary Programs: Must They Cure Students with Learning Disabilities to Be Effective?" *Phi Delta Kappan* 77 (December 1995): 300–306; Joy Rogers, "The Inclusion Revolution," *Research Bulletin of Phi Delta Kappa* 11 (May 1993): 1–6; Dorothy K. Lipsky and Alan Gartner, "Inclusion, School Restructuring, and the Remaking of Society," *Harvard Educational Review* 66 (1996): 762–96; Marleen C. Pugach, "On the Failure of Imagination in Inclusive Schooling," *The Journal of Special Education* 29 (summer 1995): 212–23.

5. The Arc, *20 Years of IDEA in America: A Celebration of the Impact of the Individuals with Disabilities Act* (1995), The Arc Files, the Coleman Institute, University of Colorado; quote is from 17.

6. National Council on Disability, *Improving the Implementation of the Individuals with Disabilities Education Act: Making Schools Work for All of America's Children* (Washington, D.C.: National Council on Disability, 1995), 75–98; President's Committee on Mental Retardation, Department of Health and Human Services, *Report to the President: The National Reform Agenda and Citizens with Mental*

Retardation: A Journey of Renewal for all Americans (Washington D.C.: Government Printing Office, 1994), 6–9; President's Committee on Mental Retardation, Department of Health and Human Services, *The Journey to Inclusion: A Resource for State Policy Makers* (Washington, D.C.: Government Printing Office, 1995), 38–48. The Department of Education issues annual reports to Congress on the implementation of IDEA under the title *To Assure the Free Appropriate Public Education of All Children with Disabilities.* See, for example, the *Nineteenth Annual Report* (1997), Section III; *Eighteenth Annual Report* (1996), 61–69; and *Fifteenth Annual Report* (1993), 16–27.

7. Carol Tashie, Susan Shapiro-Bernard, Mary Schuh, Cheryl Jorgensen, Ann Donoghue Dillon, Beth Dixon, and Jan Nisbet, eds., *From Special to Regular, From Ordinary to Extraordinary* (Durham, N.H.: Institute on Disability/University Affiliated Program, University of New Hampshire, 1993); Ann Donoghue Dillon, Carol Tashie, Marie Schuh, Cherly Jorgensen, Susan Shapiro-Bernard, Beth Dixon, and Jan Nisbet, eds., *Treasures: A Celebration of Inclusion* (Durham, N.H.: Institute on Disability/University Affiliated Program, University of New Hampshire, August 1993). For examples of parent-generated literature, see Ruth F. Cantor and Jeffrey A. Cantor, *Parents' Guide to Special Needs Schooling: Early Intervention Years* (Westport, Conn.: Auburn House, 1996), 197–206; Robert Holzberg and Sara Walsh-Burton, eds., *The Parental Voice: Problems Faced by Parents of the Deaf-Blind, Severely and Profoundly Handicapped Child* (Springfield, Ill.: Charles C Thomas, 1996), 41–52, 68, 128–32; Vicki Noble, *Down Is Up for Aaron Eagle: A Mother's Spiritual Journey with Down Syndrome* (San Francisco: Harper, 1993), 162–173; Elizabeth J. Erwin and Leslie C. Soodak, "I Never Knew I Could Stand Up to the System: Families' Perspectives on Pursuing Inclusive Education," *Journal of the Association for Persons with Severe Handicaps* 20 (1995): 136–46. An example of empirical research on parent attitudes is Karen E. Diamond and William G. LeFurgy, "Attitudes of Parents of Preschool Children toward Integration," *Early Education and Development* 5 (January 1994): 69–77. The quote about Allison is from National Council on Disability, *Improving the Implementation of the Individuals with Disabilities Education Act…,* 84; Janice M. Baker and Naomi Zigmond, "Are Regular Education Classes Equipped to Accomodate Students with Learning Disbailities?" *Exceptional Children* 56 (April 1990): 515–26; Edwin W. Martin, "Case Studies on Inclusion: Worst Fears Realized," *Journal of Special Education* 29 (April 1995): 192–199.

8. James M. Kauffman, "How We Might Achieve the Radical Reform of Special Education," *Exceptional Children* 60 (September 1993): 6–16; Douglas Fuchs and Lynn S. Fuchs, "Inclusive Schools Movement and the Radicalization of Special Education Reform," *Exceptional Children* 60 (February 1994): 294–309; Donald L. MacMillan, Frank M. Gresham, and Steven R. Forness, "Full Inclusion: An Empirical Perspective," *Behavioral Disorders* 21 (February 1996): 145–59; Michael M. Gerber, "Inclusion at the High-Water Mark? Some Thoughts on Zigmond and Baker's Case Studies of Inclusive Educational Programs," *Journal of Special Education* 29

(1995): 181–91; Richard W. Smelter, Bradley W. Rasch, and Gary J. Yudewitz, "Thinking of Inclusion for All Special Needs Students? Better Think Again," *Phi Delta Kappan* (September 1994): 38; Albert Shanker, "Where We Stand on the Rush to Inclusion," *Vital Speeches of the Day* 60 (March 1, 1984). See also Mithaug, in Vitello, *Inclusive Schooling*, 1–23.

   9. James M. Kauffman and Daniel P. Hallahan, *The Illusion of Full Inclusion: A Comprehensive Critique of a Current Special Education Bandwagon* (Austin, Tex.: Pro-Ed, 1995), ix-x, 247, 266, 307–48.

   10. Christopher Kliewer and Linda May Fitzgerald, "Disability, Schooling, and the Artifacts of Colonialism," *Teachers College Record* 103 (June 2001): 450–51.

   11. See Council for Exceptional Children, *No Child Left Behind Act of 2001: Implications for Special Education Policy and Practice: Selected Sections of Title I and Title II* (CEC, January 2003) for the CEC's evaluation of the ways in which the act will affect special education policy and practice. The secretary's quote is from pp. 7–8 of this document, which is available on the CEC website (http://www.cec.sped.org).

Index

Page numbers in italics denote figures or illustrations.